CHINA'S NEW NORMAL

Enjoy the reading

24 Sept 2019

一路平安

PASCAL COPPENS

CHINA'S NEW NORMAL

HOW CHINA SETS THE STANDARD FOR INNOVATION

Pelckmans Pro

CONTENTS

CHAPTER 2
SMART MEDIA & ENTERTAINMENT

CHAPTER 3
SMART RETAIL

CHAPTER 4
SMART FINANCE & INSURANCE

CHAPTER 5
SMART MOBILITY

CHAPTER 6
SMART MANUFACTURING

CHAPTER 7
SMART HEALTH

THANK YOU !

谢谢！

I dedicate this book to the two most important people in my life.

My wife, Annelies, who has shown alternating patience and enthusiasm throughout the 27 years of my wild China adventures. Being an entrepreneur is hard, both mentally and physically. You were my daily support and the only constant in a rich and often eventful life. Without you, I could never have gathered together the knowledge, experience and insights that have resulted in this book.

Our daughter, Amelie, who came into our lives on 11 June 2002, when she was nine months old. During the next sixteen years it was your smile and your joy that gave us the energy to try new things and to keep on moving forward. Although you are a citizen of the world, you now feel fine here in Belgium. You are the most wonderful gift that China ever gave to us.

My heartfelt thanks go to all the people who have inspired, stimulated and supported me. There are too many to name them all and I hope that those who are not among the following list will forgive my forgetfulness.

Peter Hinssen. Thank you for showing me a completely new way and for taking me along on your own journey. Since 2018, I have no longer been active as technology entrepreneur, but I have never regretted a single moment of the road we followed together. Today, in part thanks to your network, I can reach more people than ever and feel like a phoenix reborn! Your inspirational foreword to this book was, for me, the icing on the cake.

Luc De Cleir. Thank you for encouraging me to write. You were the first person to believe in me as an author. Your pen is so powerful that you continue to inspire me, time after time. After eight months of writing, your final feedback was: 'That was really not bad at all!' Thank you for your sincerity. Without you, this book would never have been written.

Elisabeth Torfs. You convinced me that Pelckmans Pro was the right choice for *China's New Normal*. It was mainly because I trusted you that I believed you, because for me all business is based on personal trust. Your team produced what you promised me they would, and for that I am enormously grateful, both to you and to them.

I would also like to thank the China experts who read through the earliest version of my manuscript: Thierry Raymaekers, Jan Van den Bergh, Jan Van Der Borght and Jan Jonckheere.

A special thanks to my friend David G. Brooks for all the long hours you spent to help me edit and improve the English version of my book. I hope, in the process, I somehow triggered you to write a book about China, as your unique China experiences and insights should be revealed to the world.

Last but not least, I would like to express my gratitude to everyone who helped me, directly or indirectly, with the realisation of this book: Jason Breen, Kurt Wang Lin, Wim Rombaut, Felix Garriau, Inge Van Damme and the whole nexxworks team. Julie Vens-De Vos, Laurence Van Elegem, Cathy Boesmans and Stephanie De Kesel deserve a special mention for continuing to give me a new podium, as do Rik Vera, Steven Van Belleghem and Nancy Rademaker-Gysbrechts for allowing me to surf on their wave of inspiration.

FOREWORD

by Peter Hinssen

A GUIDE FOR ANYONE WHO WANTS TO UNDERSTAND THE FUTURE

'The Yellow Peril'. That must have been my earliest image of China, as I grew up during the Cold War. The combination of a general fear of advancing Communism and the horror stories emerging about the Cultural Revolution had seriously coloured the West's perception of China – and that's putting it mildly! Reading the Tintin comic book entitled *The Blue Lotus* did little to set my young mind at rest!

As the young boy became a young man, I found myself living in a Europe that was trying to reinvent itself after the terror and tragedy of two world wars, out of which there had only really been one winner: The United States. Western Europe was being flooded by the commercial marketing violence of the 'greatest nation on Earth' and baby boomers bathed in the wondrous luxuries of capitalism. The United States had taken over Europe's role as the 'engine of the world', while Asia as a whole was widely regarded as a region where true innovation was dead and cheap imitation was the main way of working.

Gradually, this image was overtaken by reality. I saw 'Made in Hong Kong' on many of the cheap toys I played with as a child. For adults, this confirmed the stereotypical image of the Far East as a huge factory with dirt-cheap labour that was capable of nothing more than copying things, albeit really well. However, first Japan and then Korea slowly began to bring about a change in perception. Japan evolved from a copycat nation to a nation where world-class innovation thrived, both in technology and design. The Japanese 'miracle' saw the emergence of companies like Canon, which made the most advanced cameras in the world, or Sony, the most creative and inventive player in the field of personal electronics. In the automobile industry, Toyota and Lexus set the bar for comfort and safety higher than ever before, certainly much higher than any comparable brand in Stuttgart or Detroit.

'The Era of Asia' had begun, led by the powerhouses of Japan, Korea and Singapore, each of which excelled as world centres of innovation and growth. But China? For me, as for many others, the country remained a closed 'black box', shrouded in mystery and secrecy. Unknown and unloved.

When I started working in the 90s as a young engineer at Alcatel in Antwerp, a first wave of Belgian managers and technologists had already set off for China. When Deng Xiaoping introduced his 'open door' policy in 1978, in an effort to close the gap with the West's level of (technological) development, numerous companies were encouraged to set up operations in Shanghai. Pioneers like Julien De Wilde (later the CEO of Alcatel in Belgium) and Bert De Graeve (later the CEO of the VRT and Bekaert) seized this chance with both hands and went off to establish 'Shanghai-Bell'. They returned home with stories of huge markets and huge opportunities, but also huge challenges, huge thresholds, huge cultural differences and, most of all, huge frustrations.

For the next twenty years, I concentrated my own professional gaze almost exclusively on the West. In particular, I focused with increasing intensity on the internet revolution that was taking place in Silicon Valley and the resulting digital tsunami that soon flooded the world. For me, the epicentre was Palo Alto and it soon became clear that Europe was finding it hard to keep up with the pace of American technological development.

Over the past ten years, however, the Far East has slowly been edging its way back into the picture. The early rumours about the rapid rise of digital in Asia increasingly found confirmation in world markets. Japan was the first Asian country to fully embrace the mobile revolution, with players like NTT DoCoMo's i-mode. Korea soon followed suit, quickly becoming the world leader in broadband. Stories even began to emerge about Chinese companies enjoying previously unseen spectacular rates of growth, with Alibaba as one of the first.

For some time it had been a common sight to see Asian technologists employed in Silicon Valley. Even back then, these developers with Eastern roots were among the very best in the business. For the past few years, I have been lecturing at MIT in Boston, one of the finest technological universities in the world. It is fantastic to be part of this educational Mecca of the technological revolution and to see how the MIT continues to attract the best students from every country and continent. But a decade ago, it was a clear sign of things to come that the most brilliant students — the very best of the best — systematically began to come from China. They also began to speak English increasingly well, so that they could achieve the ambition that most of them held: to graduate from MIT, make their way *subito presto* to Silicon Valley and make lots and lots of money.

But in recent years this has all changed. Once they have completed their studies, these Chinese whizz-kids can now hardly wait to pack their bags and return home to China. If you ask them "why", the answer is nearly always the same: "Because that's where the action is." Companies like Huawei, Tencent, Alibaba and Baidu have shown that it is now possible to develop technological players of world standing in China. Entrepreneurs like Jack Ma (Alibaba) and Pony Ma (Tencent) have demonstrated to the new generation of tech superstars that you don't need to go to Palo Alto to make your fortune. Jack Ma, in particular, is now the role model par excellence for my students. He is a perfect cross between Steve Jobs and Elon Musk: larger than life, and above all, very Chinese.

In just a few years, the general perception of Chinese (digital) technology has undergone a metamorphosis. The initial idea that the Chinese players were no more than the copiers of American examples may have been correct. Alibaba, for example, was first seen as a 'Chinese knock-off of Amazon'. But it is now clear that Alibaba is moving much further and much faster than its American rival and is, above all, much more innovative.

When, not so long ago, I first went to China with my company, nexxworks, to visit Chinese start-ups and experts, just like we used to do in Silicon Valley, my eyes were opened to a whole new world. The omnipresence of digital technology, the unbelievable richness of apps and the versatility of services like WeChat were truly fascinating. But through it all shone a clear common theme: the massive innovative drive of a country in full transformation.

If you travel to China nowadays, you have the feeling that you are travelling to the future. It is very much a 'hard landing' when you return to Europe. It is perhaps an even harder landing for the American tech-gurus returning to Palo Alto. Once they led the world, but now they are increasingly being left behind. Last year, I went on a seven-day tour to Shanghai and Shenzhen, two of the absolute hotspots in terms of digital innovation. After a week's immersion in the new China, I flew directly to Silicon Valley, where I also planned a further week's stay. It was like stepping back in time. In Shenzhen, everyone uses their smartphone to pay for everything via WeChat or AliPay. Even the beggars on the streets have their own QR-code to receive money! It's a bit of a techno-shock when you then arrive back in the USA to see people still paying with paper cheques for their weekly shopping in Walmart. The contrast is huge; the difference between day and night.

Much the same is true about the respective spirit of the countries. Michael Moritz is one of my favourite risk capitalists in Silicon Valley. Today he is a partner in Sequoia Capital, but he was originally a journalist. Back in the 80s, after he wrote a portrait piece for *Time Magazine* about Steve Jobs, he decided to switch careers and try his hand in the world of venture capital. He soon worked his way up to become one of the most important financiers for Silicon Valley. Some time ago, Moritz wrote an outstanding editorial article for the *Financial Times*, in which he argued: "Silicon Valley would be wise to follow China's lead." He described the work mentality of the start-ups he had seen in China: how these companies and their hungry young lions have an aggressive drive to change the world. He compared this with the pampered nerds of Silicon Valley, who are picked up each day for work by the Google bus and treated to all the privileges of stardom, such as sushi lunches from Michelin-rated chefs. Moritz is convinced that Silicon Valley is history unless it "cottons on" — and quickly — to what is happening in China. Needless to say, the nerds were less than impressed by this prophecy.

Since time immemorial, China has been an important hub in world trade. Academic studies have confirmed that throughout the course of recorded history China has accounted for roughly one-third of the world's entire economic activity. Indeed, China's position was so crucial and so unassailable that the country came to see itself as the centre of the earth: the 'Middle Kingdom' or *Zhōngguó*.

In other words, throughout much of human history China has been the pivotal point for the global economy. There have only been relatively short periods when this was not the case. The most fascinating and most recent of these periods spans the years between 1800 and 1900, when China lost the dominant position it had held for centuries. The 19th century was Europe's century. Above all, it was the century of the Industrial Revolution, which initiated worldwide change based on new technology that was largely in European hands. This led first to the steam revolution in Great Britain, followed by the electrical and chemical revolution in Germany. Later, the United States would capitalise on these developments and scale them up to gigantic industrial proportions. While all this was happening, China stood still. The Chinese people still refer to this period as the '100 Years of Humiliation', during which they not only failed to jump on board the new technological train, but also found themselves increasingly dominated and humiliated by new world powers, such as England and Japan.

Today's China is working to erase the memory of the 'Century of Humiliation' at lightning speed. Following the death of Mao in 1976, Deng Xiaoping set his country on a new and accelerated path of transformation. The nation's new leader was not only the architect of major reform in the economic field, but also had an equally important impact on social and ideological matters. For me, the greatest monument to Deng Xiaoping is Shenzhen, my absolute favourite city in China. When Deng came to power, Shenzhen was little more than a rural village, the last railway station on the Chinese side of the border with economically prosperous Hong Kong. Deng immediately designated it as a 'Special Economic Zone', with the ambition to build a new city, alongside which Hong Kong would pale into insignificance. Shenzhen became the Silicon Valley of China, achieving amazing rates of growth based on the newly emerging electronics industry. Today, the city is the headquarters of companies such as Huawei (the telecom giant), Tencent (the owners of WeChat) and Ping An (the largest insurance company in the world).

China opened the door slightly to the West at the end of the Mao era, with the legendary visit to the country in 1972 by the American president, Richard Nixon. The US Director of National Security at the time, Henry Kissinger, has left us a brilliant description of this visit in his autobiography. At the first meeting between Nixon and Mao, it soon became clear that the Chinese Premier, Zhou Enlai, shared a passion for history with Kissinger. In his book, the American diplomat describes a later scene that took place over a glass of cognac around an open fire somewhere in the heart of Beijing. The two men were discussing their favourite subject, when Kissinger suddenly asked his Chinese host: 'What is your opinion on the French Revolution'. Zhou Enlai thought for a while, gently swirling his liquor around his glass, before answering: 'It is too early to tell.'

Perhaps this story is true; perhaps it is not. Even so, it brilliantly encapsulates the Chinese capacity for long-term thinking. The old stereotypical monolithism associated with Communist China has long since disappeared. In the meantime, China has developed with startling speed into what is now perhaps the most capitalist system in the world. That being said, the Chinese people and their leaders have not lost their ability to think and plan with something more than the immediate future in mind. The country still has a remarkable clear vision of where it wants to go and a remarkably effective way of persuading everyone to move in that same direction.

The latest evolution in Chinese thinking is the idea of China as the hub of the 'New Silk Road', an idea that finds its best expression in the famous 'One Belt One Road' (OBOR) initiative. This is perhaps the largest economic project the world has seen in the past hundred years. The Chinese government has committed itself "lock, stock and barrel" to this project, in the hope of making China the most (technologically) innovative nation in the world. The direction, planning and leadership associated with the project are fascinating to watch, although the methods can sometimes seem a little strange to Western eyes. Consider, for example, the discussion about social credit scoring: the three-figure code or score that will be given to every Chinese citizen by the year 2020 and will be correlated with, for example, their WeChat-account. This 'Big Brother' approach is frowned on or even openly reviled by many commentators in the West. But if you discuss the matter in China, people just shrug their shoulders. They regard it as the most natural way in the world to run a sprawling and complex country of 1.4 billion inhabitants.

China has become a long-term thinking machine, with a visionary 'day after tomorrow' focus and, above all, a 'ruthless power of execution'. This makes it an ideal machine for times when things are changing at a rapid pace. That is why, in this book, Pascal focuses less on China's past and more on its present and its exciting future, which is certain to have an impact on us all, the scale of which is still worryingly unknown.

At the time of writing, tension is growing between the world's two great economic superpowers, China and the United States. It is perhaps even possible to speak of a new Cold War. Concurrently, we are also living in a world increasingly dominated by a 'G-Zero' mentality, to use the phrase coined by the American Professor Ian Bremmer. Bremmer, who teaches at NYU, argues that the original function of the United Nations — thinking collectively about the future of our planet — has been devalued to the point of meaninglessness. The UN is now nothing more than a ceremonial 'talking shop' with no real power. In similar vein, the G20 has shown itself to be toothless and the G8 is equally impotent. As a result, we are evolving towards G0 or G-Zero: a situation in which no group of countries has the power to impose its will on the international agenda, so that each individual country is now required to fend for itself.

It is within the context of this economic and political free-for-all that China wishes to reassert its leadership in the world. It wants to re-establish its position as the 'Middle Kingdom'. It remains to be seen, of course, how this new Cold War will develop and what role Europe will play within it. Yet for all the uncertainty, one thing is crystal clear: this is a crucial moment for the West.

For this reason, it is vital to do everything possible to learn and understand all we can about China, about how and why it is developing so quickly and what, ultimately, it hopes to achieve. I recently led a Chinese management team from a large multinational on a tour through Silicon Valley. I was surprised by how irritated they were by the attitudes and behaviour of their former compatriots in San Francisco's Chinatown. "These are the old Chinese," they said, with a clear note of contempt in their voice, "trapped in the old way of thinking about China. They no longer know what China stands for in our modern world. This field of tension between the 'new' and the 'old' in Chinese thinking is something we need to be aware of — and learn from.

It is less than ten years since I wrote my book *The New Normal* (2010), in which I predicted that digital would soon become a normal part of our everyday lives. At the time, this idea sounded 'exotic', perhaps even a little fanciful. Surely, I was exaggerating? As a result, many people hugely underestimated the speed of the change and its impact on life, work and society as a whole. Exactly the same thing is now happening with China. Whereas the centre for digital development in the past clearly resided in Silicon Valley, the centre for the next phase, the 'Fourth Industrial Revolution' as Klaus Schwab calls it, the new cognitive era fed by AI, will unquestionably be in China. In the near future, China will become the focal point of our New Normal. This idea still sounds 'odd' to our Western ears, perhaps even a little hard to stomach or believe. As a result, and as with the digital revolution a decade ago, almost everyone is seriously underestimating the likely impact.

For this reason, this book is a must-read for everyone who is an entrepreneur, or runs a company, or is engaged in innovation, or wishes to provide his customers with a better experience, or wants to be inspired, or simply hopes to better comprehend the world in which his or her children will live. In other words, it is a must-read for all of us! After twenty years of living and working in China, Pascal knows better than anyone precisely what makes the Chinese people tick. In his own irresistible style, this makes it possible for him not only to confront us with harsh facts that we can no longer ignore, but also to show us what we can learn from China's New Normal, before it is too late.

In recent years, I have come to know Pascal as the very best of guides for everything relating to China and I am proud to regard him as my partner in this fascinating and inspirational voyage of discovery. His book is a brilliantly written manual for anyone who wants to get a grip on our uncertain future. Just forget that China is a country: it is becoming a standard.

Peter Hinssen

The Future of Go
柯洁 KE JIE
00:46:57
ALPHAGO
02:08:18

<
China's Go player Ke Jie loses on 25 May 2017 to Google's artificial intelligence machine, Alpha Go.

INTRODUCTION

CHINA'S NEW NORMAL

CHINA'S NEW NORMAL IS VERY SPECIAL

Two hundred years ago, my native city of Ghent was the very first city on the European mainland to witness the Industrial Revolution. The man responsible was Lieven Bouwens, who in 1798 managed to smuggle important parts of the spinning mule into Ghent hidden inside sacks of coffee. Much the same kind of thing happened in the United States, where the English-born Samuel Slater, known forever after as 'Slater the Traitor', kick-started the Industrial Revolution in America with the stolen designs of British cotton-making machines. In the 1960s it was Japan's turn to copy America's leading technology, although few observers at the time believed that Japan would ever develop into the world leader in the automotive industry. Similarly, 20 years later few could imagine that Korean companies like LG and Samsung would become so dominant in their sectors, largely through their imitation of and improvement upon successful Japanese methods. Throughout modern history it seems that the title of 'the most innovative place on Earth' is one that is regularly passed on from country to country. And now it is China's turn.

Xi Jinping (习近平) became President of the People's Republic of China in 2013. This event coincided with the country's first deceleration in the rate of economic growth after a nearly unbroken 35-year period of average annual GDP growth of more than 10 percent. This high-speed economic growth was the result of the 'Open Door Policy' adopted by Deng Xiaoping (邓小平) after his rise to power in 1978. Deng became the most important Chinese leader following the death of Mao Zedong in 1976 and he remained in office until 1987. The Chinese growth miracle appeared to come to a stuttering halt just as Xi Jinping assumed the reins of power. Since becoming President, Xi has had to confront an annual growth rate of less than 7 percent. In May 2014, Xi declared that China had entered a new era he called the New Normal (xīnchángtài 新常态). In doing so, he made clear to his own citizens and to the wider world that his country had entered a new phase of economic 'normalcy', during which its economic growth would be more or less in the same range as the growth rates in the rest of the world. By this he meant a more modest growth rate, linked to an improved and more balanced economic structure with growth coming increasingly from domestic innovation, rather than from exports and state subsidies.

However, China's New Normal is anything but normal! Even with a slower growth rate, China's economy is still generating around a third of the world's total economic growth each year. And there are two other important new growth normalities. China's purchasing power parity (a widely used parameter to compare the purchasing power of different countries) from 2015 onwards exceeds that of America and Europe, and by 2050 will be as great as America and Europe combined. The Chinese already have much more money at their disposal than the 'rich' West. Moreover, in recent years up to 78% of the GDP growth has been driven by domestic consumption, an increase of 45 percentage points since the advent of Xi Jinping.[1] It is remarkable that Chinese reported GDP growth in 2017 still amounted to nearly 7%, given that a large part of the economy still consists of loss-making state-run companies that are now being systematically written off, one by one.

In my opinion, China's New Normal is about much more than classical economic growth analysis, as the economy is still highly reliant on state intervention and other legacies from the past. For a future-focused analysis, I believe it to be more meaningful today to look at the exponential growth of innovation in China as the best indicator of the country's huge economic potential. If we want to view China's New Normal in its proper perspective, we need to look at the spectacular rise of innovation over the past five years. In 2018, this rise in innovation reached a tipping point, with China apparently overtaking the innovative capacity of the United States. Some key developments signal this tipping point:

- The list of the world's 20 most valuable internet companies (by market valuation) already contains nine Chinese enterprises.[2]
- China already has 149 unicorns[3], private companies that are worth more than 1 billion dollars. This is three more than the United States.
- China now spends as much on research and development (R&D) as Europe or America, whereas just eight years ago they only spent half as much.[4]
- China accounts for 40% of all the world's patent applications and is now approaching the total number of patents granted to American and Japanese companies.[5]
- Trump's firm actions against Huawei and other Chinese high-tech companies reveal new concerns for America towards the real capabilities of Chinese technology firms.
- If a comparison is made between the growth of similar technology companies in China and the West, those in China are growing nearly twice as fast, even though they are still almost exclusively active on their domestic market.

This handful of facts and figures is enough to show that the standard image of China held by most people in the West is outdated or even totally wrong. This is the image projected in 2014 by Joe Biden, the former American Vice-President, in a broadcast to the American people on national television: "I challenge you. Name me one innovative project, one innovative change, one innovative product that has come out of China." Donald Trump played on much the same theme in 2018, when he tweeted that China had already stolen 300 billion U.S. Dollars in intellectual property rights, a situation that could not be allowed to continue. The assumption remains that China needs to copy because it is not capable of generating innovation on its own. This is the stereotypical 'story' that many politicians, business leaders and journalists in the West love to tell about China. It reassures their populations that 'we' are still more innovative than 'them'. Yet while this might be a reassuring story, it is also a dangerous one, since it feeds a self-fulfilling prophecy that the West has nothing to fear from China and its dramatic economic renaissance. Nothing could be further from the truth. In this book I will highlight the trends, phenomena and examples that will shatter this outdated image of China and of the Chinese people, in the hope that this will prepare us better to remain competitive as individuals and companies in a world where

New Normal China will be a major force. I will look past the hackneyed clichés by describing the trends that stimulate innovation in China. I will explain why and how this innovation is not predominantly directed by Alibaba (China's biggest e-commerce giant) or Tencent (the country's largest social media platform) or even by Xi Jinping, but by the urgent desire of 1.4 billion Chinese to live a better life. This desire – the wish to enjoy a standard of living comparable to people in Western Europe – is unquestionably the most powerful driving force behind the Chinese innovation revolution.

My personal experience suggests that China entered the new age of innovation in 2013. This was the turning point year: the year in which the switch was made from quantity to quality; the year in which young entrepreneurs suddenly started to believe that they could become the next Jack Ma, the founder of Alibaba; the year in which consumers first recognized the huge power they possess and in which Ferrari was unable to keep up with unprecedented demand from the new class of Chinese super-rich. It was also the year in which the first major wave of Chinese experts returned from America and Europe to set up and run new companies in their homeland. The mobile digital era was their playground, and they had the ambition and self-confidence to make this playground their own. In 2013, a new and more innovative China awoke.

Was this perhaps the result of the impulse that Chinese entrepreneurs had received five years earlier when the Olympic Games were hosted in Beijing? Or was it the influence of the new standards in communication set by Tencent's WeChat product – mistakenly referred to as the Chinese Facebook? Or was it because China suddenly found itself with the largest middle class in the world? Or because the corruption trial of Bo Xilai (the Communist Party Secretary in Chongqing, the most densely populated city in China, and a member of the Chinese Politburo, the most senior political organ in China, containing the country's 25 most influential leaders) signalled the end of the era of extravagant and unprincipled self-enrichment? Or was it the appointment of Xi Jinping as President and Communist Party Secretary that provided the decisive impetus? Or was it simply because 2013 was the Year of the Snake in the Chinese zodiac, a year associated with wisdom, intelligence and intuition?

Whatever the reason, there now seems little doubt that in 2013 China turned a corner and entered a new age of innovation of a type never seen before. As a result, this book about China's New Normal also starts in that same year. Although it took Japan and Korea many decades to make the transformation from innovation copycat to innovation leader, China will achieve this in less than 20 years. These Asian countries all started by picking the low-hanging fruit that dangled tantalisingly from the tree of Western innovation. China, in particular, turned this culture of copying into its trademark by replicating almost everything that was capable of making a profit. In contrast to the experience in Japan and Korea, in China this led to the development of a production industry with millions of factories and experts: an infrastructure and a source of knowledge that the country can now exploit to its advantage as it seeks to become an innovation powerhouse in its own right. This does not mean that China will not continue to copy in the future, but the Chinese companies that are currently redefining global standards are all supremely innovative and the majority were founded less than six years ago (or else are older companies that have totally reinvented themselves over the past six years). I call these the Chinese phoenixes, in contrast to the unicorns of the West.

Unicorns, like phoenixes, are mythical creatures. But unicorns are much rarer. The desire to become the next unicorn is rooted in a Western culture that emphasises individuality and uniqueness, a dream that remains out of reach for the vast majority of entrepreneurs. In contrast, Chinese entrepreneurs want to become phoenixes. In China, the phoenix (凤凰 fènghuáng) is not only associated with the strongest virtue, strength and prosperity, but also represents yin (阴) and yang (阳), the duality of existence that gives the universe its shape and form. The phoenix also has the ability to reinvent itself, to rise from the ashes of its former self, to be reborn as a new entity. If, as an entrepreneur, you wish to be a phoenix, you need to have the mentality of a start-up and the courage to take risks (yang), combined with the wisdom that will allow you to search for the necessary resources and security that can be offered by collaboration with a larger organisation as an investor or partner (yin). Chinese phoenix-start-ups or the phoenix departments in major Chinese companies are all less than six years old. In fact, it is probably more accurate to refer to them all as start-ups. And this is what this book is about: these remarkable Chinese start-ups. But these are not start-ups as we know them in the West. They are all young companies with an enormous growth potential allied to an equally great resilience. Their race to the top is breathtakingly fast and is the result of a uniquely Chinese investment and innovation strategy.

THE S-CURVE OF WESTERN INNOVATION

In the West, innovation has been the secret to commercial success for more than 100 years. In Belgium, Ernest Solvay invented the ammonia-soda process to produce soda ash. Henry Ford developed a brilliant method for the mass production of cars. The list is almost endless.

Figure 1

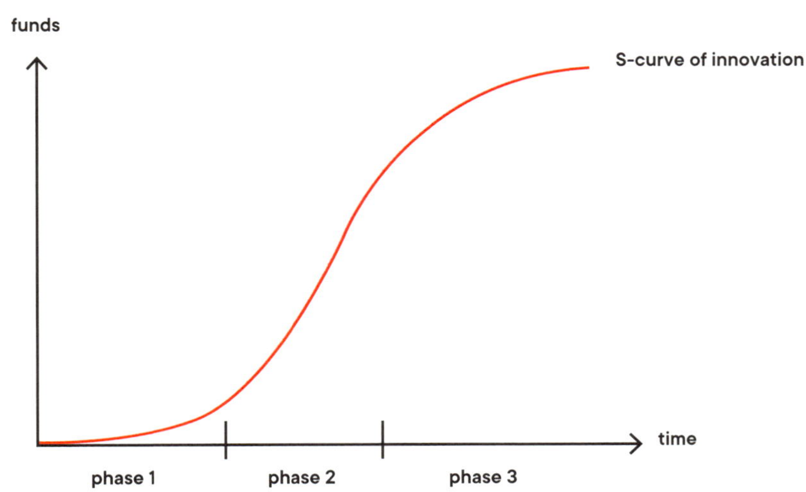

When a small team of smart people in the West start up a company, they generally want to create something unique and disruptive. First, they conceive of an idea, then they scrape together the necessary cash to build a proof-of-concept, and finally a functioning prototype. Innovation and development are usually their main objectives, mixed in with a good dose of passion, naivety and imagination, all with the intention of bringing their 'creation' to life. This is what typifies the initial phase of most Western start-ups: they are innovative and poor.

The second phase is known as the hockey stick: the phase of explosive growth. The product finds its first customers and the company (at last!) can send out its first invoices. If there is a really good product/market fit, repeat orders will start to flood in and investors will suddenly start taking more of an interest. Once they commit, they make funding available for further development and the speeding up of market adoption. This is what typifies the second phase: external money is used to take the product to market, so that the company's reliance on innovation decreases.

The third and final phase usually starts when an alternative product or competitor arrives on the market, or when trends change, or when the market simply expects something different. No matter how much time and work are now devoted to innovation, the level of profit continues to fall. This is what typifies the third phase: income slowly stagnates, eventually leading to zero growth, which the company attempts to combat by greater efforts to optimise the cost side.

This is known as the S-curve of innovation (figure 1) and it is a familiar pattern in the West. To avoid the downward pressure on growth and financial resources, it is sensible to initiate a new S-curve before the first one tails off. This can be achieved by returning to the original formula: a new focus on disruptive innovation, with a new team, a new market, a new product or a new concept (figure 2).

Figure 2

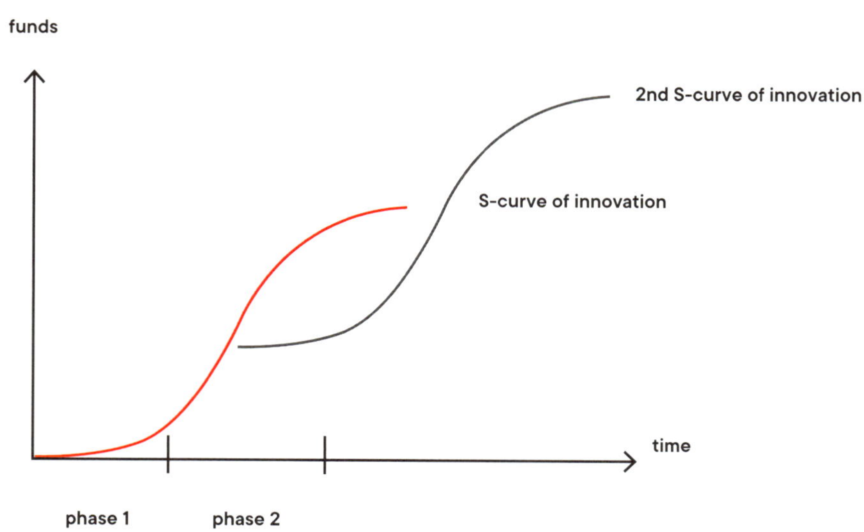

THE N-CURVE OF INNOVATION

In China, the founders of start-ups will first look at market demand and the needs of consumers. Millions of Chinese are constantly looking for ways to improve their standard of living. This forms an ideal basis for entrepreneurs who want to start a company, certainly if the founder and his friends are experiencing the same frustrations as their potential customers. The initial ideas for these companies seldom result from the founders' search for personal expression and fulfilment. The road to success is much less idealistic and much more pragmatic. The main objective is to acquire a dominant market position as quickly as possible, so that rivals are unable to topple you from your throne. In other words, it is a rat race to the top. In China, the fast fish eat the slow ones. This is in contrast to the Western world, where so far it has tended to be the big fish that eat the little ones. According to Klaus Schwab, founder of the World Economic Forum, however, in the new cyber-physical 4.0 world of tomorrow, where everything is connected with everything else, this tendency also looks set to become the new standard in the West. In China, the hunger for extremely fast growth and customer acquisition is huge. This requires lots of money and tireless non-stop execution; great attention to innovation plays less of a role. As a result, Chinese high-tech start-ups approach investors before the product/market fit has been fully proven. In the West, we are familiar with this model from internet companies like Facebook, Airbnb or Uber, but in China this phenomenon is evident in every industry. The decisions of these Chinese investors are based on their belief in the founders and the pressure they feel to act quickly, in order to avoid missing the boat. They often pump millions, sometimes even billions, into a team with an average age of less than 30, money that these disruptive gladiators desperately need if they are to have any hope of winning the battle for survival in the fiercely competitive arena. This is the first phase of the curve of innovation in China; a curve which follows an N-curve (figure 3). It is typified by the acquisition of more and more money, so that the start-up can quickly become the new market standard. This means that Chinese start-ups work outside-in — from market demand to product innovation — whereas most Western start-ups adopt an inside-out perspective — from product innovation to market positioning. I have had personal experience of this on numerous occasions during my efforts to secure investment in both Europe and China for my new ventures in China. In Europe, I was usually able to get the money I needed if I could convince the investors on the basis of a working prototype that had been developed by a top team with a clear strategic vision. In China, investors were often unwilling to part with a cent until I began to discuss my personal network, as well as customers and top brands who had already committed to the project. This changed everything, and the money tap was suddenly opened.

In the West, I have frequently noticed that whenever a new technology start-up arrives on the scene, the other start-ups adjust their own market position. It is almost as if there is a kind of unspoken gentleman's agreement to live and let live. They each want to be the best and the most innovative, but within their own clearly defined market segment. As a result, there is no clear market leader. In fact, everyone is a de facto market leader. This often finds its clearest expression on the company website, where their branding and positioning is explained in detail, supported with brochures and heaps of data for those who would like to know more. They are not afraid to display their business model — with all its strengths and weaknesses — to the world. Chinese start-ups seldom have a well-developed website. Instead, they have just a simple contact page, which explains who is behind the company and lists the awards they have won so far. Chinese start-ups are unwilling to release anything that their competitors might be able to use against them. This is understandable. In China, you have literally hundreds of competitors from day one and they are all engaged in the same fierce guerrilla warfare as you are, particularly in consumer markets. Life for a Chinese start-up is like playing a video game: you need to shoot down your well-financed and well-connected rivals one by one, before they get to you first. In this dog-eat-dog world, innovation, which takes up a lot of time, becomes one of the key limiting factors of accelerated growth. For innovative Chinese start-ups in consumer markets, this first phase barely lasts for two years, and making as much money as you can as quickly as you can is the most efficient way to ensure that you remain at the top of the heap. The winner usually takes more than 50 percent of the market, the second less than 25 percent, with the remaining 25 percent being shared between a dozen or so fast followers.

The second innovation phase of start-up growth is usually initiated once a monopoly or duopoly has been established. The battle for market supremacy will have forced down prices and forced up customer service expectations. But the handful of surviving scale-ups will, by now, also have acquired lots of customers and a fair bit of cash. Once the newly created market has stabilised, a few of the larger companies will generally try to strengthen their grip, often by investing in or even buying the smaller fast followers. This, then, is the second phase of N-curve of innovation: the phase in which the giants start fighting each other. Moreover, it is a phase in which innovation is the key weapon. Money is no longer the problem. The competitive battle is now all about quality and customer loyalty.

In China, as a result of this evolution, a dozen or so scale-ups — the successful start-ups — now commit fully to innovation, often with the help of the bigger and richer companies. They set up new research teams abroad, they hire hundreds of qualified PhDs and developers, they buy in promising foreign technology, etc. The money-customer war has now become a talent war. This phase is often the ideal moment for the truly innovative start-ups to get acquired by the major players. For the majority of these start-ups, being taken over by Alibaba or Tencent is actually their preferred exit strategy. Company founders and owners who were previously members of the management team of one of these large companies therefore generally have more chance of getting all the money they need to fund this innovation surge. This second phase sucks money out of the company with frightening speed. The reserves so carefully built up in phase one quickly drain away, but the company leaders remain convinced that this is the only way to maintain their hard-won leadership position. If necessary the big boys and their investors will continue to pump in a few extra million here and there.

They are confident that when the resulting new innovations eventually reach the market, this will allow them to grow faster than their rivals, thereby initiating a third phase of growth for these robust Chinese scale-ups, which by now are about four years old. This third phase therefore sees the deferred growth of the Chinese market leaders, comparable with the 'hockey stick' growth in Western markets. However, in China this growth curve resembles more a golf club with a shorter head than a hockey stick. This second golf club growth is much greater than anything you can see in the S-curve of Western scale-ups, because the Chinese variants start the process with lots more money, many more customers, and a wide range of innovative products and services.

This is what I call the Chinese N-curve of innovation (figure 3). The '**N**' stands for China's **N**ew **N**ormal — something that will become even clearer from the concrete cases we will examine later in the book.

Figure 3

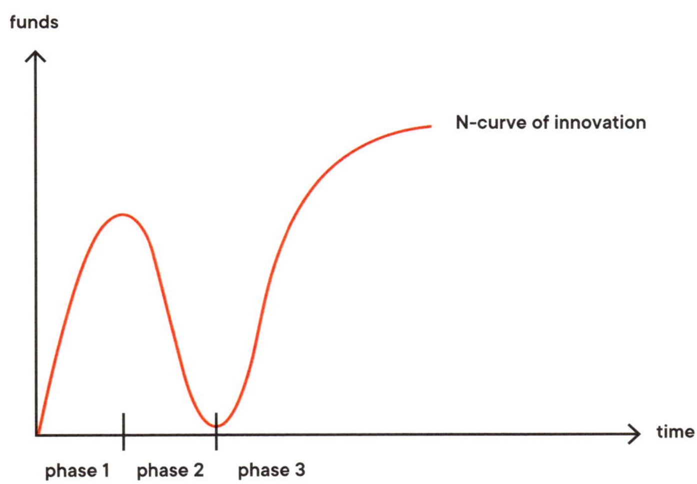

During this second and healthier period of market growth, the wise companies take steps to start up a new N-curve in a new market, either by investing in existing start-ups or by setting up their own new business ventures (figure 4). Each new market entered by one of the major players has a strengthening effect on their previous market. The markets are new but they overlap with the existing customer base, where there is still a demand for new products and services. This is why, just twenty years after they were founded, companies like Alibaba or Tencent are now active in twenty or more different sectors, including retail, tourism, music, video, car and bike-sharing, self-driving cars, mobile payments, cloud computing, navigation technology, group purchasing, e-learning, financial services, video games, healthcare, new media, etc. In the West, it is mainly Google that has this same broad range of venturing, more from a technological innovation than a market innovation purpose. But in China even the scale-ups are prepared to commit themselves to this cross-industry strategic growth model.

Figure 4

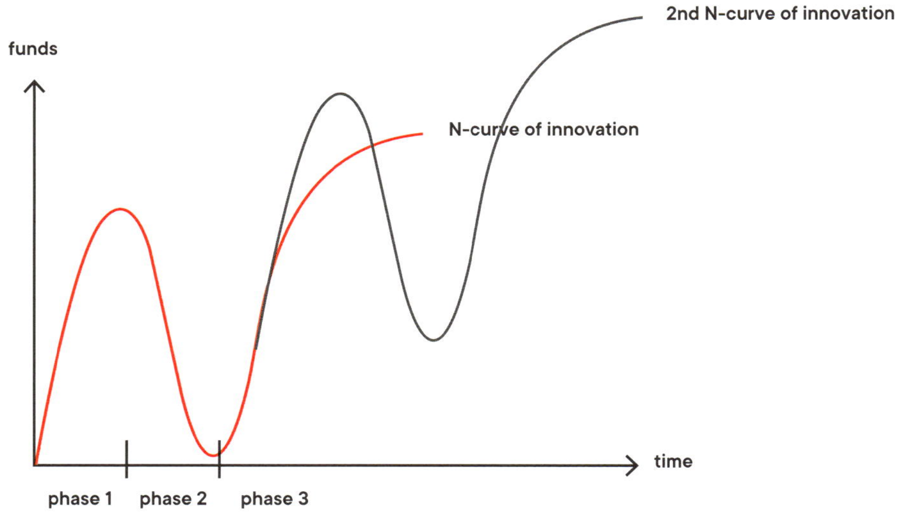

SPEED IS THE NEW INNOVATION

If you superimpose the Western S-curve on top of the Chinese N-curve, you will see that in both cases innovation has a strong financial impact on the second phase of development. However, the direction of this impact is very different; in fact, it is diametrically opposite. Chinese companies invest in innovations for customers they have already acquired. Western companies invest in the bringing to market products, based on innovations they have previously made, to new customers they do not yet have. During this second and most important phase of stable, scale-up growth, the respective objectives of Chinese and Western companies are almost a mirror image of each other. Western scale-ups spend most of their money on recruiting new sales personnel, fine-tuning their branding and marketing, expanding their infrastructure and standardising their product. Chinese scale-ups have already done all these things during their first phase of growth. As a result, they now use their available financial resources and new income to attract experts who can improve the product and optimise production processes.

Figure 5

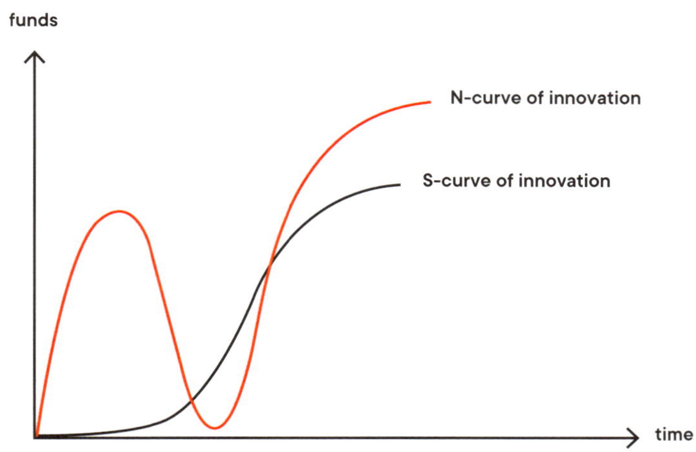

In our modern digital age, having customers and understanding them has become more important than having a factory or a product. The era in which new and ground-breaking research was able to constantly amaze the world has gone forever, or at the very least has dramatically slowed down. There are only so many new shampoo formulas you can invent that are better for your hair. At the same time, the idea that innovation can only be generated by huge multinationals who have the necessary millions is also starting to fade. Big Data and Artificial Intelligence allow for work, previously carried out over months by teams of experts and professors, to now be carried out faster and more easily with just the right amounts of test data, readily obtainable AI algorithms and cheap computing power.

Speed of availability and relevance to the consumer are now increasingly the key factors in commercial success, rather than having the best product. The biggest challenge that I foresee for the West in the coming decades is to learn how to be satisfied with poorer standards than at present. The German thoroughness, better known as *gründlichkeit*, is no longer an option in the new VUCA world:[6] Volatile, Uncertain, Complex and Ambiguous. China epitomises the VUCA concept in an extreme form and is inspiring the country's innovators to develop a new standard for their innovations. Nowadays, Chinese start-ups aim to be 'just innovative enough' for their first product releases, which are intended to do no more than win them the biggest number of customers in the shortest possible time. However, it is those same customers who then start putting pressure on the start-ups to improve on those initial products by providing upgrades. By the time European start-ups have raised sufficient venture capital (after an average of four years),[7] the high-flying Chinese start-ups have usually reached the same level of product quality, because millions of Chinese consumers have already provided an ample supply of behavioural data and are clamouring for improvements. Companies in the West run too many marathons; companies in China run relay races at the same time.

CHINA AS THE NEW NORMAL FOR THE WEST

The ambitious objective of this book is nothing less than to re-programme your thinking about China.[8] Not because your image of the country is necessarily wrong per se, but because it is most likely out of date, given the amazing speed of change currently taking place there. The journey to discover the full implications of China's New Normal has only just begun, but it is certain to be one of the most fascinating changes and evolutions of the 21st century. Those who wish to be a part of this journey must first be willing to 'unlearn' everything they thought they knew about China and then re-learn it anew, starting from square one. If they can do this, they will be among those who will be able to benefit from the opportunities that this remarkable journey will certainly create. For those who prefer to cling to the myths and legends of the old pre-2013 China, the future looks less bright. They will find themselves fighting against a powerful dragon that is only now, at long last, truly awakening from a long sleep.

Sun Tzu wrote in **The Art of War**: 'If you know the enemy and know yourself, you need not fear the result of a hundred battles. If you know yourself but not the enemy, for every victory gained you will also suffer a defeat. If you know neither the enemy nor yourself, you will succumb in every battle.' If we fail to put modern China on our radar, then the West should, as Sun Tzu predicts, be fearful of defeat. If, however, we are able to better understand the workings of 21st century China, we have a chance to reinvent ourselves and remain relevant for the future. China's New Normal innovation model first came into being in 2013, and I believe that by 2030, this model will have become fully embedded in every industrial sector in the country, eight of which I will discuss later on. In other words, at the time of writing, China is nearly half way towards completing its process of transformation. It is therefore high time that we in the West should start realigning our own business models and mindsets to reflect this new reality. The digital transformation that Western companies have undergone in recent years to adjust to the new world of 'bits and bytes' will seem insignificant in comparison with transformation they will need to undergo in the extreme VUCA world of 'data and speed'. This world will be upon us in less than 12 years' time and China is its harbinger. In other words, if you can survive in China's extreme-VUCA world of today, you can remain competitive.

ARTIFICIAL INTELLIGENCE MAKES CHINA SMARTER

In 2013, Baidu, often referred to as the Chinese Google, fired the starting gun for a new Artificial Intelligence focus in China with the launch of an active 'AI-first' agenda in the shape of its foundation of the Institute for Deep Learning. In 2014, Andrew Ng, best known as the originator of the 'Google Brain' project (a department of Google that wants to make machines intelligent, so that they can improve people's lives), opened an AI Lab for Baidu in Silicon Valley. This was followed in 2015 by the Chinese government's announcement that it intended to support plans to develop a 'China Brain', using input from Baidu. These measures represent visible signs of the huge investments being poured into AI development, and are a clear sign that China's AI revolution has already begun.

There are more than 10,000 titles referring to Artificial Intelligence on Amazon. If you haven't read any of them, you might like to start with the book that Bill Gates recommends (also seen on Xi Jinping's bookshelf): **The Master Algorithm** by Pedro Domingos. Another book that is well worth a look is **AI Superpowers** by Kai-Fu Lee. Lee is one of the most influential AI authorities in China. He once headed up Google China, but is now a venture capitalist. He has described Artificial Intelligence in the following terms:

'Many people confuse AI (or machine-learning) with what they see in science-fiction movies. What you typically see in these sci-fi movies is 'general AI', or AI that is comparable (or even superior) to humans – including reasoning, conceptual learning, common sense, planning, cross-domain thinking, creativity, and even self-awareness and emotions. But today's technology is far from this type of general AI. Today's AI is 'narrow AI', or a technology that takes in huge amounts of information from a specific domain (say, loan repayment histories) and uses it to make a decision in a specific case (whether to give an individual a loan) in the service of a specified goal (maximizing profits for the lender). Think of it as a spreadsheet on steroids, without programming, but built by making use of simple algorithms trained on big data. These tools can outperform human beings at certain tasks. This is already incredibly useful, because narrow AI is fast, accurate, works around-the-clock, and can be applied to many tasks, with substantial economic benefit. How far are we from general AI? We simply don't know enough to estimate. Because to achieve general AI will require dozens of significant breakthroughs, when the field of AI has only seen one big breakthrough in 60 years.'

Since my book is about the China of the near future, I have chosen to concentrate on narrow AI in my examples and in the trends associated with them.

We will be looking at AI throughout this book as a key stimulus for the radical transformation China is currently undergoing. This is no coincidence. Since 2013, AI has become the number one engine for the country's further evolution, a game-changer at every level of society, from companies to consumers to the government. Today, AI is the technology on which China's transformation to its New Normal is taking place. What's more, this is something that every company in China understands, which also explains why every Chinese technology company has now become an AI company. So, where does this Chinese obsession with AI come from? And what does it mean?

There are ten factors that explain why China now devotes greater attention to AI than any other country on the planet, including the United States. These factors also give us a better insight into what China might look like after it completes its transformation to the New Normal in 2030.

The Four Basic Components

There are four things you need to create an AI economy: lots of data, a server infrastructure, talent and microchips. China not only has all four elements in place, but also has the potential to become the world leader in all four segments over time.

No country on Earth has the level of data available in China — and data is the foundation of all AI. Tencent possesses the social data of more than 1 billion Chinese consumers. Alibaba has detailed information about the purchasing behaviour of half a billion people. Baidu has similar information about search tasks relating to countless different interests. Many companies also have access to the anonymised images screened by China's more than 200 million surveillance cameras, so that they can train their facial recognition algorithms, which continue to learn exponentially, as long as there are valuable tags attached to the images.

Alibaba has one of the most advanced server infrastructures in the world. China is also leading the revolution in 5G, which is vital for the development of the massive Internet-of-Things infrastructure, which in turn will develop further huge quantities of data for the algorithms to devour. In the near future, China will also be the proud owner of the fastest super-computer in the world, the Tianhe 3, and has also invested 10 billion dollars in a new quantum laboratory that will open in 2020. China is poised to lead the global race in deployment of quantum computing (Smart Security).

In terms of AI talent, China lags behind the United States, because this field of research is much younger in China than in America. But Chinese companies are now offering the same salaries as the top Silicon Valley players, so talent is now flowing in both directions. Nearly every Chinese software manufacturer has built its own AI laboratory in the Valley, so that it can attract the very best experts. At the same time, 37 percent of all STEM (Science, Technology, Engineering and Maths) students in the world are Chinese.[9] And because AI experts in China earn roughly twice as much as other IT experts, building up a massive AI talent base in a pragmatic country like China is a matter of years, not decades away.

China is also making up lost ground in an urgent quest to produce its own AI microchips. An AI microchip is constructed specifically to deal with data streams, in contrast to the traditional Neuman architecture of processors, which are expected to carry out a number of different functions, such as calculations, logic, control, storage or even signal processing. AI chips need to process huge numbers of matrix multiplications by means of parallel computations, similar to what we can already see in the graphic processors (GPU) used in video games. Thanks to the gigantic market for games, the price of GPUs has fallen in recent times, with the American company NVIDIA as the chip market leader, but they still require lots of energy and cooling. The buzzing noise you hear when you enter the room of a heavy gamer is the sound of the ventilators working hard to keep the temperature down! The challenge is to find the right balance between energy and cost, in combination with the right architecture for each specific application, since none of us would be very happy if our smartwatch or cell phone began to buzz unexpectedly or even burst into flames! The AI chip development race is taking place throughout the world, and China is one of the main contenders. At the moment, however, this remains the main Achilles heel for China in terms of further AI development. America remains some distance ahead and the American authorities are taking a more aggressive stance to block the take-over of American AI chip companies by their Chinese rivals. This has led China to set up many of its own AI chip start-ups, the most well-known of which are Horizon Robotics, Cambricon and HiSilicon.

With the framework of 'Made in China 2025' (Smart Manufacturing), almost half of all investment is being directed towards efforts to break the nation's dependence on American microprocessors. This will take time, but it is reasonable to assume that by 2030 China will have achieved parity with America, and much sought-after AI chip self-reliance.

The Chinese Government

In 2016, a Google AI machine named 'AlphaGo' created a furore in China. In March of that year, the Korean master Lee Sedol lost a game of Go to Artificial Intelligence. The Go board game was developed more than 2,500 years ago and throughout the centuries was the thinking-man's pastime of the Chinese and Japanese elites. A year later, in 2017, AlphaGo also beat the Chinese world Go champion, Ke Jie. This was a 'Sputnik moment' for China. The whole nation was amazed. All the experts had predicted that such a thing would not be possible for at least another ten years, given the great complexity of Go as a game. After the first two moves have been made in chess, there are 400 possible moves. In Go, there are 130,000. This was the moment when the Chinese government realised that with AI, America had developed a disruptive technology that posed a serious threat to China's competitiveness. By the end of 2017, China had drawn up a series of detailed measures to close the AI gap with its 'Next Generation Artificial Intelligence Development Plan'. The objectives in this plan are crystal clear: by 2020, China must be in a position to compete with the West in AI; by 2025, ground-breaking innovations in AI must have been made; and by 2030, AI world leadership must have been secured.

According to a 2017 report by PwC (PricewaterhouseCoopers), 26.1 percent of China's GDP-growth could potentially be derived from AI by 2030, in comparison with just 9.9 percent for Europe and 14.5 percent[10] for the United States. In other words, China has up to 7 trillion dollars of future GDP growth to gain depending on the success of its AI project (China's GDP was 13 trillion dollars in 2018.) This helps explain the degree of excitement and 'total mobilization' shown in China's pursuit of AI dominance. Within two months of Ke Jie's defeat by AlphaGo, the government had drawn up plans to turn China into the world centre of AI innovation, with as its target the development of an AI industry worth 150 billion dollars by 2030. This sent a clear and unmistakeable message to every Chinese entrepreneur, company and local official: if you want to get more attention from Party leaders in Beijing, you need to invest in AI. The regime backed up this 'encouragement' by announcing the construction of an AI development park in the nation's capital, capable of housing 400 AI companies, as well as setting up an AI lab at a cost of 2 billion dollars. This immediately set an expectation for how much other provinces and cities should spend proportionally to Beijing. And just in case the message had still not been understood, during the nationally televised broadcast of his 2018 New Year's speech, Xi Jinping very pointedly placed two AI books on the library shelves behind him: 'The Master Algorithm' by Pedro Domingos, and Brett King's 'Augmented'. The effect was not lost on his 800 million viewers. During the past two years China's major cities have invested billions in AI parks, AI incubators and AI funds. Some commentators regard these investments as disproportionately large, but they are only a fraction of the potential GDP gains! The key question that remains unanswered is whether China will be able to fill this impressive AI infrastructure with sufficient AI experts? The government is doing all it can to persuade Chinese AI experts working abroad to return to their homeland, while at the local level across the country city councils offer preferential policies and financial assistance to AI start-ups. As always in China, there is also a strong element of the long term in this thinking: for example, changes have already been made in the education system to better reflect the needs of the new AI society of the future.

Investment

A study of data for 2017 shows that in terms of total investment in AI, AI companies and AI talent, America spent twice as much as China, while China invested three times more than the United Kingdom.[11] What is noticeable, however, is that China is pumping much more money into companies with applications for computer vision, image processing, intelligent robots, self-driving cars, unmanned aircraft, drones and speech recognition. These are all applications that can be brought directly to market and are instantly saleable. This trend perfectly matches the N-curve of Chinese start-ups, with their aim of establishing market leadership as quickly as possible. In contrast, American AI companies are relatively more active in areas like natural language processing, machine-learning algorithms, technology platforms, defence and microprocessors. This focus is much more in keeping with the typical Western S-curve of growth, where the aim is to generate ground-breaking innovation, rather than the incremental progression favoured by the Chinese. The open question is "which of these two approaches is the most efficient?". The 'moon-shot' innovation thinking of Google X seeks to provide radical solutions to major problems through revolutionary technology, but to date the results are often slow, uncertain and incredibly expensive. The more pragmatic Chinese approach prefers to see AI as a way to earn quick money in the short term, on the assumption that any earth-shattering inventions that may be made in the West can be acquired in the long term by China with all the money they made in AI . Smart thinking? Perhaps, although in recent times Western countries have been putting up more and more walls to protect their innovation skills, so that the Chinese may nevertheless be forced to invest more heavily in some 'moon-shot' thinking of their own. Even so, for the time being AI looks like being a cash cow for the Chinese phoenix, just like the internet has so far been a cash cow for Google, Amazon and Facebook.

BATX and TMD

Of course, this does not mean that China has no interest whatsoever in long-term innovation, but it tends to be confined to the major companies: the well-known BAT trio (Baidu, Alibaba and Tencent). For example, Baidu has developed its open Apollo platform as the standard for self-driving cars. Similarly, Alibaba has created its ET Brain platform, with the ambition to become the most important AI platform by 2025. It is used today in the 'City Brain' project, which manages the control of the smart city of Hangzhou in Zhejiang Province through AI.[12] In 2016, Tencent launched its Tencent AI Lab with the slogan 'Make AI Everywhere'. Within 15 years, they hope to make natural language available via AI, which can be aligned with images, speech and actions to understand and interpret general human behaviour in both the virtual and the real world.[13] Concretely, this means that Tencent aims by 2033 to have developed NLP (natural language processing) AI at a level that approaches equivalence with human speech, so that we will no longer be able to hear the difference between people and machines. This will make AI 'invisible' and will also allow it to understand us in the same way that a psychologist or life partner might currently do, or perhaps even better. Last but not least in this list of impressive projects, Xiaomi — the 'Apple of China' — has launched its MACE platform, which integrates AI with smartphones and virtual assistants as a means to bring the Internet-of-Things to life.

In China, people talk of the BAT internet giants (or BATX, if you add Xiaomi) in much the same way that people in the US talk about GAFA (Google, Amazon, Facebook and Apple). These are the companies that already possess so much data that they are potentially capable of becoming masters of the new AI world. But China is home to three other relatively younger players who are ready to join the heavyweights' club: Toutiao, Meituan and Didi (TMD)[14]. Toutiao was founded in 2012 and is a pure AI-driven news, video and music platform, which has grown rapidly to become the largest in the world. Meituan has been in business since 2010 and is now the world's largest food delivery platform, which uses AI to integrate the online and offline worlds. Finally, there is Didi, which was set up as recently as 2015 and is already the world's largest carpool service, significantly bigger than Uber, an achievement based on an AI-driven smart mobility platform and China's enormous consumer base. These seven Chinese giants are all heavily involved in long-term AI innovation projects that are every bit as impressive as those of their GAFA counterparts.

Privacy

The biggest challenge around AI is the question of privacy. Later in the book, I will explore why Chinese citizens deal and are concerned with privacy very differently from in the West, a crucial difference that is making it much easier to integrate AI into Chinese daily life. In some ways, the concept of privacy in the traditional Confucian model of society was not far from the modern Western view of privacy, in which individuals sought to protect their social identity within the close-knit circles of family and friends. In this respect, the main differences between East and West have developed over the past hundred years. People in the West have come to believe in the autonomy of the individual, so that each person now regards him or herself as being wholly independent of others. Chinese thinking has moved in the opposite direction, so that Chinese people feel the need for a social context to fully understand and develop themselves. They still attach great importance to intimate relationships and self-discovery, and therefore also to privacy, but framed within a societal rather than a purely individual setting. Of course, another key factor that reinforces this traditional societal setting is the intrusive nature of the Chinese Communist system which always prioritizes the 'common good' over individual rights, including privacy.

Up to the 21st century, most Chinese people grew up in a small apartment or house with their extended family, comprising various generations. As a result, people were seldom alone. Instead, they were part of a community, a community in which there was always a high degree of social control. Even when you went to school or university, you shared the same accommodation with half a dozen other students! This is just the Chinese way of life. When there are 1.4 billion of you, you grow up always surrounded by people, all the time. This proximity leads to a certain familiarity. Visitors to China are often surprised by the way their Chinese hosts ask them the most personal, intrusive questions. But this seeming absence of privacy is regarded as normal in a country where, of necessity, you need to share your life so closely with so many other people. In addition, today's modern Chinese are constantly seeking to improve their comfort of living, and if providing data to the tech giants is one way to do this, most consumers are happy to share it, much more so than their Western counterparts. For them, this is a no-brainer as their comfort has been tangibly improved by these tech giants; this also helps explain why Chinese consumers are less worried by new AI applications. This does not mean that there are no ethical discussions in China about privacy. There are, but they are mostly placed in a social context.

Distrust

The moral influence of Confucianism on Chinese society is still strong. The following Confucian values form the basis for all trust: face or prestige (miànzi 面子), relations (guānxi 关系), and human feelings (rénqíng 人情).

Mianzi refers to the social status that people acquire in a societal context, which allows them to command respect and trust. In the West, people can 'lose face' too, but in China the opposite process is much more important: gaining prestige. You can invest in someone with status or *mianzi* by showing them respect and making them feel important. This is the main reason why Chinese business leaders often get involved in politics: to increase their mianzi. *Mianzi* also explains why if or when the Chinese do something wrong within the context of the new social credit system (Smart Security), there will be no qualms about publicly naming and shaming them.

Guanxi refers to the intense Confucian ties within your own circle of family and friends. *Guanxi* covers the full range of your personal relationships and implies group thinking and taking care of each other. Trust within the group is very strong and it is almost impossible to develop this trust without friendship first. *Guanxi* therefore starts with the development of trust amongst friends, even if no immediate benefit accrues. In the West, it is perfectly possible to do business through legally binding contracts without *guanxi*. For the Chinese, guanxi is a mutual obligation to help each other and to maintain each other's mianzi.

This debt of reciprocity is also known as *Renqing*. If someone does you a favour, you are under an obligation to repay it. You owe him renqing. This element functions like a bank account of favours. It is the Chinese equivalent of 'You scratch my back and I'll scratch yours'. But in China trust is based less on other people's capacities to help effectively than on the certainty that renqing will be rendered when it is due; if not immediately, then at some point in the future, more like a savings account.

Based on the interplay of these three elements, trust in China has a number of different levels, depending on the respective balances of guanxi and mianzi, and also a number of different gradations, based on the amount of renqing given and received. This helps to explain why the Chinese are the most trustworthy people in the world, according to the World Values Survey, except when they are dealing with people they don't know, when their levels of distrust are also among the highest in the world. In fact, the Chinese are generally more willing to trust technology than strangers. They know that widely used technologies have has been validated by millions of people and by their own government, and that the results are based on mountains of accumulated data. What's more, AI means that online services can now be hyper personalised. In the West, we are still more inclined to trust people than new technology. In China, that is mainly the case for people with a higher social status, like politicians.

Challenges

Notwithstanding the Chinese economic renaissance over recent decades, in reality the country still faces huge problems today. For the past 30 years, journalists and economists have repeatedly predicted that the Chinese house of cards will one day crash to the ground under the weight of these problems. Which problems? Consider the environment: hundreds of cities are confronted with levels of air pollution that are off the scale; rivers and the soil across the country have become so contaminated that 90% of the ground water in cities is undrinkable.[15] Huge areas of forest have been cut down and the Gobi Desert continues to extend its already massive expanse.

But this is just the start. China faces plenty of other problems as well. The country needs to satisfy the ever-increasing expectations of its 1.4 billion citizens. There are also huge problems relating to the rapid ageing of the population, in part due to the 'one child' policy instituted in the 1980's. Moreover, changing consumer lifestyles in modern China mean that diseases such as heart failure and diabetes claim an increasing number of fatalities each year. These developments are side effects of the remarkable social and economic progress China made in recent times, with over 700 million people lifted out of poverty. Even so, today almost 50 million people are still living below the poverty line, while the rich continue to get richer, with all the social implications this entails.[16] Inequality is not a specifically Western phenomenon; it troubles many Chinese as well. Of course, there is no disputing that the nation as a whole is becoming increasingly more prosperous. But this prosperity, contrary to what you might expect from a country run by a communist party, is far from equally divided. Since the 1980s, China's Gini index — which measures a country's level of income inequality — has risen from 0.3 to just below 0.47 on a scale of 0 to 1 (with 0 meaning everyone earns exactly the same, while 1 meaning that a country's entire wealth is concentrated in the hands of a single person).[17] With its current Gini score, China is in a similar situation to countries like Mexico and Brazil.

Due to the imbalances in the Chinese economy, the cost of apartments in the big cities is now unaffordable for the vast majority of the population, while in other parts of the country ghost cities have been built. The frenzied level of speculation on the Shanghai and Shenzhen stock markets makes them seem more like open-air casinos than financial trading institutions. Many state-run and private companies have seen stock markets as a solution to conceal their underlying poor performance, whilst at the same time making individual owners and managers filthy rich.

China knows that these problems can only be solved by appropriate incentives and monitoring as well as a fair and working legal framework to back it up. It is for this reason that Xi Jinping wants to transform China into a state where the rule of law is respected and upheld. However, my personal observation is that the government is currently focused on issuing numerous 'guidelines', many of which are open to different interpretations, rather than issuing strict and legally binding rules or laws. In a meritocracy, a value which the Chinese claim is fundamental to their political system, it is crucial that the bureaucrats make the right decisions based on good facts and with measurable outcomes. In this respect, AI could be a huge help in justifying government policies, and demonstrating that decisions are neither corrupt nor biased, important factors within the context of the Xi Jinping regime. In fact, many Chinese leaders appear to be convinced that Artificial Intelligence and Big Data are the only ways to solve the large scale problems facing the country. In other words, for China AI is not a 'nice to have'; it is a 'must have', since it has the potential both to stave off impending social and ecological disaster and to stimulate further rapid economic development. Viewed in these terms, it is little wonder that China is so keen to invest in this revolutionary new technology.

The rebooting of China

The main reason why China has committed to AI is that the new technology has suddenly changed the rules of the game in a manner that will affect every industry across the globe. This transformation will not only be technological, but will also have cultural aspects, and its effects will be revolutionary. If you take the automotive and retail industries as examples, it is already clear that traditional companies like Volkswagen or Walmart will no longer be able to rely on half a century of expertise in their respective sectors, because one day most cars will be self-driving and most routine shopping will be done online. Today it is the data-driven companies who understand consumer behaviour, such as Tesla or Amazon, who hold all the trump cards. This is something that the Chinese have internalized. They know that if they want to be a world leader, they must do it in a future market that is currently being redefined by AI. China sees the opportunity to set new standards for the largest consumer market in the world by combining AI with Internet of Things (Smart Manufacturing) and Big Data. And early signs show China's strategy is working. Over the past five years, AI has helped numerous Chinese companies seize world leadership in their industry. As a result, AI has become the holy grail for the Chinese start-ups that hope to break through the monopolies of the 'BAT' in China and 'GAFA' of Silicon Valley. Companies like Toutiao (news app), Didi (car sharing) or DJI (drones) are already proving this on a global scale. It is true that these companies are the exceptions rather than the rule, but they highlight the fact that AI is the best strategy if you want to build up your own empire or ecosystem independently.

Hardware

When AI is discussed, people instinctively think in the first place about the difference between artificial intelligence and human intelligence. In other words, they think in terms of general AI or AI that will be smarter than we are. At the present time, AI cannot exceed human capacities when dealing with data that does not conform to a fixed set of rules. In other words, AI is currently mostly superior in terms of narrow AI tasks: it needs masses of structured data to make itself useful. Most of this data is generated by the internet or smart hardware. In China, internet data is largely in the hands of BATX or TMD. Data from the physical world is collected by sensors installed in hardware: smart phones and cameras, lamps, vehicles, fridges, wearables, retail shelves, virtual assistants, door locks and so many other devices. Where are the vast majority of these smart devices made? In China, of course.

China knows that collecting more data is a question of installing and accessing more sensors. In the chapter on manufacturing, I will describe how China will become the frontrunner in the development and production of smart hardware. The biggest impact that AI will have on society in the short term will not come from better AI algorithms, but from the scale and breadth of new AI applications. These applications will come from China, but, more importantly, they will first be integrated into the Chinese industry for the benefit of Chinese consumers before spreading across the rest of the world. China is now the AI laboratory for that world; this gives Chinese producers a huge lead over their international rivals.

Robot Love

In 2016, a Chinese university in Hefei developed a robot called 'JiaJia'. What made this robot so special (or even creepy, some say) is that it is the first of its kind that looks very much like a human being. It is so convincingly humanoid in appearance that if you did not know that JiaJia is a machine, you might think it was a real woman. 'She' is programmed for man-machine interaction and has a wide range of facial micro-expressions, mouth-body movement coordination, and autonomous positioning and navigation. JiaJia has even been taught etiquette, humour and voice pitch, because her creators wanted to make her as life-like as possible. The idea is to eventually use JiaJia in the hospitality sector. It reminds me of the film *Her*,[18] in which robots with human characteristics are capable of changing the balance of relationships between people. In fact, as early as 2015 there were already documented relationships between human beings and dolls, and the step from dolls to robots is only a small one. In this domain, as in so many others, in China the future is coming sooner than you might think.

Cultural differences mean that this feels less like science fiction in China than it does in the West. As a result, Chinese manufacturers have fewer reservations about integrating the emotional aspects of robots into human reality. In mid-2018, I visited the AI company Ling.ai in Beijing. Ling has developed a companion named LUKA to help young children discover their passion for reading. One of the ways it does this is by trying to display typical human traits: it is the first intelligent robot I have ever met that farts! This might seem like a detail (a strange and amusing one at that), but for me it was the writing on the wall: it symbolises a fundamental change in mentality and willingness to ascribe human characteristics to robots. Just as importantly, this becomes the New Normal for new generations of Chinese youth. In a similar vein, a company in Nanjing has developed the iPal robot to be used as a babysitter. In return for its 1,300 US Dollars purchase price, it will teach your child maths, tell it jokes and become its new best friend. No matter what we might think about this trend, it is certain that the Chinese will become increasingly attached to their new AI companions. They are already being widely incorporated into schools and the educational curriculum. For the current generation of Chinese children, living with robots — as 'friends' — will be their New Normal (Smart Education). The close intimacy that the Chinese people have with technology is inspiring thousands of Chinese entrepreneurs to innovate in the AI field.

EIGHT NEW NORMAL INDUSTRIES

In the past few years, China's far-reaching obsession with AI has led to an explosion of innovation in eight market sectors that I intend to describe in detail in the remainder of this book. The N-curve effect is very strong in these eight industries, so that the resulting impact on the West will be greatest. In these industries all the necessary conditions exist to make the switch to innovation leader status. These industries all enjoy a huge domestic market, with consumers hungry for innovation. In these industries local competitors have already built up a large customer base and amassed know-how. From a government perspective, these are industries where change is encouraged and supported as a means to transform China from a developing into a developed country, so that the future stability of the nation can be secured. In addition, these are industries where Chinese consumers have markedly different expectations from their counterparts in the West. And finally, these are industries that already integrate AI into their products and services as a lever to secure global leadership.

I will examine these eight industries in the order in which, in my opinion, their challenge to the West will be felt. Or to express it in slightly different terms: in the order in which the West will be able to see its own future in China. Until now, the world has always looked towards America and, in particular, Silicon Valley as the cradle of innovation, especially in matters where AI is the motor for that innovation. I predict, however, that the eight industries in China which I will describe are destined to take over that leading role and will become the world's new source of inspiration for the innovation of the future.

This process began in 2013 and will last until 2030, the year in which China plans to fulfil its stated ambition of becoming the world leader in innovation. This '2030' objective is being driven by Xi Jinping himself. In fact, I believe that this partially explains his decision to have himself eligible for reappointment as President of China for life or at least until 2030 (by which time he will be 78 years old), so that he can take the credit for the successful completion of this revolutionary transformation. Be that as it may, the history over the past 40 years suggests that when China makes large-scale and important plans, it usually manages to bring them to fruition. In other words, the West would be wise to look very closely at what is happening.

1. The first industry that has managed to steal a march on its Western rivals since 2013 is **Smart Security**. This emotionally charged area, which includes China's controversial social credit system, has caused us to look again at our own values relating to privacy and security. Do we have real cause for concern?

2. The second industry is **Smart Media & Entertainment**. Since 2015, companies like Tencent and others have led worldwide innovation in this sector. But what exactly are the tensions arising in the interplay between the main actors: the generation of Chinese digital consumers, a control-oriented government and the super-powerful tech companies?

3. 2017 was the year in which the term **New Retail** was coined by Alibaba, describing a trend that has had a worldwide impact on the sector, in which only Amazon has been able to keep up with the pace of its Chinese rivals. Who is the Chinese consumer and how is he approached differently from consumers in the West? Is China destined to become the worldwide epicentre of e-commerce?

4. 2019 is predicted to be the year of **Smart Finance & Insurance**, which will require Western bankers and insurers to come to terms with a new society of ecosystems and a world without cash. Now that the Chinese people have more money at their disposal and are already accustomed to paying digitally for nearly everything, is China set to become the example for the transformation of the financial industry?

5. As early as 2021, self-driving cars are expected to be seen on Chinese roads, allowing China to provide the world with a blueprint for **Smart Mobility**. Will people in the West all be driving Chinese cars in ten years' time or will Western car brands run on China's algorithms?

6. By 2023, most factories in China will have installed next generation robots, so that **Smart Manufacturing** will have its full impact from 2025 onwards. Is China truly evolving from 'Made in China' to 'Created in China'? Will China become the smart factory for the world or is the West destined to become the smart factory for China?

7. By 2025, I also predict that healthcare in China will have been so radically transformed that it will no longer be recognisable in its present form, with a new form of **Smart Health** being available for most Chinese citizens. Can China's transformation in this field perhaps help to solve the problems of employment and service provision in our Western health sector?

8. Finally, by 2030 I expect China to have replaced its presently outdated system of education with technology-based **Smart Education**. What lessons can China,

which currently has one of the most traditional education systems in the world, teach to educationalists in the West in the years ahead?

If you look at these eight sectors in relation to the chronology of their innovative impact, you can see that China will make its society as a whole smarter in six logical steps of universal social development, starting with the basic needs of consumers, followed by their material needs and, finally, their intellectual enrichment.

1. A safe and proud country – Smart Security
2. A happy and engaged country – Smart Media and Entertainment
3. A comfortable consumer experience – Smart Retail and Finance
4. An efficient industry – Smart Manufacturing
5. Better and healthier urban living – Smart Mobility and Health
6. A more intelligent Chinese – Smart Education

In books about Chinese innovation, many other industries are also mentioned. First and foremost, perhaps, the ten industries included in the 'Made in China 2025' programme (Smart Manufacturing), which includes additional sectors such as agriculture, space equipment, high-tech ships, new materials, energy networks, energy saving and clean-tech. The 'Made in China 2025' initiative is Beijing's strategic master plan for high-tech world domination. The intent is to invest strategically focus on China's most important national industries, from robotics, space travel and bio-technology to electric cars (all sectors with a significant added value), so that imported technology can be replaced by local production. China hopes that this will allow it to develop world-leading companies that are capable of competing globally with companies such as Intel, IBM or Tesla. This ambition is, unsurprisingly, a thorn in the side of the Americans, which explains President Trump's actions in proclaiming a state of technology 'war' with China. And it is true that although China has the potential to create world-leading companies in these sectors, China's plan places a heavy emphasis on state intervention and investment to achieve this potential.

With this in mind, I have consciously chosen eight industries whose transformation is driven not only by government support, but also by market forces in the form of companies and consumers. This provides us with a strong basis for identifying the elements that truly constitute the key pillars of China's New Normal. The key question is how we, in the West, will respond to this dramatic change. Will we surf on the wave of Chinese innovation or will we be washed up on the shore of obsolescence? In my opinion, the lessons of the Chinese innovation revolution are there for the taking and offer the West a way to secure its position in the world of the future. During the past three decades, China has examined everything the West has done under a microscope. It has seen what has worked and what has not worked. It has rejected the bad and adapted the good to its own needs and circumstances. Now the time has come for us in the West to do the same to China in return. Has China made the right choices? Perhaps, perhaps not. The future will tell. That being said, China is currently making such rapid progress in a reasonably stable manner that it certainly makes sense to try and learn all we can about the new China and its strategies. There is no reason why we, too, cannot adopt things from the Chinese model that can work for us, leaving to one side the things that seem less appropriate. What's more, there is now no shortage of China experts with hands-on experience who can guide us through this process. In other words, there is no excuse for any further delay.

EGG OR BANANA ?

No, I am not talking about a diet rich in vitamins and minerals, although I wish I could make every Western company into a body builder to take on the might of the new China. No, 'egg' is the description Chinese people give to Westerners who know China 'inside-out', who have almost become Chinese: in other words, 'white on the outside, but yellow on the inside'. Of course, a banana is exactly the opposite: 'Yellow on the outside and white on the inside'. In other words, a Chinese person who has an intimate knowledge of the West or who behaves like a Westerner. And although it might seem racist for a Westerner to call a Chinese person 'yellow' or a 'banana', in fact my Chinese friends have no problem to call me an 'egg', if they want to give me a 'yellow face' in the presence of their Chinese friends and acquaintances. This is well-meaning on their part, but it has always given me a mixed feeling, because I still regard myself as being very much a European and a Belgian. But this is not always the case with a growing number of my own Western 'egg' friends in China. Many of them now boast that they could never live happily back in the slow, indecisive and complicated West. For them, everything in China is always better. That is not my opinion. At the same time, I am fortunate enough to have many other 'egg' friends who do continue to inspire me, because they know China like the back of their hand (often better than the average Chinese themselves). In my experience, China is not better or worse than Europe or America: it is just different... and often very different. A different normal? A New Normal? At the same time, sometimes it is also remarkably similar. Unexpectedly similar. After all, at the end of the day we are all people, aren't we?

Innovation is also the product of people, at least for the time being. For this reason, I will devote much more attention in this book to the motives and transformations caused by Chinese companies and consumers than to those driven by the Chinese government. I realise that as a result a number of important issues will not be discussed in depth, such as human rights, state control, expansionism or espionage. Although these topics are all relevant and the necessary questions need to be asked, in my opinion it is China's urge to innovate that we in the West need to take more seriously, since this poses the biggest clear and present threat to our economy and our way of life. That being said, we should not lose sight of the fact that the possibility of a military confrontation between China and America cannot be ruled out. We are probably living in the most uncertain era since the end of the Cold War. If America continues to taunt the Chinese dragon (Smart Security), the resulting tension might lead to military conflict. In this unimaginable situation, the resultant war, in my opinion, would not be a cold one, but the real thing. China in fact does not resemble at all the old Soviet Union, which was isolated from the rest of the world and always in an economically weak position vis-à-vis the West. If this terrifying scenario ever comes to pass, no books will be able to help us.

In the following pages I will regularly offer my personal interpretation with regard to certain objectives of the Chinese government, especially if these objectives have an impact on innovation. But I am not a political scientist, academic or military adviser, so I cannot claim to provide a definitive insight into the way Xi Jinping and/or the Communist Party are thinking. There are others better qualified to ask such questions, but perhaps that mea culpa misses the point. I believe the real question we should be asking is about China's massive innovation drive. It is this question that can mean the difference between success and failure for our Western companies and their employees during the coming decades. That is why I have made it the central theme of this book.

THE CHINESE PUZZLE

Chinese who are different from us, yet the same. A government that is strongly directive but whose message is often unclear. Confusing? Perhaps, but that is the paradox of China. I have consciously chosen to write my book in the same non-linear manner. Not logically or chronologically. That would be too much of a Western, deductive 'cause and effect' approach. No, a country where everything is in movement needs to be dealt with more fluidly and flexibly. If you want to understand the Chinese, you need to use their own inductive way of thinking (Smart Health). You must approach China as if you were a backpacking tourist, starting on a journey through an unknown country with a mind open to new ideas and new impressions. Or as an explorer, keen to discover what has previously been hidden. Or as an inquisitive detective like Hercule Poirot, anxious to solve the mystery by slowly unravelling the puzzle step by step, until the truth is finally revealed. To help you in your quest, in each chapter I will alternate stories of my personal experiences with insights into Chinese culture and the Chinese way of thinking. I will share facts and figures that suggest the directions in which key trends are moving, interesting correlations that will often lead to 'eureka!' moments, and data that makes clear the scale, speed and ambitious nature of China's plans for the future. The pace will be fast and furious, to match the tempo and intensity of developments in China, because it is important to get a sense of how the Chinese are able to survive and thrive in a world that never stands still.

In other words, it is not my intention to give a detailed description of China industry by industry, but rather to provide a general guide that will serve to show how China is positioning itself as the new standard in innovation. The Chinese themselves do not think in terms of industries or sectors, but think instead in terms of ecosystems (Smart Retail) that transcend industrial and sectoral boundaries. This is the only way to get a clear and broad view of China's new world of innovation. My hope is that each chapter will help to make the Chinese puzzle a little clearer and will prompt you to take the action that will allow you to stand your ground against China's New Normal.

Because things are moving so quickly, it is reasonable to assume that some of the facts and figures in this book will already be out of date by the time you read them. This, too, is characteristic of China. If you want to keep up-to-date with all the most recent evolutions, I invite you to follow the twists and turns of Chinese innovation with me on my website: www.chinasnewnormal.com. In the final chapter, I will offer some tips about what we in the West can learn from Chinese innovation and how we can prepare ourselves to come to terms with the new standards of innovation that China is re-defining for the entire world.

China sets the standard: from 2013 to 2030

2013

1

SMART SECURITY

The first industry that has managed to steal a march on its Western rivals since 2013 is **Smart Security**. This emotionally charged area, which includes China's controversial social credit system, has caused us to look again at our own values relating to privacy and security. Do we have real cause for concern?

2015

2

SMART MEDIA & ENTERTAINMENT

The second industry is **Smart Media & Entertainment**. Since 2015, companies like Tencent and others have led worldwide innovation in this sector. But what exactly are the tensions arising in the interplay between the main actors: the generation of Chinese digital consumers, a control-oriented government and the super-powerful tech companies?

2017

3

SMART RETAIL

2017 was the year in which the term **New Retail** was coined by Alibaba, describing a trend that has had a worldwide impact on the sector, in which only Amazon has been able to keep up with the pace of its Chinese rivals. Who is the Chinese consumer and how is he approached differently from in the West? Is China destined to become the worldwide epicentre of e-commerce?

2019

4

SMART FINANCE & INSURANCE

2019 is predicted to be the year of **Smart Finance & Insurance**, which will require Western bankers and insurers to come to terms with a new society of ecosystems and a world without cash. Now that the Chinese people have more money at their disposal and are already accustomed to paying digitally for nearly everything, is China set to become the example for the transformation of the financial industry?

2021

5

SMART MOBILITY

As early as 2021, self-driving cars are expected to be seen on Chinese roads, Ï43allowing China to provide the world with a blueprint for **Smart Mobility**. Will people in the West all be driving Chinese cars in ten years' time or will Western car brands run on China's algorithms?

2023

6

SMART MANUFACTURING

By 2023, most factories in China will have installed next generation robots, so that **Smart Manufacturing** will have its full impact from 2025 onwards. Is China truly evolving from 'Made in China' to 'Created in China'? Will China become the smart factory for the world or is the West destined to become the smart factory for China?

2025

7

SMART HEALTH

By 2025, I also predict that healthcare in China will have been so radically transformed that it will no longer be recognisable in its present form, with a new form of **Smart Health** being available for most Chinese citizens. Can China's transformation in this field perhaps help to solve the problems of employment and service provision in our Western health sector?

2030

8

SMART EDUCATION

Finally, by 2030 I expect China to have replaced its present outdated system of education with technology-based **Smart Education**. What lessons can China, which currently has one of the most traditional educa-tion systems in the world, teach to educationalists in the West in the years ahead?

117299

<
Police in China at work with the intelligent glasses of Xloong, which compares faces in the crowd with details from the national database of criminals.

1 SMART SECURITY

CHINA SETS THE STANDARD: FROM 2013 TO 2030

The first industry that has managed to steal a march on its Western rivals since 2013 is **Smart Security**. This emotionally charged area, which includes China's controversial social credit system, has caused us to look again at our own values relating to privacy and security. Do we have real cause for concern?

2013 2015 2017 2019 2021 2023 2025 2030

'UNQUALIFIED' CHINESE?

For me, the year 1998 was a turning point in my life. It was the year in which I turned thirty, got married and was selected to take part in an MBA training course organised by the European Commission in China. The idea was that each year Europe would groom 35 or so young managers in the skills necessary to negotiate with the Chinese business world. Ten years earlier, I started studying Chinese at university, but now this was to be supplemented by practical instruction in the country itself. This training took place at Shanghai Bell, a major joint-venture company of Alcatel's in China. At that time, nearly all the Belgians in Shanghai worked for Alcatel, but the 'powers that be' decided to drop me in the middle of thousands of Chinese working at their local joint-venture partner. I can remember it as if it were yesterday. In those days many of the Belgians at Alcatel-China failed to take the Chinese in Shanghai Bell seriously. In fact, some ignorantly regarded them as 'unqualified' Chinese. From the European perspective, the local partner still had so much to learn and its work needed to be checked and monitored every step of the way. If you weren't constantly looking over your partner's shoulder, you couldn't assume the work would get done correctly. Many of the Europeans tried to convince themselves that the Chinese side of the joint venture didn't have a problem with this directive approach. Since the Communist Revolution of 1949, the assumption was that Chinese employees had become used to this kind of thing and were trained to obey and copy instructions perfectly, 'just like a mimic fool'. Or at least such was the general — and highly patronising — opinion.

In contrast, I found that my Chinese colleagues had huge respect for the Belgians. They knew that they could learn from them, in the hope that they and Alcatel would one day soon provide China with the best telecommunications system in the world. At the time, the 'enemy' of Shanghai Bell was not the foreign 'invaders', but Huawei, a new Chinese company based in Shenzhen that had been engaged for years in reverse engineering of Western technology. Huawei was founded by a former military engineer, Ren Zhenfei, who in 1994 persuaded the President of China, Jiang Zemin, that a country without its own switching equipment technology was effectively a country without an army. It is ironic that 25 years later, Huawei's 5G infrastructure is now regarded as a major threat to the national security of Western countries. In effect, the roles have been reversed. But back in the 1990's, things were different. In 1996 the Chinese government decided to limit the activities of foreign communication companies and poured support into the key local players such as Huawei and ZTE. In policy documents at the time, Beijing referred to Huawei as the 'national champion' of China, a company in which making a profit was subordinated to the higher goal of serving the national interest. Over time, this gave Huawei an unfair competitive advantage over Alcatel, which, thanks to the Shanghai Bell joint venture, was the only foreign telecom provider still able to operate normally in China.

Over this period, I was working in the marketing and sales team at Shanghai Bell, which gave me the opportunity to regularly take part in customer prospecting visits. In 1999, I travelled to the four corners of China in an attempt to sell our intelligent switching system to China Telecom. No matter where I went the same scenario always unfolded. There were three of us in our team: a seller, a technician and me as the token 'big nose', [19] whose presence was supposed to underline the quality of what we were offering. We always knew that somewhere down the corridor the people from Huawei were waiting to give their sales pitch once we were finished. There were never fewer than ten people in their team, and they came dressed as though they were getting ready to go into battle, rather than into a meeting. They were able to promise a better price, better service and probably better kickbacks (which wasn't difficult, because we weren't giving any). It was as though we were trying to win the commercial fight armed with a water pistol, while they were armed with a real cannon. At the time, the Chinese team of Shanghai Bell had more expertise, a better product and a much higher standard of business ethics. On their side, backed by the government, the Chinese team at Huawei had brute force, or that's the way it seemed at the time.

Whenever we attended trade fairs, the Alcatel stand was always close to the Huawei stand. Our typical display was full of comfortable leather sofas, video screens and crates of champagne. The Huawei stand was a sprawling mess of shelves, cables and switching gear. Our slogans were all about 'listening to our customers' needs' and providing them with a 'total solution'. Theirs were more in the spirit of a door-to-door salesman selling vacuum cleaners. We regarded them as amateurs and were convinced that the customers would come flocking back to us as soon as they realised that the Huawei systems didn't deliver what they promised. But the customers did not come back, and Huawei continued to get better and better. In hindsight, the real main difference between us and them was Huawei's unrelenting will to win. Slowly but surely, the Alcatel brand disappeared from the China market, and it was our own arrogance that was our undoing. Twenty years later, I can still recognise this same arrogance in the approach of many Westerners to Chinese technology, but this time in the field of software, rather than hardware. Are we going to make the same mistakes again?

THE FOURTH INDUSTRIAL REVOLUTION

The fourth industrial revolution builds on the foundations laid by the digital revolution, which in the years following 1980 connected the whole world via computers, the internet and communication technology. This fourth revolution is based on new technologies that will not only become deeply anchored in human society, but also, in some cases, literally inside the human body: robotics, AI, IoT, 3D-printing, nanotech, biotech, quantum computing, blockchain and self-driving cars.

These up-and-coming new technologies are set to disrupt the business world from top to bottom. Just as importantly (if not more so), they are also destined to turn the existing socio-political world order on its head. China has clearly understood that the start of the new industrial revolution also marks the start of a new arms race. The side which has the most advanced intelligence in its weapons arsenal will have the strongest military apparatus. In the 21st century, this is less a matter of building nuclear warheads, jet fighters and rockets and more about the development of a commercial infrastructure for mobile communication, IoT (Internet of Things), smart factories, databanks and online recommendations. These are the technologies and fields of research that will power the most advanced weapons of the future. In this world of intelligent industry 4.0 everything will be closely interconnected, which will make the entire world more vulnerable, since both the military and the cyber-criminals will have at their disposal highly efficient commercial algorithms that can easily be used to create smarter weapons, better intelligence and non-traceable means of attack. The Chinese government sees its participation in this new high-tech arms race as part of their moral and political obligation to protect the nation. It is simply a question of national security, all the more so in an era when most technological development will always be capable of serving a dual purpose: both commercial and military.

It is already clear that China is destined to become one of the world's great military superpowers. To guarantee its own security, China is pinning its faith on three key technologies: 5G (fifth generation telecom), Quantum Computing and Artificial Intelligence. And in all three of these fields China looks set to beat the Americans, by 2030 at the latest. These three advanced technologies are capable of enriching all our lives, but at the same time it is impossible to deny their applications for military purposes. This is nothing new. Military and civilian technologies have been influencing each other for decades. After all, the internet (or ARPAnet) was initially a military invention, as were sat-nav systems, drones, radar, microwaves, digital cameras, computers and much, much more. Nowadays, however, this trend is working increasingly in the opposite direction, with commercial applications now being more frequently used as the basis for new military applications, thanks in no small measure to the availability of masses of data (for AI), almost limitless IoT communication (via 5G) and super-rapid processing (with quantum computers in the near future), all of which are already present in the commercial world on a large scale.

5G

5G networks rely on the use of more compact bundles of many smaller antennas, which makes it possible to improve the data speeds compared to 4G by between 50 and 200 times. In concrete terms, this means that it will be possible to download a full HD film in just a matter of seconds. Or that a surgeon in New York can perform a long-distance operation in Brussels. Or that hundreds of self-driving cars can make their way through the busiest of city centres in perfectly choreographed safety. Of the four companies with the best 5G telecommunication infrastructures, two are Chinese: Huawei and ZTE. The other two are Ericsson and Nokia, whose worldwide turnover in both cases is less than a quarter of Huawei's. Not surprisingly, it is Huawei that has so far concluded the biggest number of 5G agreements in both Europe and Asia. Nor should we forget that Huawei secured the deals for half of the 4G networks and 65 percent of the 4.5G networks.[20] This is not a monopoly level position, but it is a good place to start. 5G is the next step in Huawei's plan to maintain their world dominance in this field.

5G does much more than simply offer us faster internet. Above all, it is an important factor for making the world of IoT a reality, a world in which China is both the largest producer and user of sensors. Sensors of the kind that are contained in your cell phone (there are probably at least a dozen of them, ranging from temperature to motion detection) are constantly gathering all kinds of data and information. In an ideal IoT world, sensors and 5G make it possible for every person, every device, every product and even some animals to send useful data to each other without the need for human interaction. 5G opens up the possibility for a broader mobile spectrum, but the number of signal frequencies will also increase in comparison with 4G. These extremely high 5G frequencies will be able to transfer more data than in the past, but that data will reach less far and can be more easily blocked by intervening obstacles, so that more transmitters and antennas are needed to ensure effective functioning. As a result, the 5G network will be more decentralised and more complex. This offers the potential to move between the different frequencies almost undetected, which obviously has national security implications. It was this aspect of 5G technology that led the Trump administration in August 2018 to propose a ban on the use of Huawei and ZTE technology by US Government departments and contractors, as part of the Defense Authorization Act that will come into effect in 2020.[21] But the American president does not intend to wait that long. At the time of writing (early 2019), the White House has already started a witch-hunt against Huawei to persuade all America's alliance partners in the West not to purchase the company's 5G technology.

The race for 5G is hugely important and all the leading world players see it as a number one priority. South Korea and China currently seem to be head-to-head in the contest to be the first to commercially implement 5G, but America, India, Japan, Russia, the United Kingdom and France all have plans to provide 5G to their largest cities by the end of 2020. So, what is all the fuss about? The country that is first to roll out a national mobile 5G network will gain a huge advantage over the rest of the world by virtue of what Deloitte has called the 'data network effect'. This is the effect by which the 5G pioneer can generate users much more quickly, which in turn generates data in massive quantities much more quickly, which allows services to be improved, so that even more new users can be attracted, and so the cycle continues. This creates a kind of snowball effect in which China already has three major competitive advantages over its rivals: a substantially higher number of smartphone users, a clear government vision to develop a national infrastructure network as soon as possible, and a greater willingness from consumers and network operators to offer and use 5G.

In America, T-Mobile and Sprint wish to merge, in part so that they can win the 5G race. However, similar merger talks are also taking place between China Telecom and China Mobile. When rivals suddenly start working together, this is usually a sign of just how much is at stake and how serious the situation has become. According to Deloitte, China is once again ahead of the game, with three times the number of mobile telephone masts per user and 13 times the reach per square mile, thanks largely to lower material costs and fewer licensing problems.[22] China is further encouraged by the commercial war weariness of the main Western mobile network operators, who saw their turnover per user decrease by 15 percent following the introduction of 4G, whereas the turnover of Chinese operators has increased by the same amount in recent years.[23] China only rolled out 4G as recently as 2014, which made it much cheaper than in other countries, while simultaneously experiencing an explosion in the number of users switching from 3G to 4G. As a result, China currently has a total of some 1.1 billion 4G users.[24] The West is clearly facing an uphill battle — and that's putting it mildly![25, 26]

A QUANTUM LEAP

Time for some technical stuff — but I promise to keep it short. A current state-of-the-art transistor measures 14 nanometres across: that is one millionth of a metre. A transistor is a mini-electronics component that can amplify signals and functions as a switch in computers, in a manner comparable with one of the 100 billion neurons in the human brain. If we could reduce the size of transistors to just 2 nanometres across, this would mean that they would be no more than 10 atoms wide. When we are dealing with scales as minute as this, we have entered the world of quantum physics or, if you prefer, the science of elementary particles. Traditional digital computers work by processing 'bits' in just two unique states: 0 or 1. In contrast, quantum computers are not limited to these two unique states, but can store information in 'quantum bits' or 'qubits' in the form of 0 and 1, the superposition of 0 and 1. In addition, qubits are capable of entanglement, which means that they can share their state with other qubits in space. This allows them to create a kind of super-superposition, which doubles the processing capacity of each individual qubit. In a well-known experiment, the physicist Erwin Schrödinger[27] attempted to clarify this phenomenon with reference to a cat in a closed box. Given the conditions of the experiment, there was a possibility that the cat was either 100% alive or 100% dead, but you cannot know which until you open the box. Up to that point, according to quantum law and the superposition of states, the cat is a combination of both states; in other words, both alive and dead. It is only when you take a measurement — i.e., look inside the box — that the superposition ceases to be and the cat is either alive or dead. A measurement or observation is therefore required to reduce the cat to a single state. Most measurements and observations today are still done using traditional computers with traditional bits. But if you could develop an algorithm based on five entangled qubits, it would be able to do this 32 (two to the power of five) times quicker than the ordinary computer. In concrete terms, this technology would make it possible, for instance, to discover the very large prime numbers that could be necessary for the operation of the crypto-currency world, in which bitcoin is currently the best-known example. If this all sounds like 'Chinese' to you, don't worry: you are probably not alone. But on this occasion, at least, it is not the fault of the Chinese!

This sounds like science fiction and to most people it seems crazy to argue that a chair can be simultaneously in Beijing and Washington. But at the micro-level such things are observable. A quantum computer looks like a series of super-cold tubes and lasers, which slows down the speed of atoms. Lasers are also used to programme the computer. It is not yet clear what the first 'killer application' of Quantum Computing will be, nor when it is likely to be developed, but one possibility is that it will first be used for problems that are too difficult for traditional computers to solve, such as finding mega-large prime numbers, as mentioned above. In China, chemical or life science simulations with quantum computers are being researched to be used in the design of medicines and new battery technologies, for example. There is a general feeling that whoever succeeds first in using quantum computers effectively will secure a huge economic advantage. Once again, this would not only be a commercial advantage: quantum technology has the potential to analyse complex war simulations that are far beyond the ability of today's normal computers.

The stakes are therefore as high as they can possibly be. China has already surprised the world with the building of its Tianhe supercomputers, the fastest computers on the planet that approach the processing capacity of the human brain. But an efficient and more affordable quantum super-computer would take the power game to a new level that neither America nor China could afford to ignore. In fact, a breakthrough in quantum technology could mean the dawn of a new world order. For example, Quantum Computing could help with:

1. the development of a communications system that is immune to hacking;
2. a new navigation system that can operate without the need for satellites;
3. a new signal processing system that would make hostile stealth submarines and aircraft visible.

China is currently building its first mega-quantum computer in the city of Hefei with a budget of 10 billion dollars and hopes to have it operational by the end of 2020. America has responded with a proposal in Congress to invest a total of 1.3 billion dollars in quantum technology.

In 2016, China launched its first quantum satellite[28] for encryption purposes and in 2018 Chinese scientists again set new world records for multi-particle entanglement.[29]

America still has a lead in quantum research, thanks to the combined efforts of Google, IBM and Microsoft, but Alibaba and Baidu have moved up a gear in recent years, so that the American lead is shrinking. At the same time, the Chinese army is also developing a quantum compass and quantum radar. If China continues to make progress at this impressive rate, it may not be too many more years before the sleeping dragon is able to take the quantum leap that will see it replace the United States as the world's leading military superpower.

CHINA'S NEW LEADERS

Although there are hundreds of books about Chinese politics and its leaders, I believe the single most important thing you need to understand is just how much effort the Chinese government is making to accelerate progress towards the New Normal and to motivate the population to continue supporting the transition. In recent decades, more than 1 billion Chinese have made significant material progress and, in the process, have acquired a taste for more. The interests of the individual are growing stronger with each passing year and in many respects, China seems to have become the most capitalist country in the world. China's citizens have no intention of giving up their newfound freedoms, norms and material possessions. That particular point of no return was already reached some time ago. So, where does this leave the regime? Xi Jinping often talks about China's political system as being one of "Socialism with Chinese characteristics". But what does that mean exactly? My interpretation is that China is so far the only country in the world to have successfully reconciled communism with capitalism. Perhaps you can compare the Chinese system with a social 'qubit', which is permanently capable of being in more than one state. The final state is only determined once the result is verified. This is reflected in the Chinese government's obsession with data, which has much to do with the education and background of Chinese leaders in various fields of the exact sciences, often engineering. They constantly go in search of new facts and figures to evaluate things, to open the box in which the cat is contained. Is this wise? Deng Xiaoping thought so. Describing China's economic reforms, he once famously said: "It doesn't matter if a cat is white or black; as long as it can catch mice, it's a good cat." His idea was that results can often solve problems, reducing the need for ideological debate and stimulating the search for new solutions by having the courage to take action. Is China a planned economy or a market economy? For Deng, like the colour of the cat, it didn't matter. In the pragmatic Chinese approach, 'capitalism' can have a plan and 'socialism' can have a market. The Chinese 'cat' economy is more about making sure that the right resources are made available to achieve the desired outcome and less about the nature of the economic system itself.

But how are these left-brain politicians chosen in China? Put simply, local administrations are elected after nominations have been made through a recommendation process known as 'three ups and three downs',[30] in which a list of electable candidates is drawn up after three rounds of debate. This list is then submitted for final choice to the eligible voters (whose numbers are relative to the size of the district). In contrast, the upper echelons of the People's Congress, the most senior organ of political power in China, are chosen indirectly by the members of the echelons immediately below them.

In a highly simplified graphic below (figure 6), you can see how the Chinese electoral system works from the bottom up, starting with the ordinary citizen. But it also shows how the balance between the local administrations and the higher reaches of government is maintained through a process of dialogue and debate. In principle, this means that citizens can have their say and are able to influence decisions, through consultations with their local administrators, who have an incentive to listen if they wish to be re-elected and move higher up the political ladder. The consultative nature of this model is designed to bring positive change to the local population and to measure the progress made. Contrary to what many Westerners might think, strikes and protests are common in China, but they usually take place at this local level, so that they remain much less visible, and even less widely reported. But this does not make them any the less effective in creating pressure for change. It is this bottom-up advisory and top-down advice-seeking model that allows China to act so quickly. I call it the Chinese 'political yo-yo model', because it is constantly in motion and its own momentum makes it possible for the leaders to constantly make new spins.

Figure 6

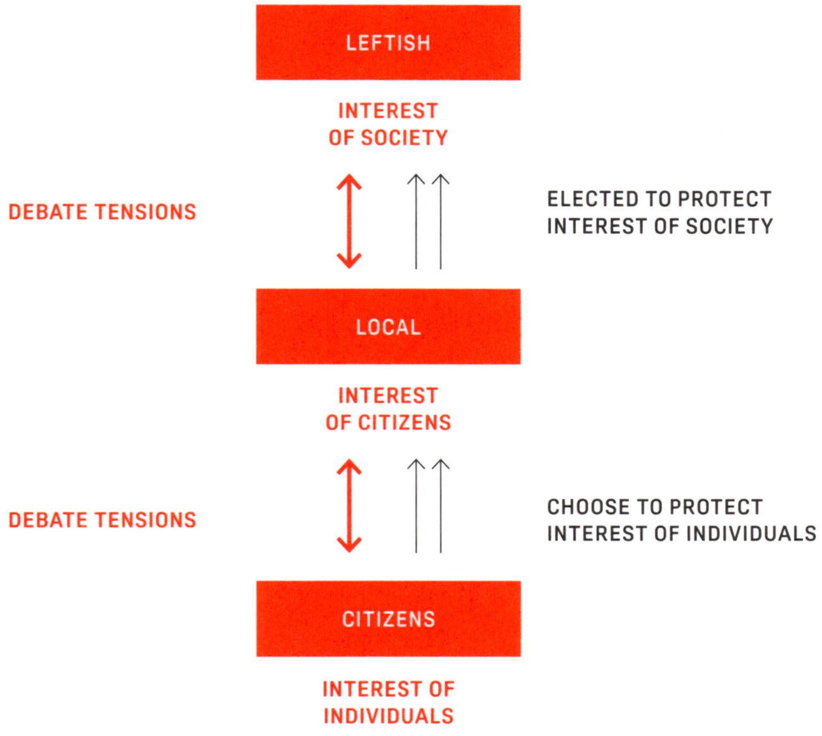

Western politicians often have a background in political, social or legal studies, in which debate and argumentation are central pillars of the political process. In this system, the person who is most convincing to more people has the highest chance of being elected. This has both advantages and disadvantages. As soon as politicians are in power, they debate on a number of matters that are eventually converted into legislation. This continues until the next set of elections comes around. Viewed from a Chinese perspective, this seems like a political version of Newton's cradle. A constant swinging movement back and forth, where the politicians need to absorb each other's often negative energy and push it in the opposite direction. Once the leaders are chosen, the people can continue to exert pressure through demonstrations and petitions, but this, paradoxically, often tends to slow down decision-making instead of speeding it up — certainly compared with the speed and decisiveness of China.

Figure 7

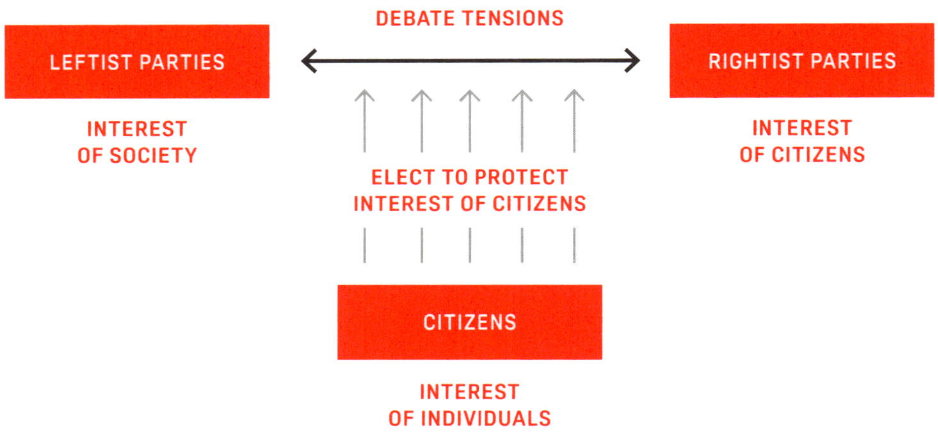

Every country believes that its own system is the best. But it is certain that China could never have become the country it is today — a country which has managed to lift some 700 million people out of poverty since 1990 — under a democratic system. This was only possible thanks to the fast-moving top-down yo-yo model, which has the ability to accelerate societal action while still keeping it stable — at least for the time being.

CHINESE NATURE LOVERS

After my time at Alcatel, I started my career in 2000 by joining a medium-sized Belgian company that made an operating system for signal processors, the MS Windows equivalent for more complex applications such as intelligent telecom, security cameras, sonar and radar. My time at the Shanghai Bell joint venture had given me a list of useful contacts. The sectors in China that showed most interest in our products were, unsurprisingly, the space, air and maritime industries. For each sale of a package of software and hardware we needed an export license, even when we were selling to a university, since our technology always contained some American components. For me, it was already clear 20 years ago that the United States wanted to control who could benefit from its technology and who could not, and the Chinese were not on their wish-list.

At the start of the new century, China's technology learning curve was only just beginning to turn upwards. The vast majority of its present legion of scientific researchers were still at their teaching desk in one of the country's many universities or research institutes. During that period, I travelled the length and breadth of the Chinese countryside and met many incredibly smart Chinese. The institutes all had a number, but no name, and I knew at least a hundred such numbers by heart. Those were very different times: back then, you could easily make an appointment to see the president of the No.1 Space or Sea Institute and they were happy to meet you and show you everything they were working on. With great passion they explained to me, for example, how they had developed a super-sonar with 600 of the world's most powerful signal sensors, so that they could track whales in deep seas. Or how they were building unmanned aircraft to prevent forest fires or predict earthquakes. Whales, forest fires, earthquakes...? Had the Chinese suddenly become nature-loving environmentalists? Even at the time, I didn't think so; the ulterior motives were not hard to find.

EXPENSIVE IS BETTER

Back then, the Chinese also had a different way of communicating about business. Our other international customers knew exactly what they wanted, but not the Chinese. If a Western customer was researching the possible purchase of a new 3G telecommunications system, we would have weeks of discussion about which hardware platform would best serve their requirements. The customers knew our products in detail before they bought them and, as a result, bombarded us with relevant questions. In contrast, the Chinese simply asked us what we had in stock and then went off to find the budget that would allow them to purchase our most expensive products. Money was seldom a problem and we were always paid up front. In China, you often sold more if you increased your prices. This was a tactic that (among many others) Nokia certainly used back then. If the sales figures for a specific product were disappointing, they simply hiked up the price and sales started to grow again, according to my friend Dan Wong, a former vice-president of Nokia in China. The best strategy was straightforward: to make everything as dear as possible. As a result, these were boom years for companies like GE, IBM and Siemens. However, this process also worked to the benefit of the Chinese army today, since for 20 years they bought and had access to the most expensive — and therefore the best — Western technology.

Our company also provided one of these expensive products to lots of professors at the Chinese universities, and I consequently had to give training to hundreds of Chinese students. Some days we felt more like professors sharing knowledge than technology suppliers. It was during this period that I chose my Chinese first name BOSI (博思), which literally means 'many thoughts', primarily because it sounds like the word BOSHI (博士 BOSHI), which means 'professor', although it is written with a different character. My full name in Chinese is KEBOSI (柯博思), an onomatopoeic form of Coppens. At this time, there was still no inkling that China would one day overtake the technical expertise of the West. By then, I was valued by the company as our top salesman in China and as someone who knew the country inside out. In 2001, to make use of this sales skill and my China experience I was rewarded with a transfer to the company headquarters in Silicon Valley. And so, I briefly left behind China, at that time still a peacefully sleeping dragon.

MILITARY CATCH-UP

By 2006, I was back in China, where our company was now selling a similar product to the one I had sold earlier in 2000. But now my Chinese customers suddenly wanted much more from their suppliers. Suddenly, they were willing to pay for applications and for expertise. However, I was no longer able to visit these customers in their institutes and when we met, they were careful to never mention a word about what they were doing, not even about the whales! Since our company was unable to supply any applications — that was the business of our customers — selling became difficult, notwithstanding all the good relationships I had built up in the past. By 2010, our sales had fallen almost to zero. Slowly but surely, and in all quietness, the Chinese had caught up with us.

The Chinese military apparatus is very different today from the way it was in the year 2000. During the past two decades it has emerged from the shadows and overcome its inferiority complex. Twenty years ago, you could see this complex everywhere in China's technology sectors. For years, Korea had almost exactly the same complex about Japan. It is not that the Chinese lack confidence in their belief that they will one day become the biggest and the best, but they have been extremely cautious up until recently about making this claim too openly. However, the turning point in this process is now approaching rapidly, with growing nationalist sentiment as a result.

Today, the Chinese military have no reason to be anything but confident. Thanks to the catch-up operation of the past 20 years, they are now strong and powerful. What's more, China's display of military power is backed by the entire Chinese population. Defence spending in China has increased nine-fold since the turn of the century, from 26 billion dollars to 228 billion dollars in 2017. This is four times more than India, Saudi Arabia, Russia, the United Kingdom or France, but still three times less than the massive 661 billion US Dollars spent by the United States. This new Chinese military power goes hand in hand with economic power. Inside China, it is increasingly being mentioned that the country must be able to defend itself. This inward-looking perspective and the associated fear that outsiders may once again attack China has been a constant in Chinese history for more than 2,000 years. It was not without good reason that the ancient Chinese built a 21,196[31] kilometre-long wall to keep out the 'barbarians'. And more recent history — with the Opium War and European dominance in the 19th century and the bloody invasion of China by Japan in 1937 as the twin low-water marks — suggests that such fears may not be groundless, at least in Chinese eyes.

MILITARY EXPANSION

What does this new military balance of power mean for the West? This is a question I am often asked. Should we be afraid of China's renewed military might? Certainly, in the past I never saw China as a 'conqueror' of other countries; as the Chinese like to explain, expansion is not historically part of their genetic make-up. China's first considerations have always been defensive rather than offensive. But there are signs that this is changing. In 2017, China set up a military base on the Horn of Africa in Djibouti, a country with fewer than 1 million inhabitants and no natural resources. The main aim was to protect their commercial investments that are channelled through the major port there which is the gateway to China's wide-ranging economic interests in the African continent. If another country had the same level of interests in Africa as China, setting up a military base in Djibouti would be seen as a logical step (for this reason, the Americans and the Japanese already have one). But for China this is something new. It seems that defence of China's national security is now to be extended to defence of China's overseas commitments. This implies the use of a blue-water fleet operating throughout the world's open seas. Yet another New Normal that the West will need to accept.

There are, of course, some other areas that China does wish to physically reclaim; namely, the island of Taiwan and approximately 90 percent of the islands in the South China Sea, where there are important reserves of gas and oil, as well as several main international shipping routes. China wants these areas under its sovereignty, and, if necessary, is willing to wait a hundred years to get them. However, the situation is complex. The main danger is that the Americans will want to play 'war games' with China in the South China Sea, which might easily escalate into a real conflict. China shows no signs of being willing to back down and has significantly boosted its naval strength in recent years, which now includes sixty or so submarines, some of them nuclear, which are clearly not intended just to search for whales. In response, the Americans have pushed up their defence budget to new record heights, increasing it by 13 percent to 716 billion dollars in 2019. Confident in the technological superiority of their arsenal, it seems as though Washington is trying to goad Beijing into an arms race, particularly since the 'war on terror' has now come to an end, allowing the US to refocus its attention on the more traditional rivals of Russia and now China. The official American National Defence Strategy almost says this in as many words. If the Americans succeed in their intent, this will force the Chinese to further ratchet up their investment in their military-industrial apparatus, which, illogically enough, will result in further innovation of the kind that already has the US so worried! The outcome will be a bipolar military world as our new common reality.

FACIAL RECOGNITION

By 2010, I was convinced that China would become the new centre of the technological world. It was then that I decided to sell Chinese products outside of China. My first idea was to sell a product from the security sector, since it seemed clear to me that China was destined to become the market leader in that sector. Put simply, I planned to sell the products developed by my former customers! Professor Stan Z. Li[32], a good Chinese friend of mine from Beijing, was head of the National Biometric and Security Institute, which formed as part of the Chinese Academy of Science. I was fascinated by all the applications he and his team had developed, such as the facial recognition system used at the 2008 Olympic Games in Beijing and the 2010 World Expo in Shanghai. Stan was the reference in China in the field of image and pattern identification. He advised the Chinese government, had written several books on the subject and had already achieved his first commercial success earlier on when working for Microsoft in Beijing. My vision was correct, but I forgot that it is sometimes not wise to attempt to launch commercial products onto the market in collaboration with a passionate academic. After three years of hard but not particularly fruitful work, we decided to call it a day.

Since 2012, projects focusing on biometric applications, such as pattern recognition in faces, fingerprints, objects, irises, walking patterns, palms and voices, have been the target of huge funding by the Chinese government to drive research developments and commercialize practical uses. In 2013, for example, Stan was given a team of almost one hundred PhD students and facilities near Shanghai to create the next generation of groundbreaking algorithms. All free of charge, courtesy of the State. Given this level of resource commitment, it is little wonder that China has taken over world leadership in biometrics. Of course, commercial and military developments go hand in hand (as seen in the American model). Today, China has almost 200 million cameras in use in public locations and it intends to double that number within the next few years. Beijing has made its preference for this technology abundantly clear and the yo-yo effect has passed this message effectively down the line. Local administrations and public security institutions are now purchasing face recognition software and high-resolution cameras in large quantities. What's more, Chinese companies have few limitations or challenges when selling this kind of security technology, while people in the West are still debating about how and when it can 'properly' be used.

A FACE-LIFT FOR THE FUTURE

A handful of Chinese unicorns, like Sensetime, Megvii, Yitu and CloudWalk, can now justifiably be called the world leaders in face recognition applications.

Sensetime was founded in 2015 and by 2017 it was already profitable. In 2018, it became the world's most valuable AI start-up, with an estimated value of 4.5 billion dollars. The first phase of their N-curve was given added impetus by the government's stimulation of market demand: Sensetime works primarily with local government authorities to guarantee safety in China's cities.

A second start-up, Megvii, has been working closely with Beijing since 2011 to develop a nationwide surveillance system and has helped the police to arrest hundreds of criminals. The company wants to build new 'eyes' and new 'brains' for every city in China and their open-source application Face++ is already being used by more than 300,000 programmers.

Yitu has already won the world's top two awards (NIST and IARPA) in the biometrics field[33] for its algorithms that have a high rate of identification accuracy. The company has a database containing more than 1 billion faces and has successfully launched banking applications where a facial recognition scan replaces identification by card.[34] With its large R&D teams in Silicon Valley and Singapore, Yitu looks set to conquer the world.

China is therefore well on the way to capturing half of the global market by 2025 and it is possible that the fourth company, CloudWalk — the first to break through Apple's Face-ID monopoly[35] — might be the single largest world player one day.[36] They are investing massively to achieve 3D-facial recognition that not only exceeds an accuracy rate of 99 per-cent but will also cut the recognition time from a few seconds with 2D-algorithms to a few milliseconds with 3D.

The Western media often exaggerates the capabilities of China's facial recognition technology, certainly when it comes to the 200 million security cameras installed around China. Above all, there is a wild overestimation in terms of the progress made by facial recognition algorithms. We humans need a certain degree of light and subject immobility to be able to make a good identification, and it is no different for machines. Of course, these inaccurate claims make great headlines for the newspapers that like to warn us how everyone and everything in China is continually followed and monitored. It means the end of privacy, or so we are told. This kind of 'Big Brother' dystopian thinking is a long way from the reality of the situation. The algorithmic capacity run on even the very fastest servers is not capable of processing and screening all the data from thousands, never mind millions, of cameras. What's more, most of the ordinary cameras in China are positioned at the regulation height of 2.8 metres, which is too high for most of them to recognise a face. And what do the Chinese think of it all? Most of them are much more bothered if their car number plate is identified in the context of a traffic violation. A city like Shenzhen is however going one step further with experiments with high-definition cameras to better identify civilians involved in traffic violations. So far, most people see this more as a law and order issue than a privacy one.

COMFORT OR CONTROL?

At the same time, there is still a general underestimation of the level of disruption — in the positive sense — that this technology will cause in China in the long term. I am not talking here about control; I am talking about comfort. People outside of China often have no conception of just how much easier life will be for the average Chinese person as a result of these technical breakthroughs. In China you can already quite literally pay with a smile at

McDonalds and KFC. You can also open a bank account with your face, as well as check into your hotel, board your flight, enter a secure office, pay your car park ticket, get money from a cash machine or even request more toilet paper in public conveniences. All you need to do is look at the screen and smile. And as soon as 5G becomes fully operational, these types of application will be rolled out commercially across the entire country. Your face will become your new passport, replacing the need for wallets and bits of paper. In this way, the Chinese concept of mianzi, whereby every Chinese man or woman is constantly capable of losing or gaining face, is given a very concrete and practical form of implementation. What's more, this 'face-lift' disruption will enable dozens of other new applications in areas like self-driving cars, finance, social media and healthcare. With all these evolutions in the pipeline, it is certain that by 2025 China will be light-years ahead of the West in terms of the integration of biometric recognition into social and commercial life. This is a deficit Europe and America will never be able to make up. For young Chinese tourists, unable to understand why they need a passport, cash and train tickets to travel, the West will increasingly seem like a museum of outdated technologies.

Another aspect of these developments is the so-called social credit system, which is the new apparatus being constructed by the Chinese state to improve general societal security at the expense of some elements of individual privacy. By 2020, China's central government intends to introduce a system that will allow it to better judge and manage its citizens. If you are a 'good citizen', you will be rewarded; if you display 'bad' behaviour, you will be punished. The Western media are keen to portray these plans as the start of some kind of Orwellian 1984 nightmare or a scene from Black Mirror, often because they conflate the Chinese national credit score with the social credit system, whereas in reality they are two separate systems (see the following paragraph). The first image that forms in Western minds is one that sees China as some kind of artificial planet of the future, where 'Big Brother' controls all its citizens, so that people's right to live their lives as they choose will become a thing of the past. Of course, this mental picture says as much about the West as it does about China, with China's social credit system (or score, as it is usually described) being cast in the role of villain in our own discussion about the necessary balance between freedom and security. In this sense, the credit score is more a mirror for Europe and America than for China. Although this new reality may indeed lead to stricter state control of some aspects of Chinese life (at least when viewed from a Western perspective) and although we are right to maintain a critical stance, it is nevertheless important to separate what is really happening in China from our own demons and fantasies.

THE CRISIS OF SOCIAL CONFIDENCE

Recent decades have seen an unprecedented economic explosion in China. In fact, the economy has grown much too quickly, so that the measures needed to ensure sustainable economic foundations for continued healthy growth have not kept pace. Every stable and flourishing economy is founded on confidence and trust. To make this possible, the countries of the world rely on effective legal systems to keep everything in balance, effective financial systems that calculate every risk, and responsible parents who teach their children the difference between right and wrong. Unfortunately, in China the legal system is still in its infancy, notwithstanding the pledges made by Xi Jinping to create a state governed by the rule of law. Similarly, the banks know far too little about the creditworthiness of their customers and young parents are surrounded by countless examples of people who simply want to get rich quick, often in a dubious manner. If you lend money or rent an apartment to someone in China and if they are unable to pay, you can certainly pursue the defaulter through the courts and you will probably win your case. However, the likelihood that you will ever see the money you are owed is small, because it is difficult for you to prove that your debtor actually has enough money to pay you back. In other words, China is currently facing a crisis of social confidence. There is a negative balance of trust.

In the West, it is possible to obtain an accurate credit history for almost every private citizen from the National Bank or from private companies like Equifax. When I returned to Belgium from China and asked my local bank for a loan to renovate my home, I was told: 'Sorry, you are not creditworthy!' Because I had spent most of my working life in China and had been paid there, I had no recent credit history with the National Bank. This gave me a good idea of what many Chinese citizens experience, because many of them do not have a credit rating, or even keep their money with a bank. There is a huge amount of 'black money' (not to mention fifty shades of grey money) in circulation in China, much of it belonging to people who are extremely creditworthy, but are unable to get bank loans for much the same reasons I couldn't. This is the inevitable result of a situation where the economy and its entrepreneurs are moving forward more quickly than the country's legal and fiscal framework.

Given these circumstances, Chinese consumers sometimes no longer know what a good citizen is supposed to be or do, who is really creditworthy and who is not, and whether the legal system will protect them if things go wrong. In the first instance, they generally put their trust in their friends, but this is obviously not a model that can be scaled up. The government is aware that it needs to deal with this situation with urgency, otherwise there is a risk that the Chinese economic miracle will be derailed. You might say (admittedly with some degree of exaggeration) that the Chinese economy would have grown even faster if strangers were prepared to trust each other. Now that China's growth is starting to slow down, the government sees the social credit system as a dual remedy, serving both as a gas pedal for renewed growth and as a safety net to restore confidence and trust.

Of course, it was not possible for Beijing simply to copy the credit rating systems employed in Western societies. Something different was needed and so China has developed the concept of a social credit system, the basic idea being to trace everyone's purchasing and other behaviours to assess whether they are creditworthy or not and whether they are a 'good citizen' or not. In other words, there are two elements to this trust system — one dealing with financial credibility, the other with social responsibility — both of which the government hopes to implement by 2020. The financial credit rating system will be based on a score, similar to models widely used in the West. The social responsibility system will be in the form of a blacklist, again just as it is in the police network in the West. This said, the limitations in people's freedom to those who end up on the blacklist is more far-reaching than the West, such as the well-known example of travel bans. Unfortunately, the media in America and Europe often conflate these two rating systems, saying that all Chinese citizens will be given a score to show how socially responsible they are, just like in an episode of Black Mirror. In fact, the system for determining the creditworthiness score is not so very different from the system used by data giants like Amazon to identify the behaviour patterns that allow them to serve us better. In essence, it is a system designed to give people credit options. Similarly, the social responsibility credit system is not so different from the way in which internet companies and banks use private data to inform the government of people they suspect of terrorist or other criminal activities. Where China is different, of course, is that the bar for defining what is 'anti-social behaviour' could be set much lower than in the West, and the consequences for such behaviour could be much greater. In an effort to strike the right balance between these different elements, pilot experiments are currently being conducted throughout the country. These experiments are frowned upon in the West, since they often compromise our Western norms of privacy. But again, that is not always how many Chinese people see things. One of the best-known examples of the system at work is the use of facial recognition technology to identify and impose fines on jaywalkers in the city of Shenzhen, who are also publicly named and shamed on the internet. Strange as it may seem, until now all other measures to persuade people to obey by the normal rules of the road have failed (the Chinese can often be fairly cavalier about such matters). But this new system seems to be working, not only cutting the number of pedestrian accidents, but also significantly reducing the stress for Shenzhen's many drivers. Viewed in these terms, the implementation of the social credit system can be seen as a new barometer for the norms in present-day Chinese society. The trick, of course, is knowing where to set the boundary. If the system is too stringent, China will find itself heading towards social revolt. If the system is not stringent enough, it will achieve nothing. This is the crucial balancing act that the pilot projects hope to solve.

THE BLACKLIST

Even after the pilots, the question will remain: what is acceptable? If you fail to repay a debt, it does not sound illogical for your name to appear on a blacklist. That is already the case in China. It nearly happened to me when I wanted to close one of my companies in Shanghai in 2016. As a result of a number of procedural errors, I received a letter from the arbitration court saying that one of my former employees was suing me for compensation. In my best Chinese, I explained to the judge that the company no longer had any business activity. We came to a compromise: providing there were no further transactions on the company's bank account, I wouldn't have to pay the compensation claim. Unfortunately, at the end of that month the tax authorities made a final automatic deduction from the account. The result: a second enforcing court judge phoned me and said that I would now have to pay the claim and would not be allowed to leave China until I did! As it turned out, at that moment I was on a visit to Belgium, but against the advice of the Belgian consulate, my lawyer and even my wife, I booked a ticket on the next plane back to Shanghai, so that I could speak to the judge in person. Everyone was worried that I would end up in prison; in which case I might have written a different book.

After two months of weekly visits to the judge and hours of tedious discussions, I managed to resolve the matter. That is one of the great things about China: everything is negotiable, as long as you remain sincere. Just before my third visit to the court, I couldn't resist the temptation to test out the system, and so I booked a flight from Shanghai to Hong Kong. The first thing the judge asked me during our next meeting was: 'Why did you book a flight to Hong Kong? I told you that you are not allowed to leave the country!' I have no idea how she knew about the flight (I hadn't paid for the ticket), but she did. It is clear that companies have no qualms about forwarding information to the authorities when your name is on a watch list. Fortunately, I had my answer ready for the judge: 'But Hong Kong is a part of China now, isn't it? Anyway, that's where I have my money in a bank account.' Problem solved and confidence restored! Telling a white lie to allow someone to save face is not uncommon in China. The judge knew that I was lying, but it suited her purposes, since she would ultimately be judged on her ability to settle the conflict. My travel ban was eventually lifted after three months and, fortunately, my name was never added to the blacklist. As you might imagine, I am not a great fan of this blacklist and the limitations it can impose, but one thing is certain: it is very effective: no doubt about it.

OPEN SESAME

Central to the social credit system was the need to create a database that could store huge amounts of data about people so that the credit score and the blacklist could be maintained as accurately as possible. The government turned in the first instance to a company that had been dealing with counterfeiters for years and already had half of China in its own database: Alibaba. Although the state-led social credit system has nothing to do with Alibaba's Sesame score, which is really a kind of advanced loyalty system, it was certainly a source of inspiration and expertise. In 2015, the Sesame score was launched as a first kind of individual credit score in China. As an Alibaba customer, you have the option to take part in the credit system (or not), which links your transactions to numerous special offers and other benefits. Hundreds of millions of Chinese consumers love this system. With a good Sesame credit score, you can get small loans, avoid the payment of guarantees and advances, defer paying for your purchases, borrow free umbrellas and battery chargers, get VIP treatment at airports, take a test drive in a Ford or even obtain a visa for Singapore. The aim of countless Chinese is to reach a Sesame score in excess of 650 and then to share this good news with their jealous friends!

TRANSPARENCY

In a country where millions of people are huge fans of the Sesame score system, it is hardly surprising that the vast majority of Chinese people have few problems accepting the idea of the government's credit score or even a citizenship score. In general terms, 83 percent of the Chinese population trusts its government, in comparison with around just 50 percent in Western countries.[37] Chinese internet users (netizens) sometimes discuss the social credit system online, but the overall impression is that it is not a subject that keeps them awake at night. The words most commonly used on Sina Weibo (the Chinese Twitter) are security, harmony, trust and comfort.[38] Most Chinese see the proposed new system as a kind of 'karma' or 'law of cause and effect': what you sow, you will eventually reap.

Of course, in addition to dealing with tax fraud and criminal activities, the social credit system has the potential to be used in other ways. If, for example, you buy lots of baby milk powder for your new-born child, it might be possible to conclude that you are a responsible person, whereas someone who only buys video games might be seen as less trustworthy. The implication? If you are a fervent games player, you might need to think about buying some milk powder as well, just to be on the safe side.

It is understandable that we in the West are quick to write off this new system. But at the moment the Chinese government has not come up with a better alternative to deal with the problems it urgently needs to tackle. These problems — whether it is another baby milk scandal, fake goods, jaywalking or something else — are so huge and the Chinese are so inventive at getting around the rules that only large-scale and 'drastic' measures have any chance of success. In general, the bulk of the population supports measures to ensure that individuals and companies are held to account for their actions. People are tired of endless scams and non-stop corruption. As a result, ordinary men and women in the street are willing to support an effective scam blocker: a system that will allow law abiding citizens to show that they are to be trusted, so that they can borrow money, rent a house, get a job, travel, or even get married. A transparent and honest system that screens everyone and screens them well, including civil servants, the police, judges and companies. In other words, a true social credit system.

THE MASTER PLAN

China's social credit system can be traced back to a Chinese master plan that dates back to the Han Dynasty some 2,000 years ago, the main purpose of which is to ultimately create a Confucian *datong* 大同 society,[39] based on the idea of common 'goodness' or 'The Great Unity'. China is currently at the level of what Confucians call a *xiaokang* 小康 or 'Moderately Prosperous' society, which has not yet achieved full 'unity' or 'goodness', but is nonetheless approaching the ideal.

China's objective is simple: by 2021, a century after the founding of the Chinese Communist Party, the country will have reached a higher state of *xiaokang*, which will see every Chinese citizen provided with education, paid work, sufficient clothes, enough to eat, access to medical and elderly care, a roof over their heads and a certain degree of material comfort. Seen in this context, it is no coincidence that China intends to launch its social credit system in 2020.

By 2049, when the People's Republic of China will celebrate its 100th anniversary, it is intended that China will have progressed to the middle level of *datong* — in other words, the middle level of a developed country — in economic, technological and social terms. To achieve this last objective, the Chinese government believes it needs to implement a national social credit system. In other words, they have another 29 years to get it right.

As outlined in even longer-term plans, by 2121, China hopes to have attained a higher form of *datong*, in which its people are highly educated, strongly developed, prosperous and ready to accept responsibility to the benefit of the common good or 'The Great Unity'. In other words, a more ideal society in which everyone is cared for and no-one need fear the depredations of thieves, deceivers or invaders.

This will be the end result of an upcoming century of refinement of the social credit system, which is in its infancy today. Put simply, we will need to wait another 100 years to see if the system effectively leads to a better society or whether in the meantime it will have been abandoned under pressure exerted by the Chinese people or by outside influences. As a plan, however, there is something both wonderful and terrible about it. Speaking personally, I have only one word to describe it: 'Terrific'.

What to Remember?

1 → **The world is becoming bipolar.** The United States is no longer the only military superpower. China is on the way to achieving parity with America by 2030, thanks to its superiority in 5G telecom, Quantum Computing and Artificial Intelligence. If we extrapolate on the basis of China's recent technological past, this looks set to become the new reality for the Western world.

2 → **The Chinese leadership model seems to be based on a yo-yo movement** of information and ideas up and down, so that decisions are communicated quickly and efficiently to local administrations and, ultimately, the Chinese people. The question is whether our Western pendulum model is still truly democratic, bearing in mind that socialist China is creating progress and prosperity for the average Chinese citizen at a much faster pace than in the West. Can China give our Western politicians new insights; for example, in dealing with the environmental crisis?

3 → **China is catching up militarily** and the still large gap with superpower America is narrowing all the time. China is building a new and high-tech 'Great Wall' to defend itself, but also now has the confidence to take its first expansionist steps, using sea power to protect its overseas interests. Is a war with China a real possibility?

4 → **China is taking its place as the world leader in facial recognition technology** and it is not difficult to imagine that super-intelligent Chinese products will become the New Normal in the West. Chinese consumers will be the new global trendsetters for the integration of biometric applications into everyday life.

5 → **The Chinese social credit system is been created** as the answer to the crisis in social trust in China. While the West sees this as a 'Big Brother' solution, the average Chinese citizen sees it as a transparent form of 'karma' that will create balance in a society that otherwise threatens to derail. By 2049, the Chinese government hopes to use this social credit system to achieve the same level of economic, technological and social development as Western Europe.

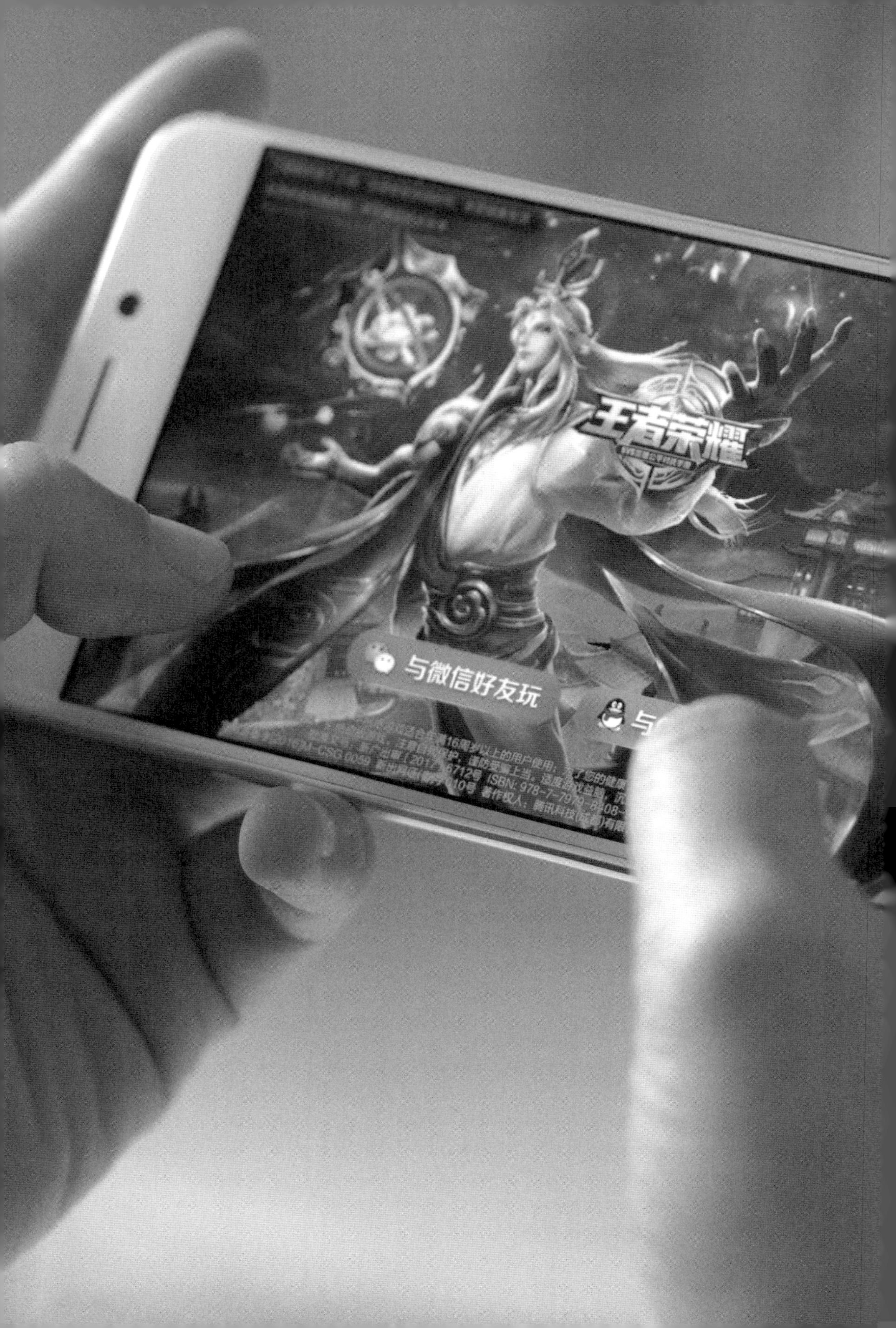
王者荣耀
与微信好友玩

<
A Chinese mobile game player plays Tencent's *King of Glory* (or *Honour of Kings*) on his smartphone.

2

SMART MEDIA & ENTERTAINMENT

The second industry is Smart Media & Entertainment. Since 2015, companies like Tencent and others have led worldwide innovation in this sector. But what exactly are the tensions arising in the interplay between the main actors: the generation of Chinese digital consumers, a control-oriented government and the super-powerful tech companies?

2013 2015 2017 2019 2021 2023 2025 2030

CHINESE FUN

On a festive Friday evening at the end of January 2013, Adidas held its New Year's reception in the five-star Shangri-La Hotel. Some 900 of its employees gathered together in the largest ballroom in Shanghai, having travelled there from all over the country. Everyone was dressed for the occasion in colourful costumes and each was welcomed by one of the thirty hostesses, who searched for the guests' name on an iPad list and took a photo before they entered. Within 30 minutes, hundreds and hundreds of smiling faces had been captured by their digital cameras. The entire evening was a perfectly orchestrated entertainment show, ranging from emotional Adidas stories to a series of dance numbers performed by some of the personnel. But the highlight of the evening was the lucky draw, with hundreds of valuable prizes to be won. You could feel the tension rising as the moment to announce the winners approached. At last, the Director of Adidas China mounted the stage and stood in front of a large red button, whose purpose until now had been unclear. With a fine sense of drama, he brought his hand down on the button. Suddenly, all the photos that had been taken during the registration two hours earlier now began to flash across a thirty-metre wide screen. The enthusiasm of the audience, already at fever pitch, now reached new heights. Everybody arose from their seats and stood on the tips of their toes, hoping to see their own picture. When the series of flashing images stopped on the face of a winner, you could tell instantly where he or she was located in the room, simply by the crescendo of noise from their table. In many ways, it was moving to watch and the experience is one that I have never forgotten.

Just a year earlier, I founded a new start-up called Letsface. We had developed a new iPad-based event registration and ticket application, which allowed visitors and guests to get to know each other via a mobile app with photos and data of all guests. We quickly realised, however, that the Chinese were more interested in the entertainment possibilities of the system than its more practical networking uses. Suddenly, we were an entertainment software company — and that is how we ended up being used at the Adidas reception! Conclusion? The Chinese really like to enjoy themselves and that insight was the real basis for the success of Letsface.

DATA

Our concept at Letsface was simply but effective, and was a big hit at a wide range events for companies ranging from Ikea to Cartier. The idea was to collect visitors' data via interactive digital entertainment. With Europeans, this can sometimes cause raised eyebrows (or even curled toes), but not with the Chinese. They regard their data, such as their e-mail address, photo or telephone number, as a means of payment or, perhaps more accurately, as a means of exchange. Exchange for what? In our case, in exchange for fun. Over five years, we digitised thousands of events and collected a huge amount of valuable data. In 2014, we took our software to the Belgian market, but it was not a great success. In fact, we were actually forbidden from using the lucky draw application in Europe, because it falls under the legislation relating to games of chance. This made it clear to us that Europeans view such things in a very different light from the Chinese.

Data is the lifeblood for Artificial Intelligence (AI) based solutions. As the internationally famous Chinese AI researcher Andrew Ng[40] puts it: 'AI is the new electricity. Just as electricity transformed almost everything 100 years ago, today I actually have a hard time thinking of an industry that I don't think AI will transform in the next several years.' Given how easy it is to collect data in China, where almost a billion people spend an average of four hours online each day, it is not difficult to imagine why the country has become the largest experimental laboratory for Artificial Intelligence on the planet.

The biggest harvester of data in China is Tencent. At the start of 2018, it was the fourth most valuable company in the world, in part because it is a data farmer on a massive scale. The Tencent story began just 20 years ago with the development of a simple messaging application (QQ), which worked on the cheapest 2G data plans of the Chinese cell phone operators. In this way, Tencent became the standard means of communication in China. But that was not all: the company had the brilliant idea to make each customer's cell phone number their log-in ID for chat, e-mail, social network and other Tencent applications. Ease of use is always a decisive factor in China and the Tencent system couldn't have made things any easier! By 2012, Tencent had 800 million QQ users and 600 million visitors to its related QZone social network.[41] With its more recent and updated product, WeChat, the company has now comfortably passed the magical barrier of one billion users.

MEDIA

Entertainment and media are perhaps the most fascinating sectors in China, not least because of the way they interact with the 'field of tension' that exists between the government, the people and the companies.

Think back, if you can, to the times when media channels were limited and we all stayed at home to watch our favourite shows on the television. These were the days when in Belgium, for example, the entertainment offer consisted of a single regional broadcaster and a few foreign channels. It was an age when the key media were compartmentalised, organised along the fault lines that ran between the different political groupings. Today, this is unthinkable. In our secular, decompartmentalised society there is now, if anything, too much choice, leading almost inevitably to choice stress or, worse still, choice apathy and inertia.

In China, media content is still strictly controlled by the government. The largest media channels, like CCTV (the state TV broadcaster), People's Daily (main state newspaper) and Xinhua News (official state news agency), have close links with the Party. As a result, there is a uniform offer on television, in print, and even in cinemas. Until the beginning of the 21st century, this helped to create a fairly closed society, an image of China that is still often perpetuated by many outsiders. However, this view is now hopelessly out of date. As this chapter will explain, the face of the new Chinese media is very different from the grey uniform days of the past. The technological progress made possible by the internet (from 2005 onwards), mobility (from 2010 onwards) and online media (from 2013 onwards) has broken CCTV's previous monopoly for the provision of news and entertainment. At the end of 2018, there were more video-streaming subscribers than cable television subscribers in China. At the same time, still strict government regulations limiting access to media offers from the West remain in place. The insistence that only a maximum of 30 percent of foreign films can be dubbed into Chinese and screened on the local market has stimulated a huge increase in the production of home-grown film content of a very high quality.[42] From 2020 onwards, many more top-class TV dramas and films will be available for viewing on television and in Chinese cinemas. Over the years, much has been written about the 'Great Firewall', an all-encompassing process of media censorship that many outsiders see as cutting China off from the rest of the world. And indeed, it is hard to dispute that freedom of opinion and freedom of information are to some extent restricted in China, but primarily when viewing things from a purely Western perspective. That is not how I experienced it during the many years I lived in the country. Nor is it the experience of my many Chinese friends. The crucial question is, of course: what is freedom?

To answer that question, we need to look back into history. Forty years ago, Deng Xiaoping[43] set China on a new course, opening China to the world. One of the great symbolic moments was when Coca-Cola was allowed back into the Chinese market in 1978. This was followed a short time later by the creation of the first Special Economic Zone in Shenzhen, where companies were permitted for the first time to pursue profit in keeping with Western market-driven principles, stimulated by more relaxed government regula-

Figure 8

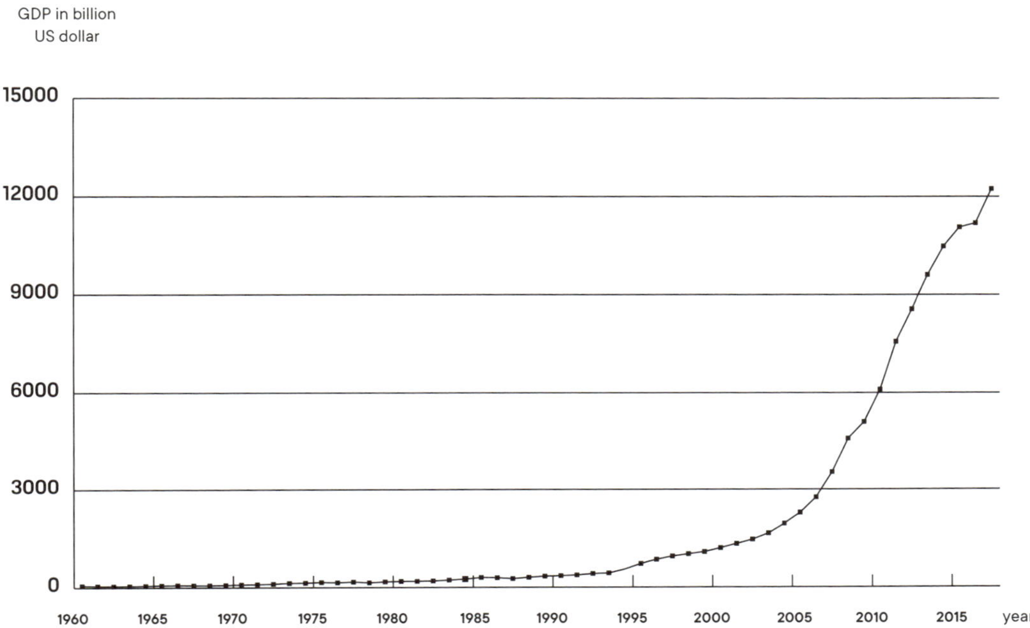

tions. As a result, the one-time fishing village of Shenzhen has been transformed into a metropolis of some 12 million inhabitants. The ever-pragmatic Deng believed that what the West had achieved through the processes of economic competition could also be made to work in China, and he was right. The curve in figure 8 illustrates the rate of economic growth of the People's Republic of China over recent decades. But one can also regard this as the curve of freedom.

When people talk about modern China, the idea of greater freedom is not something that immediately springs to mind. It is however indisputable that since the 1980s a huge segment of the Chinese population has enjoyed the freedom that comes from being released from poverty. This, in turn, has meant the freedom to enjoy an improved standard of living, greater material prosperity, increased property ownership, better education, more employment opportunities, better healthcare, more free time, more things to do with that free time, more freely available travel destinations, more private initiatives, more public safety, more information, more pleasure, and even more religion; more, more, more. In many respects, the quality of life of the middle class in China is today far higher than in America. Until recently, the social and political values of freedom so cherished in the West have not been a matter of great concern to the ordinary Chinese man or woman in the street. For the time being, most people still regard the progress they have made in terms of economic freedom as far outweighing the less tangible benefits of 'democratic' freedom. Will it stay that way? Only time will tell. But it is certain that the vast majority of the Chinese people feel much freer than they did — and much freer than we in the West might suspect — just four decades ago.

Deng's Open Door Policy was only the first step. Around the turn of the 21st Century, a new wave of openness (or freedom, to use another word) was heralded by the arrival of the internet. This was a revelation (and a very popular one) to China's 1.4 billion citizens and, notwithstanding a continued high level of media control by the state, it soon became the most powerful instrument in their search to discover a new identity. Paradoxically, China's internet policy is seen in the West as a serious limitation on human freedom, whereas most Chinese people will tell you that they had never known such freedom before the internet. As a result, Big Data and Artificial Intelligence are seen as posing less of a societal threat in China. In contrast to the West, these developments are regarded as symbols of progress both for society and the individual. True, Westerners also regard these things as signs of progress, but we remain much more wary for the intrusion of the all-knowing state and unscrupulous businessmen into our lives. This said, since 2019 many more Chinese are increasingly concerned too.

In addition to the advent of the internet, there were three other transformations taking place at the start of the new century that helped to sharpen the sense of freedom among the general Chinese population: mobile first, digital natives and living apart from mum and dad. This unique cocktail of trends helped turn China into a nation where technology is nearly universally accepted as the silver bullet to create and maintain a smarter society.

Mobile first, mobile only. In the years after 2000, the Chinese very quickly made the transition to mobile internet, while we in the West continued for much longer to surf on ADSL lines. E-mail was quickly ditched and replaced by QQ chat. For most Chinese people, and certainly in the countryside, their 2G cell phone was the first personal communication device they had ever owned. This led to the rapid evolution of the mobile network in China, as well as stimulating the growth of a new industry for the manufacture of cheap mobile phones.

Digital natives. The first decade of the new century was also the moment when a new generation of digital natives (people born after 1980) entered the labour market. This was the first generation of 'freedom seekers', who had grown up in what was still a simple and strongly traditional China, with limited prosperity and limited access to information. This is the biggest difference this generation of Chinese have in comparison with digital natives in the West. These Chinese adolescents were pretty naive, but were constantly searching for a new China and, above all, a new 'me'. The internet was the ideal answer to satisfy both their insatiable curiosity and their drive for personal improvement. It was as if a magical well of information had suddenly sprung up in the desert, a well from which every Chinese citizen was allowed to drink.

Separation from the family. Traditionally, the Chinese live in close-knit family units. At the start of the century, however, the fast-growing Chinese middle class now wanted to send their children to the best possible universities their entrance exam results would allow. This often meant universities on the other side of the country. Wealthier Chinese even began to send their offspring abroad to complete their education. At the same time, there was a similar trend at the other end of the social spectrum, but now it was the parents who were on the move, as men and women left the countryside and headed for better paid employment in the big cities, leaving their children behind in the care of grandparents. For both rich and poor, the 2G cell phone was the perfect way to maintain the close family ties that have been a characteristic of the Chinese way of life for centuries. And the mass purchase of mobile phones prompted by this familial separation further helped to spread new information across all China.

ARTIFICIAL COUNSELLORS. A DIGITAL SPARTA

To illustrate a point about China, let us briefly return to the golden age of Ancient Greece, the cradle of Western democracy. The two main Greek states — Athens and Sparta — had very different views about government. Athens was run by what could loosely be termed a democratic assembly. Sparta was ruled by two kings, supported by a council of elders (*Gerousia*) and a democratic forum of privileged citizens (*Apella*). The council of elders (*Gerousia*) approved laws but otherwise had little real power: it was a purely advisory body. According to Aristotle, the Sparta model was an ideal mix of democracy, aristocracy and monarchy. But what if the *Gerousia* was not a body of wise old men, but a machine driven by smart algorithms? And what if this machine could give consistently better advice than the wise old men, because it has at its disposal much more data, which allowed it to make more reliable judgements? In this way, the men in charge, whether kings or modern-day politicians, would be able to make better informed choices, based on improved societal outcomes rather than political or personal agendas. Would this not be, to paraphrase the Aristotelian formula, an ideal mix between technocracy, democracy and autocracy?

This is how I see China evolving in the century ahead: into a kind of digital Sparta. Is it possible that China will one day become a democracy? Perhaps, but I believe only in the Chinese sense of the word, or as Xi Jinping refers to it: 'a consultative democracy'.[44] By this he means a system of consultation meetings on a national scale to test the level of public consensus and to provide answers to any questions that the people may have. This could at least be called a semi-democratic form of society, and far removed from the autocratic, rigid image that many Westerners have of the Chinese political system. Is it possible that in the long run this Chinese semi-democracy might prove more resilient than our own full-blown version? Once again, only time will tell. Whatever the outcome, it is already clear that China is focusing strongly in the media sector on the development of Artificial Intelligence, not only as a propaganda mechanism, but also to better understand the real concerns of the population, so that the government can respond to these concerns quicker and more effectively.

At the present time, information in China is collected on behalf of the government by a veritable army of researchers who take samples of data content, mainly from the sites of internet companies. However, at this time (according to those in the know) the Public

Security Service (PSB) simply does not have the resources to do this on a deep or wide-scale basis. True, there are 'informer' hotlines, where concerned citizens can pass on information or make complaints, but this is not scalable. Consequently, it is expected that in the years ahead AI computers will become the nation's new censorship police, civic watchdog and civic participation adviser all rolled into one. That things are already moving in this direction was made clear by the appearance in 2018 of the first-ever AI newsanchor on the state-run Xinhua News channel.[45] Should we be worried by such developments? There are those who argue that democratic legitimacy is not simply a matter of elections but can also be achieved through systematic public consultation on issues of importance, so that elections actually become less necessary. And to follow that argument, is it not the case that in many Western countries elections have already become too static an instrument to properly reflect the dynamism of our 21st century society?

SOCIAL CONTROL

Investment in AI in the Chinese media sector is set to increase dramatically in the coming decade because the Chinese government is convinced that society will require more 'direction'. AI is seen as the best way to strengthen the necessary processes of censorship and control. Each dollar invested in Artificial Intelligence in the media sector therefore has a double function: the 'push' of propaganda and the 'pull' of information for more efficient communication. Contrary to what many observers in the West believe, there is an on-going social debate in China about the limits and effectiveness of state control and questions are being asked by some about the new social credit system (Smart Security). But these are not the most burning issues of the day. Why? Because the actions of the government are broadly in keeping with the Confucian idea of the importance of social control and, as a corollary, of a social safety net. In other words, the government's plans are nothing new in Chinese society, simply an upgrade made possible by improved technology. The increased economic freedoms now enjoyed by the majority of Chinese citizens can sometimes seem to contrast sharply with the increased 'interference' by the Chinese government. This is one of the paradoxes in China that is most difficult for outsiders to understand. Without wishing to minimise the problem, you can perhaps best compare it with the debate about whether a child is likely to have a better future if he or she has strict parents or indulgent parents. In practice, the raising and education of the young is often a matter of both 'carrot' and 'stick'. In this sense, providing a better future by ensuring a better structured society can also be seen as a form of freedom. After all, is that not what every parent wants for their child: a better future?

There is also a perception outside of China that the nation's social framework is extremely rigid. But is that really the case? Over the years, I have increasingly come to view China as a being in a non-stop state of flux. The country and its people are a bit like a swarm of starlings, birds which are constantly in chaotic individual motion but nonetheless move together in the right general direction. There is something essentially bird-like about the Chinese: nimble, quick and light, or to express it in business terms, agile. As a result, it feels to me less like the Party is orchestrating 'everything,' and more like a concerted common effort to fly as fast, as far and as high as possible. The whole effect only becomes visible when you can see it as the sum of the individual parts.

This is my answer to the question of why Chinese companies have a much tighter relationship with the government than in the West: the Chinese Government and the Chinese business community are constantly working together to move in the same direction: forwards. There is much more shared thinking and harmony between the government and business leaders than you will generally read about in the Western media. Of course, it goes without saying that government censorship and interference are not always welcomed by China's citizens, but the Chinese media and internet companies have become expert at flirting with the boundaries of what is permissible and what is not. Every starling in the system can marginally influence the direction, but no-one will be allowed to push the swarm as a whole from its chosen course.

THE NEW MEDIA

Today, China has some 800 million mobile internet users whose demand for news and information is insatiable.[46] Bearing in mind the censorship exercised by the state, you would be forgiven for assuming that the internet environment in China is limited and boring. But nothing could be further from the truth! There is much more diversity than in the West. Every niche market in China is as large as a national market in Europe, which has driven up the number of websites and apps exponentially.

In addition, Chinese netizens also actively create much more content of their own, whereas in the West we are largely passive consumers of content. As early as 2012, 76 percent of the Chinese online population was creating content — posting photos, blogs, vlogs, reviews, ratings, etc. — in contrast with just 23 percent in Europe.[47] Europeans use the internet to search for information; the Chinese use the internet so that they can be searched for (and found) by others. This is an important difference, because you often hear it said that the Chinese are not a creative people. The statistics prove that this is certainly not the case as far as their online behaviour is concerned.

The most popular social media platforms in China in 2018[48]
(Western version in brackets)

Tencent: WeChat (all-in-one): a combination of Facebook and Whatsapp on steroids, with games, online shopping, financial services and much, much more. 1.08 billion monthly active users (MAU) and 10 million applications. The most complete and most popular social media platform in China.

4. **Tencent: QQ (messaging):** the second largest Tencent site, one which few in the West have ever heard of. 803 million MAU. It is a kind of WeChat for younger people that is linked to QZone, Tencent's blogging platform with over 600 million users.

5. **Sina: Weibo (Twitter):** a combination of Facebook and Twitter. 446 million MAU, most of whom are highly-educated. Popular with brands for the recommendation of their products.

6. **Tencent Video, Youku-Tudou, and iQiYi (YouTube):** the three competing online video channels of the BAT: Baidu (iQiYi), Alibaba (Tudou-Youku) and Tencent Video. Together they have 600 million MAU.

7. **Baidu Tieba (Reddit):** a search machine forum. China's largest keyword-based discussion forum with 665 million MAU, with specific and content-oriented communication.

8. **Douban (social lifestyle app):** a review, rating and discussion platform around lifestyle topics such as books, music, film and events. 300 million MAU. Particularly important for brands for Word-of-Mouth marketing.

9. **Zhihu (Quora):** probably the most reliable information site in China, primarily used by better educated urban dwellers. 160 million MAU. High-quality content and images that are superior to Quora in many respects.

10. **Meituan-Dianping (Yelp):** with 60 million location reviews, this is the largest review and food delivery application in the world. It is the all-in-one app for restaurants, bars, gyms, hotels, etc. for the offline world. 382 million MAU, older than 20.

11. **Momo and Tantan (Tinder):** the two largest dating apps in China. In addition to pure dating, they integrate mobile gaming, online video and much more. Each app has 100 million MAU, making them ideal location-based advertising platforms for brands.

12. **Meitu, Tik Tok and Red (Instagram):** the three most popular video-sharing applications. Meitu is known for its selfie beauty functionality, Tik Tok for its lip-sync applications and Red for social e-commerce (see later). These are the favourite platforms for Chinese influencers and they have between 100 and 450 million MAU.

But I believe the online company that has most fully embraced the future trends in media is Toutiao (头条), whose name literally means 'headline'. Toutiao makes use of Artificial Intelligence to quench its readers' thirst for news and entertainment. Toutiao does not have its own newsroom, but instead works with more than 4,000 internet partners[49] and uses AI algorithms to provide its subscribers with personalised news bulletins and hyper-relevant advertisements. These algorithms learn the online behaviour of each user and can update this information in real time. In other words, Toutiao aims at the hyper-personalisation of your online reading habits. In contrast to other content on social media, this information platform operates in a dual dataset environment. It is not only what you read that determines what appears on your screen; what you write also influences the recommendation algorithm. In short, this neural network knows you better than your own best friend! Toutiao is one of the darlings of Silicon Valley and at the end of 2018 was valued at 75 billion dollars.[50] Such is its dominance that at the start of 2018 Buzzfeed, its American counterpart, decided to enter into collaboration with Toutiao, seeing its platform as the only effective way to spread their content in China. It was a classic example of 'if you can't beat them, join them'. Toutiao is equally confident of maintaining its position against domestic rivals. In 2017, there were rumours that the powerful Baidu was planning to buy Toutiao. The Toutiao management replied light-heartedly that the rumour-mongers had clearly got the buyer and the seller mixed up! This confidence is not misplaced. Since a massive investment made by Sequoia Capital in 2014, Toutiao has employed a growing army of data scientists in Beijing to develop the very best AI algorithms. Broadcasted, published news reports, which are the largest online open data bank, provide the best input for the further optimisation of these algorithms. That being said, Toutiao's hunger to explore new ground is insatiable, as witnessed by its purchase in 2017 of the live-streaming app Musical.ly and the video creation app Flipagram.

The head of the Toutiao AI lab, Dr. Ma Wei-Ying, says that the world is moving from a digital era to a semantic era. Dr. Ma is already living in this world of the future, where content creation and curation will be revolutionised. For instance, Toutiao is teaching its algorithms to write fake news. I can almost hear you all tut-tutting in disapproval, but it is not what you think! Toutiao has developed two bots, one to write fake news and a second to analyse and identify it. These two bots are in permanent competition with each other, almost as if they are playing some kind of high-tech super-game. One is brilliant at deceiving; the other is brilliant at detecting. Let's hope that the second one wins! That, at least, is what Toutiao intends. Other examples of their AI revolution? Toutiao translates all their articles from Chinese to English and then back to Chinese, with the aim of refining their translation technology to new levels of nuance and sophistication. They also use algorithms to predict if certain content will go viral or to help writers by suggesting titles for their articles that are likely to attract more readers. What's more, Toutiao goes much further than just text. Images are compressed by object and pattern recognition software to allow the addition of personalised metadata on top of the images. Imagine that you are watching a football game online. From an analysis of your viewing behaviour, Toutiao will already know your favourite player and will consequently zoom in more on him or her, while continuing to show you images of the game and at the same time giving you a personalised live commentary, supplemented with the right captions — all automated by technology. Toutiao is a perfect example of how the new China 3.0 is emerging as a consumer-driven society.

SPORT IS GOOD

This brings me to one of the most interesting growth markets in China: sport. Some years ago, the Chinese sport industry was in bad shape, in part due to the exposure of a number of corruption scandals involving match-fixing in football. But all this has now changed and sport is destined to become 'the next big thing'. The sport industry is unique in China because its broadcasting is subject to much less censorship. The government continues to invest heavily in sport, with the aim of transforming the sector into a 290 billion US Dollar industry by 2025, which will be equivalent to one percent of that year's expected Gross Domestic Product. In recent times, China has been frantically searching for new industries that can help to maintain its overall rate of economic growth. In this context, sport is seen as a potentially important growth pole.[51]

As a result, in 2014 sport was designated for the very first time as a priority industry by the central government. That same year, President Xi Jinping — in a move not unlike that of Chairman Mao in 1952, when he proclaimed that table tennis should become the national sport — decided that everyone in China needed to get fit. With this in mind, the intention is to double the capacity of China's sporting facilities (nearly all of which are in the hands of the government) by 2022. Sport is also seen as the ideal medium to create new Chinese heroes and to demonstrate national pride, not only for domestic consumption but also on the world stage. This latter aspect was very clear, for example, during the 2008 Olympic Games held in Beijing. In other words, sport is seen as a growth motor both for the Chinese economy and the Chinese identity. It will be interesting to follow this trend and see whether China can indeed emerge as a top sporting nation or whether the sector will continue to be used primarily for propaganda purposes.

Local companies like Alibaba, Li-Ning and Lenovo have understood the significance of these developments and are pumping billions of dollars into the sponsoring of sporting events worldwide, grabbing costly advertising space from under the noses of Western giants like Coca-Cola and McDonalds. Alibaba recently became a worldwide sponsor of the International Olympic Committee to the tune of 800 million dollars, as part of its overall plan to increase its income from sales outside China from 6 to 50 percent. Sport does indeed have the potential to be the conductor through which Chinese brands become known to the world. All that is now necessary as the icing on the cake is for China to improve its sporting results at the top international level.

THE NEW CHINESE HEROES

Although China currently does not have the best athletes in the world's most popular sports, like football, basketball and cricket, they are streets ahead of the competition in the virtual world of gaming. E-sport in China has developed with remarkable speed and is now played on a massive scale. Tencent and Alibaba both organise gaming competitions in football stadiums that are sold out in minutes and also broadcast live online for the millions of fans who cannot get a ticket. In China, gaming is more than a trend; it is the mother of all trends — much to the annoyance of the government, which sees gaming as a corrupting influence on the spirit of the young. With this in mind, Beijing decided in 2018 to review all the gaming licenses, a decision which immediately sent Tencent shares into free-fall. However, the government already seems to have had a change of heart, since the amount of lost income and lost jobs is potentially huge. In fact, the level of addiction to gaming in China is so massive that not even the Party has much chance of being able to reverse what has effectively become a national obsession. So, how did this obsession originate?

China was the first country to recognize internet addiction as an illness and to open rehabilitation clinics to deal with it. The roots of the problem can be traced to the reality that Chinese society is extremely competitive. The importance of 'performing' is drummed into children from an early age and parents set them a 'good' example by working long and hard to improve things for their families. In these circumstances, many children feel anxious because they are not able to live up to the huge expectations placed upon them. For these children, the internet is often a form of escape, a place where in games they can become the heroes they are unable to be in real life. What's more, the advent of the smartphone has meant that this addictive form of escapism in now available anywhere and anytime. Such is the importance of the internet in general and gaming in particular in Chinese life that the very best online players have acquired a kind of pop-star status. For many, these addicted digital natives are the new heroes in China, acclaimed with the same praise as a Steve Jobs or an Elon Musk in the West! Of course, this has also worked to the advantage of the large Chinese internet companies, for whom gaming has become a cash cow. This is in contrast to the US, where it was advertising revenue that turned Facebook and Google into giants.

At Tencent, the largest internet company in China, more than a third of all income comes from games. Their most popular game — 'Honour of Kings' — has 50 million daily users. On average, the Chinese spend more money on online gaming and virtual goods than any other country in the world. They are also fanatical gamblers. There is a popular anecdote which says that China has 1.3 billion people and 1.2 billion gamblers. In fact, gambling is forbidden in mainland China, which immediately explains why the casinos in nearby Macao are always overflowing and the world of virtual gambling is flourishing. Many of the most popular gambling websites have been set up by Chinese 'entrepreneurs' in the Philippines, much to the annoyance of the government, which is constantly trying to block them, with only partial success. As a result, gambling addiction continues to be a real problem, although at the same time it also reveals an important aspect of Chinese society that often remains hidden: as far as money is concerned, the Chinese can never get enough of earning it or, preferably, winning it. Of course, not all Chinese are like this, and now that people in general have greater prosperity and more free time than ever before, many are turning their attention to other and more worthwhile pastimes. This does nothing to alter the fact that the pursuit of money is still the highest priority for the majority for now.

RESPONSIBLE GAMES

Mid 2018 Tencent decided to require all its game users to register with real and verifiable names and to limit the amount of time they can play each day (the younger the user, the shorter the time limit). This is evidence of a recent positive trend in China, which has seen an increasing number of major companies adopting a more socially responsible attitude. These steps are being taken not necessarily because they are being pushed by the government, but primarily because they wish to keep their business model sustainable and to prevent the negative reputational damage that might otherwise ensue. In China, it is the internet companies themselves that bear the final responsibility for online censorship, which means that they have an obligation to block harmful and unacceptable content on their social media platforms, if they wish to avoid heavy State fines or more dire consequences. As a result, these companies have become adept at dealing with data and content more sensibly and more proactively than in the West. It is not that they apply higher moral standards per se, but rather that they are confronted with problems of this kind on an almost daily basis and know that they will be harshly sanctioned if they fail to take the action expected of them.

For example, Alibaba and JingDong (JD.com) now have thousands of employees who check the origin and authenticity of the goods offered for sale on their sites, to ensure that no fake products slip through the net. In this context, Alibaba checks and approves more than 1,000 new online shops each day. Because some Chinese have an irresistible urge to earn more and more money, often illegally and online, and because a growing number of consumers are no longer prepared to tolerate this, the Chinese e-commerce giants have now decided to step in with a number of concrete actions. Today, Big Data, Artificial Intelligence and blockchain are all being used to prevent abuses and to drive the criminals off the internet. In part to pre-empt government intervention, the founder of Alibaba Jack Ma has also persuaded the government to toughen up the legislation against forgers and falsifiers. Of course, to carry out this kind of control you need relevant data, and lots of it, but this is less of a problem in China than in Europe. As we have already mentioned, the Chinese people are much more willing to make public their personal data than their European counterparts. This is for three main reasons:

1. The government already has insight into this data, if it wants it.
2. Chinese companies offer bigger benefits in exchange for the release of personal data. Sharing data is often a transaction that involves much more than simply ticking an 'I agree' box.
3. The large Chinese internet companies are better equipped and better trained to guard against data abuses, and are therefore more careful about sharing data with their customers and partners than, say, Facebook or Google.

In short, China has more data, more accurate data, and better protected data, which can be used in the algorithms that will create and run their smart new world.

POLARISED HARMONY

In the West, the media situation in China is often presented in a one-dimensional way, as though President Xi wants to concentrate all power in his hands and turn China into a kind of 'Black Mirror' society, where his word — and his word alone — is law. In this scenario, everything is directed from above and Artificial Intelligence will be used to ensure that the Party maintains its iron grip on all aspects of Chinese life. The reality, of course, is much more complex, since the pressure being exerted from below is also increasing. In fact, in my experience this pressure from below is actually greater in China than in the West; it is simply that it is much less visible to us

As we have just discussed, Chinese consumers love entertainment, with social media allowing them new freedom to express themselves in ways that were not possible in the past. Even so, no Chinese citizen forgets that he or she is acting within the framework of a strong social context. In this respect, social media are also a medium through which people can confirm their membership in society and seek ways to improve it. This helps explain why the Chinese are so active and so articulate on social media. As soon as something happens in China that is deemed unacceptable, a veritable storm of protest will break out online, a storm that is capable of damaging the reputations of companies and the government alike. This was the case, for example, with the Wenzhou high-speed train accident in 2011, when 40 people died and Beijing was given the blame fairly and squarely by the country's public fora. Dealing with this pressure from below is a constant challenge for the government. If they attempt to exercise too much control, they may provoke a damaging reaction. But if they exercise too little control, there is a risk that China might run of the rails. An example of such an escalation can be seen from the enormous amount of fake goods that Chinese have made to earn money quickly, and until the current battle against fake goods, and zero-tolerance policies from companies like JD.com, it was impossible to contain it regardless of the warnings made by Alibaba and JD.

To cope with this delicate balancing act, the government hopes to use of Artificial Intelligence to better identify and assess the 'how, what, when and where' of potential areas of risk. But will a smarter government lead to a smarter society?

There is a similar field of tension within the business community. Remembering the story of Nokia or Kodak, it is obvious that consumers can harm or even kill a company that moves too slowly to innovate. In China, in contrast, the companies attempt to offer consumers new degrees of freedom and ease at such high speed that trends become irreversibly established, even before the government has the chance to do much about them. Consider, for instance, the recent examples of mobile payments and the sharing economy for bikes and cars. CEOs like Pony Ma of Tencent or Chuanwei Lu of Didi (the Chinese Uber) have successfully changed consumer demand to such an extent that they have also acquired an increasing influence in government circles with regard to the way Chinese society is organised and improved. What's more, these are the richest men in China, and are therefore looked up to and respected by the entire population, which makes them difficult to ignore. This complex combination of factors often makes it difficult to know what the Chinese government is really thinking. Is it acting proactively or reactively? Is it acting willingly or in response to pressure? One thing, however, is certain: the increasing influence of both the public and the companies is prompting Beijing to try and centralise more and more power in its own hands. This has been a very clear trend since Xi Jinping started his second term of office in 2018.

I believe the new Chinese consumers and the tech companies are the real drivers of innovation and progress in China. And the government? In contrast to most governments elsewhere in the world, where the general reaction to technological advancement is cautious, organised and plan-based, the Chinese government, to its credit, is pro-technology, pro-experimentation and pro-speed. In short, Chinese consumers, companies and the State apparatus are all spurring each other on, creating an innovation process and ecosystem the like of which the world has never seen.

What to Remember?

1 → **The Chinese are inquisitive, like to gamble and have fun,** so that there is a lot of money to be made from the entertainment industry. At the same time, the internet companies have been forced to innovate in order to prevent abuses from creeping into the system. Sport is the domain where the transformation to a smart industry is most likely to take place most quickly.

2 → **Chinese companies have more data than anywhere else in the world** and Chinese consumers share their data more often because the companies offer them a better life experience in exchange. Chinese consumers usually give priority to ease of use above brand loyalty and the use of integrated technology in making a purchasing decision will soon become standard.

3 → **The Chinese government is a partner of Chinese companies.** The companies serve as catalysts in the field of tension that exists between the government and consumers. The media sector is the gateway both for the cat-and-mouse game of avoidance on social media and for state censorship and propaganda. This dual situation is becoming more complex all the time and is the motor for far-reaching innovation in the media industry via a 'push and pull' effect

4 → **Social media platforms are the voice of the people.** Companies like Toutiao are building ever smarter algorithms to give consumers personalised content. Because the Chinese create so much more of their own content and entertainment than in the West, China will probably win the race to develop the personalised internet, on which every individual will be offered the content that is most relevant to him or her at all times and in all places.

24:00:00
天猫全球狂欢节
十周年
天猫双11
成交额
Global Shopping Festival
billion
213

<
Alibaba's CEO Daniel Zhang addresses the public after the 24-hour long Alibaba e-commerce festival on 11 November 2018 (Single's Day). The online sales that day amounted to 213.5 billion yuan (30.7 billion US Dollars).

3

SMART RETAIL

CHINA SETS THE STANDARD: FROM 2013 TO 2030

2017 was the year in which the term **New Retail** was coined by Alibaba, describing a trend that has had a worldwide impact on the sector, in which only Amazon has been able to keep up with the pace of its Chinese rivals. Who is the Chinese consumer and how is he approached differently from in the West? Is China destined to become the worldwide epicentre of e-commerce?

2013 2015 2017 2019 2021 2023 2025 2030

CHINA FOR ALIENS

In 1991, I went on a two-month long trek through China. The first city I came to was Guangzhou. My Lonely Planet travel guide directed me to the little island of Shamian on the great Pearl River, a perfect mini-city within the city, where most foreigners stayed in those days. The island had been a foreign enclave since 1685, and there were moments when it felt as though I had been transported back to that time.

The first Chinese who spoke to me knew only one sentence in English: 'Fake student card?' Taken a bit by surprise, I mumbled 'Yes' before I realized what I was doing. A photo was taken on the spot and ten minutes later I was 10 dollars poorer but now the proud owner of a seemingly brand-new student card that entitled me to 50 percent discounts in many locations. This meant that my journey became 50 percent cheaper, so that I could now afford to travel twice as far! This was my very first lesson about China: the customer is king and sellers are highly inventive and flexible when it comes to providing 'personalised' services.

Back in those days, you could only exchange your European and American banknotes for so-called Foreign Exchange Certificate (FEC), not for the RMB banknotes that the Chinese population used. The FEC were only valid for use in designated hotels, cafés and shops for 'aliens', the official term for all foreign visitors. This double currency system neatly kept the outsiders separate from the Chinese people.

However, because China badly needed to attract large-scale foreign investment, it was important that foreign experts living in China could buy their favourite products from home, such as coffee, cheese and Marlboro cigarettes (how times have changed!). These types of products were not encouraged for import, and so the government set up special 'Friendship Stores', where you could only pay in FEC and where the local Chinese population was physically not allowed to enter. China being what it is, there was soon a flourishing black market for FEC, because many Chinese also wanted to buy these imported luxury products. Strange as it may sound, the illegal changing of money was perfectly safe and open at the time. There were even cashiers in the banks who helped to check that the notes being exchanged were genuine! That is how I remember China in the 1990s: every Chinese I met was far too busy trying to make money for himself to check or control what others were doing.

A TWO-SPEED CHINA

In the 1980's and 1990's, most of the retail shops (not just the Friendship Stores) were state-run. They also had a very unusual system for payment. Each shop had a hundred or so separate retail counters. Behind each counter were two sales clerks, offering their various wares. One sold socks, another ties, a third teddy bears, and so on. Nearly all the articles for sale were produced in state-run factories. If you wanted a particular article, the sales clerk wrote down your order on a piece of paper, which was then attached to a moveable rope on a complex pulley system hanging from the ceiling. In the middle of the store, high up against the tall ceiling, sat a woman in a sort of crow's nest, which was connected to every counter by the system of ropes and pulleys. The order and your money were reeled up to her by pulley and your change and a stamped note (proving you had paid) was then reeled back down. If you wanted to buy ten different articles from separate counters, this process had to be repeated ten times. There was a constant swish of money and orders flying non-stop through the air, making for a fascinating shopping experience.

For me, this now vanished type of retail shop symbolises how Chinese innovation management works in practice: there is one person with final responsibility sitting above a distributed system that allows everyone to look after their own 'shop', with much less middle management than is the case in the West (Smart Manufacturing).

During that two-month tour, I also came across something else that still strikes me as being characteristically Chinese. I can remember the scene as if it were yesterday. I wanted to buy a new coat. I could see the coat hanging on the rack, but the sales assistant told me it wasn't available, as though she was talking to a blind person. Because I really wanted that coat, I waited and patiently began to tell her my life story and of my travels around her country in my broken Chinese. Two hours later, by which time most of her colleagues had also joined in the conversation, we were the best of friends — and the coat was mine.

People often say that everything happens super-fast in China, but that is not really the case. Things can only happen quickly on two conditions: one, the decision-taker is convinced that the matter is important or opportune; and two, there is a well-grounded personal connection with the people responsible for carrying it out. That is a lesson that you need to learn in China if you want to get anything done.

E-COMMERCE

Given this background, it is not hard to understand why e-commerce has really taken off in China. The old way of shopping in China was archaic, inconvenient and highly inefficient. The retail industry was small, immature and weak. Today, this industry only has an average of 2.4 shopping malls per million inhabitants, in comparison with 12 in America. In addition, the physical shopping market is the most fragmented in the world. In China, the 100 largest retail brands account for just 6.4 percent[52] of consumer sales. The comparable figure in America is 40 percent.[53]

Such an underdeveloped retail environment was the ideal setting in which to launch a new selling paradigm: e-commerce. In 1999, Jack Ma launched Alibaba Online. Because there were only around 8 million internet users in China at that time, Ma knew that it would take a while before the Chinese started to buy massively online. For that reason, Alibaba's first product was a business website for foreign companies that wanted to find Chinese companies and goods.

It is often said that the big Chinese internet companies like Baidu, Alibaba and Tencent are just copies of the American giants Google, eBay or AOL. That is simply not true. In fact, the environment in China was wholly unsuitable for a 'search and reapply' of the American online models, so the Chinese entrepreneurs needed to adapt and re-invent everything about these new models to suit China's unique conditions.

That is why Jack Ma is seen as the true genius of Chinese e-commerce. He introduced four concepts that were wholly unknown to eBay and these allowed him to transform Alibaba into the empire it has become today.

1. **Trust.** Credit cards were never popular in China. Chinese society was strongly cash-driven, not least because credit cards were subject to charges as high as 15 percent. There was not a single bank in China willing to help Jack Ma obtain a banking license, because none of them believed in the internet. Jack was convinced that e-commerce without trust simply would not work, and that it must be possible to guarantee the security of the transactions. To solve the problem, he decided to set up a payment system called AliPay – at the time totally illegally and with a real chance that he might end up in prison. He made deals with the banks and the Chinese postal service so that their clients could open an AliPay account. Through a guarantee system that Alibaba set up, the seller on Alibaba would only get the money due to him when the goods were confirmed as being accepted by the buyer. In this way, Alibaba was able to gain the trust and confidence of millions of consumers.

2. **Rewarding your customers.** In the West, most business models are built by first having a good product, which you then launch to potential customers with a strong marketing campaign. In China, customers tend to be much more pragmatic: if you don't give them a good discount or find some other way to reward them,

they will hesitate for much longer before making a purchasing decision. Even in the street markets in China, you can often see how obviously wealthy customers are content to haggle for minutes on end to get a marginally lower price. In the West, we not only weigh our valuable time against a potential discount, but also against the effort it costs to gain that discount. But not in China. For that reason, Chinese companies think much more about how they can find ways to reward their customers. In terms of the internet companies, this translates into a wide range of 'special actions' that allow customers to sign up for free extras like taxi rides, meals or call credit. At Alibaba, the customer focus has always been on small self-employed businesses and individuals who want to sell things on-line. Jack Ma allowed online listings free of charge (which is not the case with eBay), resulting in a platform with a huge variety of products and a robust and loyal customer base. Alibaba made its money not from these small-scale sellers, but from the sale of advertising space and keyword placements to the larger brands. The buyers were also given discounts in return for feedback, which made the reliability of the sellers in the marketplace more transparent. In this way, both parties to the transactions — the buyers and the sellers — were rewarded by Alibaba.

3. **Comfort-as-a-service.** For a country led by a communist party, it is surprising how customer-oriented modern China has become. Private companies in China understand the importance of keeping customers satisfied better than their international peers. For example, at CTRIP, the largest online travel platform in China, they promise to pick up the phone within 20 seconds — and they achieve this. If I phone my bank in Europe, I often have to wait for many minutes before I finally get someone on the line. In the West, customer service is seldom a core activity of the company, as a result of which call centres are a complex labyrinth of menu choices that take an age to negotiate before you can actually speak to a real live person. Alibaba introduced 'Aliwangwang' as early as 2004, an instant messaging system to better connect buyers and sellers. Alibaba recognized early on that business is personal, something that takes place between individuals. Consequently, they organised online business training for sellers, as well as a special code system to facilitate the management of all the many different online stores. At the same time, every returned product was covered by a seven-day repayment guarantee, something that was revolutionary in its day. In this way, Alibaba set the standard for customer service in China, a role it still fulfils today. Its recently introduced Sesame credit score may be criticised by some (particularly in the West), but the vast majority of customers love it!

4. **Ecosystem thinking.** Alibaba has moved away from positioning itself as a pure e-commerce player, in part because its focus has always remained firmly on the customer. Alibaba continues to search for solutions for sellers and buyers to simplify the transaction process and provide each side with a more positive

purchasing experience. This basic philosophy has led to a dramatic extension of Alibaba's range of activities. For example, it has set up the Alimama advertising platform, following the Google model. Similarly, Taobao Ke was launched as an external sales team for clients. Video and mobile options have been integrated into Youku-Tudou. Ali Micro Finance facilitates small-scale loans. The smart logistics network Cainiao has become the ideal partner for sellers, thanks to its Big Data network that can make optimal delivery choices. And this is just the tip of the iceberg of the rapidly expanding Alibaba ecosystem.

These four important areas of differentiation — which made it possible for Alibaba to force eBay out of China in 2006 — now form the four pillars on which the strength of successful Chinese online companies is based.

Chinese companies **always take the customer as the starting-point for their thinking. How can we make customers trust us?** In the West, we too often take this for granted. **How can we reward customers?** In the West, we are much less concerned with win-win. **How can we better help customers?** In the West, customer service is not seen as being 'cool'. **How can we make the customer's life easier?** In the West, we are more concerned with making our internal processes easier.

Of course, there are also companies in the West that are highly customer-oriented, like Zalando or Amazon, but they tend to be the exception, rather than the rule. In China, customer service always takes precedence over product innovation. This is seldom the case in Europe and America, although in recent years increasing attention has been devoted to customer-centricity. This focus on the customer is unquestionably the greatest strength of the Chinese online companies, especially since product innovation is no longer primarily the preserve of the West and can just as often come from China itself.

Thinking in terms of ecosystems also makes China unique. Every Chinese company belongs to an existing ecosystem or tries to build one of its own. This is typical for a market that is already immeasurably large, yet continues to grow rapidly. In this environment, it is no longer about trying to capture someone else's market share, but is more a question of growing faster than the market by constantly re-inventing yourself. In China, businesspeople are convinced that major problems can only be solved if the entire ecosystem works together. For this reason, smaller Chinese companies are generally willing to attach themselves to bigger ecosystems until they are large enough to attempt to go it alone. And even if they are small, by belonging to an ecosystem, they can nearly always quickly find money, talent, partners and, above all, a market and customers to help them grow.

This is why I believe that in the years ahead the Alibaba and Tencent ecosystems will win the retail battle with Amazon, certainly in the southern hemisphere, probably in Europe, and perhaps even in America over time. Or to use the words of Jack Ma: 'Amazon is as an empire, and Alibaba is an ecosystem. We want to empower others to sell, to service, to make sure that other people are more powerful than us. Making sure that with our technology and innovation, our partners and 10 million small-business sellers can compete with Microsoft and IBM... We think, by using our technology, we can make every company become Amazon.'[54]

Chinese businesses see their **market** as the greatest source of value for the company: their customers, networks, sales figures, market size, number of offices, speed of growth, competitiveness, reputation, number of services, variety of market segments, customer loyalty, etc.

Businesses in the West see **knowledge** as the greatest source of value for the company: their people, technology, intellectual property, research, culture, leadership, business model, strategy, shareholders, partners, innovation, etc.

Managers in the West are typically searching for a 'blue ocean', the creation of new markets by offering something unique, being the first, generating previously unknown value. Managers in China are happy to swim in red oceans, where there is already an existing market, existing demand, plenty of money and plenty of opportunities. Plenty of competition as well? That is something they are willing to accept as a fact of life. This mentality also means that on the rare occasions when a blue ocean market does appear in China, it is almost immediately coloured red, since there are soon dozens of fast followers willing to take their chances in a new growth environment. Put simply: Westerners want to be 'unique'; the Chinese want to be 'important'. It is possible to be unique without becoming relevant. But if you are important, you are nearly always relevant —and if not, the Chinese government is there to lend you a helping hand along the way.

In the West, companies try to find customers for their technology or products; in China, companies try to find technologies or products for their customers.

This is the greatest challenge for Americans and Europeans who want to work together with the Chinese. Each side wants something different. Western companies want to sell their technology to Chinese customers, whereas Chinese companies simply want more and better customers, for whom they will eventually — through research and investment — find a technology that matches.

This is increasingly seen as a sound strategy. In today's software-driven market, there are already several important examples where technology no longer necessarily makes the key difference to success in the market. Uber, Airbnb and Amazon are all cases in point. Customer ease, speed of execution and ingenuity are now often more important ingredients in a winning business model than technological inventiveness. And it is precisely where the Chinese excel.

CONTEXT

Big Data and Artificial Intelligence are the next advances that will give a huge boost to e-commerce sales. As you might expect, the key ingredient, data, is in the hands of the internet giants. Alibaba and Tencent have at their disposal the data generated by almost 1 billion daily users, who, thanks to mobile payment systems, are 90 times more active than Western consumers.[55] More than 50 percent of all online sales in China are made via cell phone; even up to 90 percent on Alibaba's Single's Day.[56, 57] And lots more data means lots more useful insights. In China, every time that you search for something, buy something, pay for something, like something, post something, share something or recommend something, Alibaba and Tencent will know just that little bit more about you. And it is not just a matter of internet use. Every time you buy something in a shop, pay for a taxi ride or for a bike hire, have something delivered, go to the bank, make a journey, visit a sporting event or the cinema, the two internet mastodons are capturing the data, waiting to further refine their already extensive profile of who you are and what you like. In this way, almost every moment of your life is slowly mapped. By comparison, Facebook, Amazon and Google start to look like internet dwarfs alongside Alibaba or Tencent.

Every user that logs in on one of the two ecosystems is recognized by the same identification number, irrespective of the context or the application that he/she is using at the time. This means that both of the big data harvesters are able to make a full 360-degree profile of your preferences and habits. This is a bit like what Amazon does with its recommendations system, but it happens with every single app used by the Chinese both online and offline. Of course, this has privacy implications that in the West would immediately lead to dire warnings that we are heading towards a zero-privacy society. But I think that conclusion misinterprets the situation, as you can read in the chapter on Smart Health. Even so, there is no denying that the Chinese internet companies do indeed possess huge amounts of data about almost every Chinese citizen.

Over the years, retailers in the West have used various data systems, which work more or less independently from each other: marketing, sales, e-commerce, processes, logistics, offline, customer loyalty, analyses, etc. Retail experts have been saying that this all needs to be integrated into a 'multi-channel' strategy. But in China this kind of centralised ecosystem already exists, in the shape of just a handful of internet companies, with Alibaba and Tencent (with JD.com, Alibaba's biggest competitor) taking the lion's share of the market.

This centralisation of data in two huge ecosystems helps brands gain better insights about their consumers. In this way, for example, Alibaba can assist a company like P&G to find the ideal markets and target groups in China (and increasingly elsewhere) for a new product or can offer advice about the best promotion and communication channels, all thanks to its Big Data. At the same time, the data can also reveal useful insights for niche players about specific sub-segments or interest groups.

With Artificial Intelligence, it is possible to take things a step further. Alibaba and Tencent can make recommendations about which product packaging is most likely to appeal to which target group. Or what the ideal supply chain should look like. Or which trends need to be watched more closely. Or even how products can best be designed. It is no coincidence that Alibaba and Tencent are both investing so heavily in AI, because this means that they will become the unavoidable point of contact for every strategic decision of literally every brand and retailer. This signals the inevitable demise of strategic consultants, market research and advertising bureaus. In the future, the powerful AI machines of Alibaba and Tencent will be able to do everything quicker and better.

THE MODERN CHINESE CONSUMER

Even though Alibaba and Tencent have both invested heavily in nearly every market that has something to do with retail, the two internet giants are very different in terms of focus and culture. Alibaba's main activity is e-commerce and the company thinks like a property developer. In contrast, Tencent's main activity is social media and the company thinks like a risk investor that wishes to ensure gains for its partners. It is this social aspect that makes Tencent so unique, even in comparison with Alibaba, if you want to understand the true nature of new Chinese retail consumers.

Chinese consumers born after 1990 differ very little from Western millennials: they want to have a good time, share experiences, live in the 'here and now', be unique, etc. Even so, traditions continue to play a prominent role in China, especially if you wish to manifest yourself as an individual. This underlying conformism is strongly coloured by Confucianism, a system based on a social and ethical philosophy that is focused on achieving harmony, respect and goodness in society. Although more than 2,500 years old, this is still the manner in which Chinese society wishes to be ordered, an ethos firmly supported by both the people and the government. The result is a community in which your position and your responsibilities stand in relation to your immediate environment and society as a whole, which implies a high regard for the elderly and the wise, and, of course, the state.

At the same time, Chinese consumer expert Tom Doctoroff[58] has identified a conflicting quality in Confucianism that is mentioned much less frequently: the urge and ambition to excel, together with the need to be recognised for the contribution you make to society. He refers to this as the internal conflict between 'projection' and 'protection'. The field of tension that exists between strict social regulation and the desire to move up the social ladder makes every purchase in China a curious mix of social conformity and an expression of powerful individualism. Although this might seem highly contradictory to Westerners, the two motivations are not mutually exclusive. In advertisements for Nike in the West, it is the individual who stands as the central hero, whereas in China Nike's advertising is about team spirit and the contribution the individual can make to the whole. This social context can either completely suffocate the individual objectives of consumers or, alternatively, give them wings. The Chinese want to achieve personal advancement, but not at the expense of the team or what they have already built together in the past. The greatest difference between Western and Chinese consumers can therefore be reduced in its essence to the difference between a 'me' identity and a 'we' identity.

The Chinese concept of 'projection' and 'protection' is also of great importance in the business world. If you want to do business with the Chinese, you will need to try and understand whether your prospective partner views your relationship from a 'projection' or 'protection' perspective. The mistake that nearly all Westerners make is to approach the Chinese too defensively, partly because they do not really trust them and partly from a desire to 'protect' our knowledge, intellectual property or investment. When this happens, the Chinese are automatically also pushed into a 'protection' frame of mind, so that the chances of successful collaboration are very slim. My advice to Western managers is to approach the Chinese with a more positive 'projection' attitude. Talk about the future, about your common dreams, about what you can build together, about the money you will be earning together. In this way, it is much more likely that you will win the approval and support of your Chinese partner's decision maker. Once you have this top-level alignment, you can let your accountants and lawyers loose on the more 'protectionist'-minded middle managers of the Chinese company, who in a professional context inhabit a very different environment from their boss. In this sense, the Chinese sometimes seem to be 'qubit people', who adjust their frame of mind to the manner in which they are assessed or approached.

SOCIAL E-COMMERCE

Chinese consumers are constantly searching for affirmation, for which they usually turn to social media. Tencent excels in providing this to its users. For example, on WeChat you can share brand products with your friends on your moments (like with Facebook), but with just two more clicks your friends can order those brands and have them delivered to their home.

An application that has become extremely popular in recent years is the purchase advice site RED (xiǎohóngshū 小红书). It was started in 2013 as a social media platform to share personal shopping experiences online. The site makes it possible for you to easily share and recommend products and brands that match your lifestyle, as well as offering more general information about new and upcoming products. In just four years, the platform grew to become one of the largest e-commerce sites in China, with more than 100 million users.[59] In addition, it is almost the only social media platform in which both Tencent and Alibaba are shareholders, which clearly underlines the importance of social e-commerce. What sets RED and similar platforms apart are the close social media communities that develop spontaneously, thanks to the original content of the users.

This is a business approach that is very different from the practices of the large e-commerce sites, like Tmall and Taobao of Alibaba or its biggest competitor JD.com (JingDong). Consumers never feel that RED is trying to push products on to them, but instead is genuinely concerned to provide them with genuine shared experiences and sound advice. RED's success can be attributed to the idea that on this site (unlike many others) the Chinese feel able to make their own choices, which automatically increases their belief in the reliability of the information. RED does almost no marketing, believing that its sharing of genuine content and highly relevant purchase tips is marketing enough. Their clear objective is to improve their consumers' lives. In this sense, their site visitors are more trend-followers than buying customers, many of whom end up buying on their site anyhow.

Another interesting site in this respect is the luxury e-commerce site Secoo, whose motivation is not directly socially oriented, but which has nevertheless built up close ties with Tencent to follow every phase of the customer trajectory, starting with the sharing of products with friends on WeChat and ending with the final purchase of those products on the Secoo site. In collaboration with Tencent, Secoo uses smart algorithms to search for and identify the motives that prompt potential buyers to make a purchase. In other words, they do not look at the followers of brands or the products that are shared, liked and bought. Instead, they try to identify patterns of social behaviour that correspond with different communities. These searches have revealed, for example, that rich people in China do not necessarily follow the brand 'Gucci', or golf or even the stock exchange, but prefer football, playing video games and listening to music on iQiYi. Using these correlated insights, Secoo can then build relevant micro-communities for its customers, who it can charm with its 'butler customer service'. In this way, like RED, Secoo can win the trust of millions in a way that takes Alibaba or JD a lot more effort.

Different in nature but equally impressive is the PDD (拼多多 pīnduōduō) site, which emerged from nowhere in 2015. PDD rewards users for buying things together. You might think that this sounds very much like Groupon, the inventor of social e-commerce, but you would be mistaken. The two online stores are very different. Groupon started in the pre-smartphone era, sending out temporary special offers from brands and restaurants via newsletters. And then they had to wait: wait and hope that lots of people who were previously unknown to them would sign up for the deal. In contrast, PDD makes use of WeChat, where the users themselves can encourage each other to make communal purchases, all in the same app. The actual purchasing happens in real time via the smartphone and you can receive discounts if you can persuade your friends to join in. There is also a strong element of competitive gamification in the PDD model, which appeals to the Chinese mentality. In 2018, Tencent invested three billion dollars in PDD and catapulted the company to super-unicorn status, so that it now represents the biggest threat to Alibaba's e-commerce dominance.[60] In China, even a market leader like Alibaba, with more than 50 percent of all e-commerce transactions, can never feel safe.[61]

This new type of internet platform, like RED, Secoo and PDD, unites groups of customers in communities or tribes, providing them with relevant interactions that result in greater customer trust. And now these Chinese social e-commerce platforms plan to take things a stage further by using Artificial Intelligence and Big Data. Sites like Secoo are today already capable of offering a personal service to more than 300,000 customers. It is the social context within which trust is sought and given in China, in combination with a natural distrust of strangers and companies in general, which has led to this development of a flourishing social e-commerce in China. If you want to understand the communication world of tomorrow, with its transmission of individual and personalised content for very large numbers of customers who have the fullest confidence in your site, then China is the place to be.

Western business leaders often say, (not without some justification) that the Chinese, notwithstanding their other achievements, are unable to make good presentations or tell great stories. Pointing to companies like Disney, they claim that in reality, Westerners are still the masters of communication and storytelling. In my opinion, this may be true, but it is becoming less relevant. Perhaps we were the best marketeers in the 'old world' of push-marketing, but almost imperceptibly the Chinese have become masters in the 'new world' of communication: a 'connected contextual world', in which communication is driven by individuals in contact with other individuals of the same tribe, with the brand facilitating their communication. I am increasingly worried for the Western marketing conglomerates and managers who still have a false feeling of creative superiority.

CONSUMER TO BUSINESS (C2B)

Since Taobao, the Chinese eBay equivalent, first launched its site in 2003, China has been flooded by a tidal wave of starter-entrepreneurs. Today, the country has almost 10 million online Taobao stores, which are primarily operated by private individuals who often have another full-time or part-time job. Because a growing number of non-authentic products were eventually being sold on Taobao, the website acquired a bad reputation, so that many store owners lost their new source of income.

Until 2014, there was no real alternative to Taobao. However, in May of that year Tencent launched WeChat stores, which encourage small companies to sell their products online via the site. In fact, even if you don't have a company as such, you can still offer your products via your own WeChat moments to 5,000 connections, so that you can earn some extra private cash. And because your WeChat followers are the friends of your friends, the levels of authenticity and trust are high. What's more, the system requires no investment, no stock and payments are made through the reliable WeChat Pay. It really couldn't be any easier, as a result of which 'playing shop' has become something of a rage in China. At the same time, it is a trend that has brought out the hidden artist in many Chinese. Countless people suddenly began to design and fabricate their own things or offer their own services, from self-knitted caps and fancy cupcakes to 'at home' manicure and tattooing services. WeChat has transformed the Chinese consumer into a businessperson, making well-known brands now buying into the online design and services of their own customers. This is a great example of moving from B2C (Business-to-Consumer) to C2B (Consumer-to-Business).

DAIGOU

Because many fake and unsafe products are still sold in China, in recent years many Chinese have been turning to products from overseas. This demand launched a new trend that has since become a part of the Chinese way of life: daigou (which literally means: 'buying on behalf of someone').

Daigou participants are Chinese who buy foreign products abroad and then bring them or send them back to China via a parallel (and often illegal) circuit, a practice that is also sometimes known as 'grey trade'. It is estimated that there are as many as 100,000 daigou sellers in Australia. These are often Chinese students who search via WeChat for products that are in high demand with their family and friends back home, such as baby milk powder, vitamins or cosmetics. They buy these things in their own name and then send them home by post, in order to avoid import duties. Since many Western brands often set their prices higher in China than elsewhere, the profit margin for the daigou trader is often a good one. In fact, the daigou have acquired such influence that they are actually in a position to make or break Western brands in China. The major international companies are now aware that as much as 50 percent of their sales in the country now pass through this parallel circuit and it is fortunate for them that in 2018 the government finally decided to crack down on this grey trade. With effect from 1 January 2019, new e-commerce legislation has come into force that is intended to change China's reputation as a land where fake products abound. This legislation is aimed primarily at the daigou,[62] who now need to register with the authorities and pay tax on their activities — unless they want to risk a 290,000 dollar fine. This should bring in considerable additional revenue for the State, which in return has added more products to the list of goods that can be imported tax-free into China, as well as increasing the limit of the permitted maximum value per traveller. This is another classic example of the way in which the Chinese government can cleverly convert a problem into an opportunity.

The power that the Chinese consumer today has acquired over brands is frightening for brand owners, especially if they are still living in the old push-communication world. Trends in China provide a glimpse of the future: a world where consumers, thanks to the daigou, PPD or WeChat, have brands at their mercy, are able to create and market their own alternative products, check product quality and share the results, provide their own marketing communication and even give a social dimension to the whole buying and selling process. This is a full-blown C2B business model, and one that the Western B2C companies will need to learn to live with. But how exactly? How can they reach these new, all-powerful consumers who have a very short attention span and expect a high-quality personalised butler service?

KOL – KEY OPINION LEADERS

Key Opinion Leaders (KOL) play a central role in communication and trust between consumers and brands. KOLs in China are very different from their Western counterparts, the 'influencers' with whom we have become familiar through YouTube or Instagram. These Western-style online celebrities are known in China as wanghong (网红). Chinese KOLs focus primarily on lifestyle, and usually offer strong educational angle in their content. They generally have expertise on a specific theme and have frequently built up a relationship with their public over a long period. The wanghong are also widely known through the internet, but their opinions are not always trusted by Chinese netizens if they directly recommend products. For this reason, the real Chinese KOLs do not like to be referred to as wanghong. KOLs have a much wider impact than Western influencers. To a large extent, the KOL trend has been able to blossom in China because the country's heavily censored state television and press have been unable to provide young people with answers to many of the questions that most interest them. How can I date a girl (or boy)? How can I look my best? What is the healthiest way to feed my baby? Nowadays, tens of thousands of KOLs are ready and willing to offer helpful answers. They are top entertainers, who, like their influencer colleagues in the West, know how to keep their followers on a string.

It has been calculated that a KOL in China only needs 1,000 superfans who share content, trust the KOL implicitly and often buy what he/she recommends in order to generate the same turnover as an online influencer in the West (like a YouTube star) with 1 million followers. 70 percent[63] of Chinese consumers born after 1995 feel wholly comfortable with buying via social media, in comparison with just 44 percent in the rest of the world in the same age category. Consumer brands are constantly searching for the right formula to create and keep loyal customers. In China, the KOLs enjoy a high degree of loyalty from their followers, which Western brands are now trying to exploit by investing in KOLs on a large scale.

In my view, it is no longer possible to optimally reach Chinese consumers without a viable KOL strategy. The interesting thing from the perspective of the brands is that the KOLs make use of brand products to demonstrate to their followers how they can improve the quality of their life. For this reason, the brands are happy to give KOLs free samples or products, in the hope that they will use them and talk about them positively. This lucrative business model, which regularly sees top brands like L'Oréal or Michael Kors paying court to successful KOLs, has led to the setting up of more than 200 KOL academies in China, where promising Chinese influencers can be groomed for KOL stardom. And it really is big business. The best KOLs earn tens of thousands of US Dollars each month or even more, and the academies are sometimes willing to invest as much as a million dollars in a single KOL. Is it just a bubble that will one day burst? Perhaps, but KOLs who offer honest, authentic content and genuine, passionate opinions will never disappear completely from the retail scene.

At the present time, there is no question that the KOL trend is turning the advertising world in China on its head, a phenomenon that is now making its way to the West, and known as nano- or micro-influencers. And perhaps this is not so surprising: at the end of the day, people prefer to interact with other people rather than with brands. It is this human element that is the real strength of the KOLs, who have now, in effect, become their own brand. They are starting to design and market their own creations, selling them to other consumers and stores. The retail world of tomorrow is destined to be a mix of C2C (Consumer-to-Consumer) and C2B (Consumer-to-Business), with the KOLs and their new products, services and innovations playing the central role. This future is already a reality in China.

SHORT-VIDEO

Every day, the KOLs livestream from their webcams in improvised home studios for hundreds and sometimes even thousands of followers. They tell a story via video streaming apps like WeChat, Sina Weibo (Twitter), Youku (YouTube) or the popular Yizhibo, Kuaishou, Inke or Meitu (Instagram).

The most successful of the recently emerged short video apps are Musical.ly (2015) and Tik Tok (2016).[64] If you have young children, you don't need me to tell you just how addictive these two music video platforms can be. Like many people, perhaps you think this phenomenon originated in America? Wrong: it is pure Chinese. Tik Tok is the No.1 most downloaded app on iPhone worldwide. What's more, since 2018 both platforms belong to the same company, Bytedance, which earlier had a huge success with the news app Toutiao (Smart Media and Entertainment). Bytedance is now merging the two apps into a single super-app, combining the compulsive lip-syncing, video creation skills of Musical.ly with the powerful AI recommendation algorithm of Tik Tok, which analyses interests and viewing habits, all with the purpose of making even more compelling short videos.

The way in which the Chinese earn money with these apps is also fairly unorthodox; namely, through the sale of virtual presents.[65] These are fun emoticons, like flowers, a heart or a car, each of which has a different price. The live-streamer can make a gift of one of these emoticons during an online session in a manner that is highly visible to everyone. The receiving KOL or wanghong can then exchange them for cash. This is the '5 minutes of fame' that the celebrities offer their followers, and it is a real money-spinner. The average Chinese man or woman spends a huge amount by Western standards on virtual presents, which are actually a unique form of entertainment experience that perfectly matches the prevailing social context in China. You can compare it with getting an autograph from your favourite pop star after a concert, but in this case it happens online and against a micropayment.

The American social media companies have not been able to make a breakthrough in China. Google was never able to fully reconcile itself with the internet censorship practised by Beijing, while Facebook and Twitter were both blocked because they were seen by the Chinese government to be enablers of public protests. By the same token, Chinese social media powerhouses like Tencent or Sina have not truly broken through in the West, although it is now possible that Bytedance may become the first Chinese social media player with a truly worldwide reach. In just two years' time, Tik Tok has racked up 500 million active monthly users, a figure that took Facebook seven years to achieve. If you add to this the fact that in 2017 Tencent also bought into Snapchat (12 percent) and Spotify (7.5 percent), it seems inevitable that the influence of Chinese media companies will increasingly filter through to the West. We had better start preparing ourselves for the world of KOLs, short video and social e-commerce: because, like it or not, they are all on their way.

OMO-SAPIENS

The behaviour and lifestyle of young people today is heavily influenced by the 'stickiness' of social media: the desire for social validation and comparison, and fear of missing out (FOMO). Of course, pure egocentrism and healthy curiosity also play important roles. Social networks fulfil our need to define ourselves within a particular social context and form an extension to our physical world, which, for the time being, is regrettably limited in time and space.

But what if that physical world was suddenly no longer limited in time and space? In my view, the moment is fast approaching when the boundaries between online and offline will first blur and then dissolve. I am not talking about a Matrix-like science fiction movie, in which parallel worlds can exist simultaneously alongside each other at the quantum level. No, I mean a world in which people no longer make a distinction between the world of atoms and the world of bits. This will happen when we have a digital environment which is so realistic that it can be experienced as reality, through virtual or augmented applications. Or we have a physical world that is so digitally connected that every object and every person is a smart receiver and transmitter of data via the Internet of Things (IoT), 5G and Artificial Intelligence. A world in which people, things and data form a single unity. This is what Kai-Fu Lee[66], the CEO of Sinovation Ventures, calls the OMO world. OMO stands for 'Online-Merge-Offline'. A new world in which the frontier between online and offline will slowly but surely become blurred.

Kai-Fu Lee believes that this futuristic world will arrive sooner than we think, and that it will first be discovered in China. Lee claims that China has an important lead over the West in the four key elements that are necessary to build this new world.

1. **Everyone is connected.** China is currently the country with the most smartphones in the world (713 million in 2018),[67] and is destined to stay in the lead. All these phones are equipped with a GPS system and sensors. As a result, China is the most connected and most mobile country on the planet. In fact, the smartphone has significantly reduced the huge size of China in both time and space. Everyone is constantly in motion but they are always available, no matter where they are. This is only possible because the Chinese have a very different relationship with their cell phones from Westerners. In China, it is not impolite to check your WeChat messages during meetings, or to conduct phone conversations out loud in a restaurant, or to leave a personal voice mail message while you are in a crowded lift. The Chinese do not talk about the need for a 'digital detox' and the social acceptability of mobile technology is seldom a subject for discussion. China may not have a high enough level of freedom of expression, but it has an extremely high level of freedom of communication.

2. **Ease of mobile payment.** 85 percent of all smartphone users in China have already used their device to make payments, whereas the comparable figure in most Western countries hovers around 25 percent.[68] According to the President of PayPal, an aver-

age Chinese citizen opens his or her mobile payment app between 30 and 40 times a day, whereas with PayPal the figure is between 30 and 40 times a year.[69] The transactions are instant and cost-free, with no strings attached, and are used to make person-to-person payments without the need for a bank or other financial intermediary. When the cashier tells you the price in China, people's first reaction is to reach for their smartphone. In the West, our first reaction is still to reach for our wallet or purse. This phenomenon is already so ingrained in China that it has stimulated a whole new wave of offline markets, which has made China the world's top innovator in mobile payment applications, both technologically and from the perspective of user-friendliness. Think, for example, of the car and bike share industry, the courier industry or autonomous stores (Smart Mobility).

3. **Internet of Things (IOT).** China is today by far the world's largest producer and user of electronics, such as sensors, microprocessors and other electronic devices. The country is also the front-runner and the No.1 test market for new products and new locations where sensor-based technology can be employed. These factors will soon give China the ability to trace the movements and collect the data of most of its nearly 1.4 billion consumers, in a manner that goes far beyond what is currently possible online. In Shenzhen, products are already being manufactured with IoT concepts as a standard functionality, so that IoT is set to become an inherent part of China's maker-ecosystem in the very near future (Smart Manufacturing).

4. **Artificial Intelligence.** For an OMO world, it is vital that online and offline data can be further aggregated to allow Artificial Intelligence to give much more accurate real-time recommendations with much greater customer-friendliness and to enable much more efficient logistical and supply chains. It is AI that will open up the real possibility of dissolving the boundary between the physical and the virtual worlds, creating a whole new plane of experience. This will not only bring huge economic benefits, but also improve the comfort of our lifestyle immeasurably. And as already mentioned, no country is further ahead in the race to develop AI implementations than China.

Kai-Fu Lee refers to the new citizens of his merged online-offline world as **OMO sapiens**, people who will opt for the advantages of the new OMO world and, consequently, will automatically and almost unconsciously cross the border between what is man and what is machine. I predict that China will be the first country to have genuine **OMO sapiens consumers**, thanks to the speed at which its domestic environment is already changing and will continue to evolve. The power of the human brain and the power of data collected by smart products from smart locations will be integrated into a decentralised and more collective pool of intelligence, which will no longer have the properties and the qualities of intelligence that we today ascribe to homo sapiens.

NEW RETAIL

Given all these different developments, it is hardly surprising that China will also be the pioneer of a new retail world, in which online and offline will become a single unity. One of the first examples of this can be seen in the Hema (pronounced Huh-ma) fresh food stores recently launched by Alibaba (which have nothing to do with the Dutch discount retailer of the same name). Jack Ma has developed what he calls the concept of 'new retail', which goes far beyond the existing omnichannel model. The idea is to build an entire ecosystem around Alibaba applications and platforms, driven by data that is used to understand the thoughts and wishes of the customer in the best possible manner.

These Hema supermarkets give us a glimpse of how the Chinese OMO sapiens consumers of the future will shop. To begin with, you need to register for membership of Hema via Alibaba Taobao or your AliPay account. In the store itself, every product is perfectly packed and super-fresh. By scanning the product bar code with your app you can find all the information you need: price, origin, date, weight, sell-by date, etc. You scan in everything you want to buy, pay with a single press of a button and make your way home, where your purchases will be delivered within 30 minutes, providing you live within a three-mile radius. You prefer to take your groceries with you? No problem! The stores are equipped with staff-free check-outs, similar to those used in the Amazon Go shops in the US. And if you fancy a bite to eat before you leave, one of the chefs will be delighted to cook anything you purchased from the store for you in the open kitchen, with your meal delivered to your table by a sushi-style conveyor belt. You will still see plenty of staff in the Hema stores, but they are not there to help the physical customers (because all their needs are met digitally). Instead, the staff's task is to complete the online orders. Again, the products are scanned, bagged and carried by a belt system to a waiting chain of motorbike couriers for delivery to your door, a process you can follow by the Hema app on your cell phone. What's more, you can be certain that the goods are fresh, because they come from a source where other customers in the store have already validated the quality ahead of you. The process is completely automated and fully transparent.

When you are standing in a Hema store, you have the feeling of surfing on Amazon.com, but in a physical environment. And if you order from home, you have the feeling that you are in a real store! One main difference with the more widely known Amazon Go is that you can also eat on site, adding a special offline bonus to your shopping experience. And because Hema's delivery system is so super-efficient, you also have a sense that you have just downloaded something online! This is a great example of the OMO world, where online and offline merge seamlessly.

In 2018, Amazon opened nine Amazon Go stores, where you can shop using the Amazon Go application, which allows you to walk in, pick up the groceries you need and walk out again without waiting, with payment being made automatically as you pass through the exit door. In that same year, Alibaba opened almost a hundred similar stores with staff-free cash desks. Both companies say they hope to have thousands of these stores by 2021, but only Alibaba seems to be making serious progress on the project. Curious as it might sound, they are assisted in this process by the existence of hundreds of competitors, who all believe firmly in the concept of new retail. This results in a constant stream of new initiatives, greater integration of sensors at an increasing number of locations, and a much closer level of collaboration between traditional retailers and the online platforms like JD.com and Tencent. As a consequence of all these 'acceleration' factors, it is reasonable to predict that within the next two years 50 percent of all the stores in a city like Shanghai will be partially or fully automated. 'New retail' is not a hype, but the real and very tangible re-invention of an industry. So be warned: no matter how big an online or offline retailer you are today, unless you allow yourself to be inspired by this new Chinese model there is a good chance that you will be going out of business within the next decade.

SHOPPING IS FUN!

In this volatile environment, no retailer is safe. Consider, for example, the case of Starbucks, which over the past 20 years has been wildly successful in introducing coffee culture to the new Chinese middle class. Today they have more than 2,000 coffee shops in 136 different cities across China. This represents a huge achievement in a country where the traditional drink is tea. At the end of 2017, the company opened a new flagship 'experience store' in Shanghai, where the entire coffee production process can be experienced on-site, from the roasting of the beans to the serving of the piping-hot beverage in the cup. Walking into this 3,000 m^2 store is like walking into a fairy tale, where all your senses are stimulated via a unique interactive coffee experience, translating a story that not only has history, craft skills and refinement, but also augmented reality, 3D printing and digital comfort for product ordering. Alibaba was Starbucks' partner in this venture and was responsible for the full digitalisation of the concept. So far, so good.

In 2018, the Luckin coffee start-up made its first entrance into the market. Luckin is not a Starbucks copycat, and it believes in a very different type of customer experience. Whereas Starbucks concentrates on a more authentic experience, Luckin seeks to create a fully mobile experience. In other words, they want to be the 'new retail' of coffee. If a customer wants to enter a Luckin coffee store, he first needs to download the Luckin application. Why? Among other reasons, because you can no longer pay with cash at Luckin, only with WeChat Pay. You also need to order your coffee on your smartphone, typing in what you want, where you want it delivered and when. In terms of the range and quality of the coffee on offer, Luckin can compete with Starbucks, but its prices are 30 percent lower, because they are aiming to capture the coffee-on-the-go market and so do not need to pay huge rents for prime inner-city locations. In a period of just nine months Luckin has opened in more than 500 locations and after just one year of existence it is already worth 2.2 billion US Dollars. In the meantime, Starbucks has entered into an alliance with E.le of Alibaba to provide delivery services from their stores: yet another example of how Western companies are being forced to copy or adapt to Chinese models. It is something we will need to get used to in the years ahead. To be clear, I am not saying that Starbucks has done anything wrong in China. I am saying that Western businesses, even famous and successful ones like Starbucks, will need to look carefully at emerging consumer innovations in China and replicate them in their own domestic markets. In 2018, Starbucks CEO Kevin Johnson said: "The pace of innovation is faster here than any part of the world. It's called 'China speed'. We are going to leverage those learnings and apply them into the world, including the United States."[70]

In China, everything revolves around the experience of shopping, and not the actual buying, which you can either do online or offline, according to your preference. Nowadays, almost every shop has been turned into a kind of mini-theme park. Shopping malls are the favourite place for friends and young couples to spend their free time. For ease of access, they are usually situated next to a metro station and they offer just about anything you can possibly think of. You can shop for groceries in one of the supermarkets, eat a meal in one of the dozen or so restaurants, pick up some street food from one of the numerous stalls in the food court, buy a Gucci handbag, sample a Godiva chocolate, varnish your nails, watch a film, read a book, play in the games hall or even arrange to have your wedding photographs taken! The Chinese expect shopping to be a pleasant way to pass the time and not necessarily (at least not in the first instance) a way to buy things. Shops in China have evolved into places that are intended to inspire or to give potential consumers the chance to feel and experience products first-hand.

Each store tries to develop its own concept to immerse people in its own unique world. Some opt for a 100 percent technological approach, with virtual reality and 'magical' fitting mirrors. Others prefer to organise special events and activities that will live in their visitors' memories. Some rely on the pampering of a personalised butler service, while yet others focus on the authenticity of their story, which they tell in a decor oozing with elegance, beauty and nostalgia. Irrespective of the theme, it is clear that this kind of theatrical 'staged' approach is only possible in symbiosis with the digital world, where all the relevant information about products can be found and where, if desired, also be purchased, either on-site or for home delivery.

During the annual Alibaba online shopping festival in November, the B2C e-commerce site Tmall puts on a four-hour fashion show under the title: 'See now, buy now'. During this mega-event, famous brands from Zara to Victoria's Secret allow their latest designs to be presented to the Chinese public by a team of more than 200 fashion models. It is a unique combination of top brands, e-commerce and interactive amusement. In short, the cross-fertilisation of online and offline. Whether you are one of the favoured few invited to attend at the catwalk or are simply watching from the comfort of your own home, everyone sees the same show and has the same opportunity to buy everything instantly (with guaranteed swift home delivery, of course!) The live video stream is seamlessly integrated with the Alibaba e-commerce platform, but is also linked with seven other channels run by Youku (YouTube), Weibo (Twitter) and the television broadcasting network. If you see something that interests you, you can arrive on the product page of the brand in question with the press of a single button on your mobile phone. Wherever you are sitting, it still feels as though you are following the show live and can buy the clothes directly 'on site', even though in the vast majority of cases you don't even need to step outside your own front door!

Alibaba is the clear leader of new retail in China and looks set to fulfil the same role worldwide over time. By 2035, Alibaba aims to have a massive two billion customers, which means that one billion of them will need to come from outside China. In this context, Alibaba is making skilful use of China's status as a developing country within the World Trade Organisation (WTO). If you order something in Belgium from AliExpress, Alibaba pays for the delivery of the package until Liège. If someone in China orders something on zalando.com, Zalando pays for the delivery of the package until Shanghai. In both cases, the local delivery is done by the local postage service free of charge. This is a worldwide arrangement for developing counties, which currently still includes China. In other words, the tax-payer in the West subsidises the cheap delivery costs of AliExpress, which allows the platform to remain highly competitive. This is one of the main reasons why President Trump recently helped the US Postal Service to leave the Universal Postal Union (UPU).[71]

This current WTO status is certainly a significant factor in Alibaba's expansion plans, but it would be wrong to imagine that because of this WTO status the West will be flooded with primarily cheap Chinese products. If Jack Ma is able to make his dream come true, by 2030 the impact of new retail on consumers in Europe and America could be comparable with the impact Facebook products have on our lives today.

Looking in the opposite direction, during the next five years the West, perhaps without even fully realising it, will have the biggest opportunity it has ever had to influence what Chinese consumers think about and buy. Alibaba and JD.com are currently investing billions in Europe and America. This is not because they wish to flood our markets with cheap rubbish, but because they hope to satisfy the hunger of the billion Chinese who are fascinated by the West, adore foreign brands and want better quality products, especially in the food sector.

I believe the next five years represent a final, one-off chance for Western brands to win the hearts and minds of Chinese consumers. The Chinese people want what we currently have, because we in the West are still seen as the cradle of progress, quality and stability. But this situation will not last indefinitely. If our Western leading consumer brands and retailers fail to understand and embrace the nature of the new Chinese OMO consumer, social e-commerce and the other pioneering trends emerging from China, this golden opportunity risks being lost, and with it the hope of survival for many of our leading brands.

What to Remember?

1 → **E-commerce in China has grown exponentially in recent years** as an alternative solution in an immature offline retail market. The innovative model of Alibaba has become the new norm in China: the development of an ecosystem that has the full confidence of consumers and can both reward them and enhance their living standards. Chinese companies regard their customers as their most important asset, not their technology or their teams. This obsession with the customer will see China emerge as the leader in retail innovation in the years ahead.

2 → **Alibaba and Tencent already have so much data about every Chinese that they now know all their customers intimately.** This allows them to place each individual in the right social context, so that they can make the best possible personal recommendations, using the power of AI. In a parallel development, the traditional Chinese distrust of companies means that they often rely on the opinions of their circle of family and friends when making purchasing decisions. This has led to the creation of several very popular social e-commerce platforms, a phenomenon that makes China's innovation in this field unique.

3 → **Chinese e-commerce already has a new way of looking at the retail world,** which sees consumers being grouped together in social tribes that have power over brands via social networks. Consumers often seek out people they can trust to find the inspiration or quality they need. Key Opinion Leaders (KOL) have become a key communication medium and the creative partners of the brands. In this context, new AI-driven short video social media from China have come into existence and are now spreading worldwide.

4 → **Chinese consumers are evolving towards OMO (Online-Merge-Offline) sapiens.** This new OMO world will first be built in China, because China already has a lead in the four major building blocks: digital connections, mobile payment, IoT and AI. The term 'New Retail' was first coined by Jack Ma and Alibaba's new Hema stores are a first expression of the OMO philosophy, where shopping is intended, above all, to be fun, thanks to the perfect integration of the digital and the analogue, the virtual and the physical, time and space, and story and content.

<
Alibaba's founder, Jack Ma (right), and the founder of Tencent, Pony Ma (left), are recognised by the Communist Party of China for their exceptional contribution to Chinese growth.

4

SMART FINANCE & INSURANCE

CHINA SETS THE STANDARD: FROM 2013 TO 2030

2019 is predicted to be the year of **Smart Finance & Insurance**, which will require Western bankers and insurers to come to terms with a new society of ecosystems and a world without cash. Now that the Chinese people have more money at their disposal and are already accustomed to paying digitally for nearly everything, is China set to become the example for the transformation of the financial industry?

2013 2015 2017 2019 2021 2023 2025 2030

HNWI

It was two o'clock in the morning. We had already been waiting for over an hour in the lobby of the exclusive Peninsula Hotel in Shanghai. Out of sheer boredom, I looked through the window and saw Chinese tourists taking selfies alongside a flashy McLaren sports car that had been parked in front of the main door. What were tourists still doing on the street at two o'clock in the morning, I asked myself? But I was more interested in how much longer we would have to wait before the event manager of the hotel put in an appearance. The next day, our popular 'photoscreen' product was scheduled to be used for a VIP event organised by the Swiss luxury watchmaker, Jaeger-Le Coultre (JLC). We had been told that we could set up our equipment from three AM onwards. By then, all the hotel's rich Chinese customers would be safely tucked up in bed, so that our preparations would not disturb them. I thought back to my first visit to China in 1991, when only foreigners were allowed into the expensive hotels: how times change.

This was not the first event we had digitized for JLC in 2015; we had already done several and so our team knew the routine blindfolded. Every Sunday, the luxury brand invited its biggest customers, their partners and friends for a day of pure pampering at JLC's expense. HNWI is an acronym that you quickly learn in the luxury sector: 'High-Net-Worth Individual'. In other words, people with money, lots of money. The event was more than just a big party. One of the highlights was a workshop, in which ten of the wealthy invitees, usually ladies, were shown how to take apart a JLC watch and put it back together again. This workshop was personally led by a top watchmaker who was flown in especially from Switzerland. But that was not all. While one guest dismantled a watch, another received careful attention from a make-up artist, while a third was restyled by a fashionista and a fourth enjoyed an hour of relaxation with a head massage therapist. Every need and whim of those ten guests was catered to by a team of twenty staff members - only in China! Our task was to take as many professional photographs as possible and make them available digitally via our software, so that the HNWI ladies could share them with all their friends on social media — because that was the object of the exercise: to make even more rich Chinese fall in love with an exclusive house brand that had already existed for 185 years. At the end of the afternoon, white gloves were used to place the fabulous JLC watches in a display — and you really don't want to know just how many millions of dollars were put on those few HNWI wrists that day!

TRUST ME WITH YOUR MONEY

The top one percent of Chinese citizens control almost one-third of the nation's wealth.[72] Fifteen million super-rich, who have sufficient liquidity to invest large sums of money. In the past, wealthy Chinese investors did not trust asset managers, preferring instead to buy shares on the stock market themselves, a practice that proved to be increasingly lucrative until the international banking crisis broke in 2008. China survived this financial crisis and the subsequent world recession much better than most other countries, notwithstanding a sudden fall in exports to just 45 percent of their previous level. China's successful handling was due in large measure to the government's injection of 500 billion dollars into state-run industries. It was the British economist John M. Keynes who first proposed this strategy in the 1930s, as a means to combat the effects of the Great Depression: significantly expand state spending and cut taxes. In June 2015, China experienced a second major stock exchange crash. Following an increase of 68 percent in the preceding five months, there was a fall of 49 percent over the subsequent six months.[73] The creation of this particular speculative bubble was blamed on the activities of individual Chinese investors, who saw the stock exchanges in Shanghai and Shenzhen as their new casino. The problem was that they saw too few other places to invest their money. At the time, there were not enough large-scale investment funds, pension funds or insurance investments available and there were too many capital restrictions on the number of foreign shares and bonds they could buy. In other words, they didn't know what to do with all their cash. What they did know is that they were not keen on asking for advice from professional investors. The 2015 crash was a hard lesson. It taught wealthy Chinese investors to spread their investment portfolios over a range of different products and geographical locations, often through clever financial engineering. This marked the opening of a new age for asset managers in China. Suddenly, they were back in favour, with plenty of new and better investment opportunities to offer their clients.

This increasing market demand coincided with the technological revolution of machine learning, which gave Chinese investors access to lower-cost and in their eyes more 'objective' asset management advice. Because China's asset management sector is still in its infancy, China is confident that its early promotion of AI and mobile investment apps will allow Chinese investors of all income levels to make better investment choices, as well as helping asset managers with their digital transformation via the development of new types of investment platforms. In this way, for example, Alibaba's Ant Fortune open platform has brought together a total of 100 asset management companies, which now have 90 percent of all Chinese funds and most of the Chinese banks as customers[74]. In particular, the AI-driven Caifuhao business account on Ant Fortune has been a popular success. According to Alibaba, after just one year the account was able offer its first 27 fund clients immediate benefits including a 70 percent increase in operational efficiency, a 50 percent cost reduction, ten times more visitors (including three times more returning visitors) and an increase of 89 percent in the investor holding period. Even if we regard these impressive figures as the result of a one-off period of hockey-stick growth in the new financial industry, it is still worth noting that in just three years' time (the platform was first launched in 2015) Ant Fortune has been able to offer a range of more than 4,000 investment products to tens of millions of customers. AI has clearly disrupted the savings and investment habits of the rising Chinese middle class, who have greater confidence in AI-based advice than the sage advice of grey-suited state bankers. The West continues to cling to an outdated 'people expert' model, but may find itself paying the price if or when our financial institutions are placed under increasing socio-economic pressure.

INNOVATION IS TAKING RISKS

According to the 2019 Hurun Global Rich List,[75] China has 658 US Dollar billionaires, which is 74 more than America. In 2017, China had 819[76] billionaires, which was 40 percent more than America at a moment when the US dollar was weaker and the Chinese stock market had reached an all-time high. By comparison, in 2006 there were only 18 Chinese billionaires.[77] In 2018, the Chinese billionaires had at their disposal assets worth a combined total of 2 trillion US dollars or 16 percent of China's GDP. In addition to real estate, it was primarily in the manufacturing and technology sectors where they made their wealth. Admittedly, in some cases these billionaires got rich through corruption and state connections, but China nevertheless now has more self-made billionaires than America, while 80 percent of female self-made billionaires in the world are also Chinese. These hundreds of self-made billionaires, who like most phoenix innovators who have worked themselves up from nothing, are now investing heavily in the technology sector.

In the first six months of 2018, Chinese venture capitalists (VC) invested 56 billion dollars in start-ups, against a comparable figure of just 42 billion in the United States.[78] The first wave of professionalization in the Chinese VC industry occurred around 2010, with investments of some 4.6 billion dollars, nearly all in hardware. By this time, Silicon Valley had been professionally active for more than 25 years, investing larger amounts, mainly in software. Today, the picture is very different. In 2017, China invested 4.9 billion dollars in 19 AI start-ups, against just 4.4 billion in America, spread over 155 AI start-ups[79]. In 2018, these amounts were doubled, both in the US and China. Clearly, the investment race is on!

The main difference between the Chinese and American technology investments is in the profile of the start-up founders they target. In Silicon Valley, VCs prefer to invest in companies with a great team, led by between two and four strongly technology-driven founders, who each have roughly the same number of shares in the company. This is typical for our Western management style, which is focused on consultation and complementarity to achieve the right investment decisions that will lead to the discovery of a new blue ocean. In contrast, Chinese VCs invest in start-ups with a single founder-leader, who holds a majority of the shares. This is better suited to the necessity of being able to take rapid decisions in response to the N-curve during the innovation battle, since it means that all power and responsibility; not only for technology, but also for marketing, recruitment, sales, new investments, etc. is concentrated in the hands of just one person. Chinese founders have broad shoulders; Western founders are often two hands in one glove.

TICK, TICK, TICK, TICK, ...

In the not too distant future, the world will have a thousand Chinese billionaires, millions of Chinese millionaires and hundreds of millions of new middle-class Chinese citizens: over a billion Chinese who have been able to enrich themselves in a single generation, 700 million of whom have been raised out of real poverty. In other words, a huge number of 'new rich' are emerging, who are able to spend more and invest more than ever before. During this same span of a generation, 50 percent of the people in America now have to make do with a share of just 13 percent of the national income, in comparison with 20 percent just thirty years ago.[80] In Western Europe, the lower middle class is also now at greater risk of falling back into poverty than it was three decades ago. Viewed in these terms, it is easy to think that China is getting richer, while the West is getting poorer. Of course, this is not wholly correct, because China is also sitting on a time bomb that one day threatens to explode.

1. **State debt.**[81] China has a national debt of 34 trillion US dollars, which is equivalent to 299 percent of the country's GDP. In particular, the level of debt increased dramatically after the financial crisis of 2008, at which time the debt amounted to 'only' 171 percent of GDP. In 2018, Xi Jinping announced measures to tackle this problem more seriously: the largest conglomerates were encouraged to acquire loss-making state companies; government expenditure was cut; shadow banks were more carefully regulated; new debts in the private sector were curbed. Because the central government maintains tight control over the country's banks, the foreign exchange market and the flight of capital, China is better able to manipulate its financial system and better manage its debt than the West. This government intervention stands in sharp contrast to China's earlier promises to move towards a freer and more open market, promises that were recently reiterated under pressure from President Trump. This results in a very delicate balancing act, but in my view this will not lead to an explosive crisis as long as consumption on

the domestic market continues to grow. Even so, the risk remains that the Chinese debt situation might put the brakes on world growth. Some of the more pessimistic commentators think that it may even spark off a new global financial crisis.

Figure 9

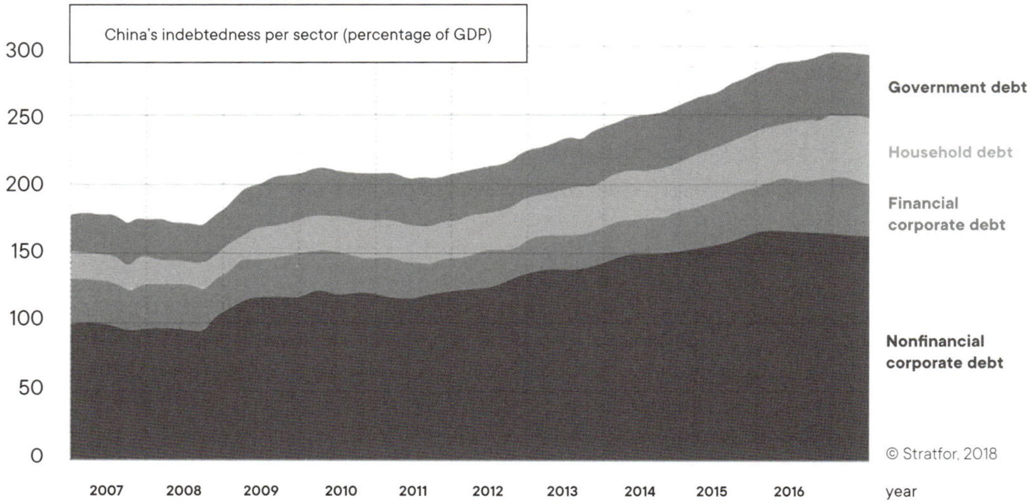

2. **State companies.**[82] China has 150,000 State-Owned Enterprises (SOEs), or 5 percent of the total number of companies. Theoretically, they are allowed to make money, but they also have a clear social and societal purpose. Collectively, they hold 40 percent of all the nation's assets, employ 11 percent of all workers, represent 25 percent of the GDP and are responsible for half of all bank credits and national debts.[83] Western countries often complain about China's SOEs, arguing that state loans gives them a huge and unfair competitive advantage, resulting in price-dumping, among other issues. SOE's do have access to much more financing than their activities or creditworthiness can ever warrant. The central government even encourages overinvestment, such as in the Belt and Road (BRI) initiative. For quite some time now, the government has turned its attention to much needed SOE reform. Zombie SOEs are being declared bankrupt, mergers are being encouraged, the biggest polluters are being closed down and the number of central SOEs reduced. At the same time, a major strategic shift to become a more innovation driven economy is also being encouraged with guidelines such as 'Made in China 2025' (Smart Manufacturing). The result so far has been generally positive, leading to more efficient production in many SOEs. Despite state support for SOE , 60 percent of China's GDP still originates from the private sector. Today, private Chinese companies find themselves in the middle of a profitability squeeze,

as a result of higher costs (including labour), intense competition, higher investments in innovation and tighter enforcement of environmental laws. This is good for Chinese society, but not so good for the private companies concerned. China now wants to help these companies, but without lessening its focus on SOE reforms. Over time, it is envisaged that Beijing will gradually allow foreign investors increased access to SOE-dominated sectors like finance, telecom and energy, while protecting sensitive industries like aerospace, aeronautics and microelectronics, where China wishes to become more self-sufficient. According to the European Union and the United States, this transition is taking far too long. But if you are trying to dismantle a time bomb, doing it slowly is perhaps wiser than going at it too fast.

3. **The Real Estate Bubble.** Running parallel with the growing national debt post-2008, people also suddenly found it much easier to borrow money, with interest rates falling below 5 percent, leading to a boom in property prices. House prices are already 38 percent more expensive in China than in America, despite the GDP per capita in the United States being 3.6 times higher.[84] In Shanghai, an apartment with a surface area of 100m^2 can easily cost 780,000 USD[85] or 50 times the average anual salary of the city's population. With an urbanisation ratio in China of 60 percent increasing by 1 percent every year so that it will soon rise to 80%, matching developed Western countries, developments like the high-speed train network and the expansion of the metro networks are more than welcome, because the standard commuting time is already more than two hours. The government employs various policies to try and counter the effects of this real estate bubble, but Chinese property buyers do not seem deterred and prices in many cities continue to rise. Ownership levels are rising too. According to Nomura Securities, 21 percent of Chinese property owners already have a second home. In total, 90 percent of Chinese families own their home, in comparison with just 65 percent in America. In part, this is related to the Chinese tradition of regarding a house as a form of life insurance for the future, with the entire family of three or even four generations often living in the same dwelling. And because the entire family pools it resources to make this major purchase possible, the tradition is helping to keep the bubble in check.

4. **Those Left-Behind.** Inequality in China continues to increase. According to the Gini index, which measures income equality throughout the world, China currently occupies the 29th place, in the company of various African and South American countries. The United States ranks 39th place. China's level of inequality is however twice as large as in Belgium, which occupies 147th position. Inequality particularly affects many young Chinese, who were unable to surf on the wave of the economic boom. As a result, many young people find themselves on the wrong side of an ever-widening gulf between rich and poor. Many are unable to find work, which also means they can instantly forget about buying a home or even getting married.

Many of them ended up in this situation as they had the bad luck to become the victim of their own overinvestment impulses; others moved from the countryside to the city but were never given the same opportunities in terms of education and residency as 'officially registered' members of the urban population. These are not people you will find described in the pages of this book about innovation, simply because they are not part of the innovation process. Is it possible that new business models created by AI, such as the sharing economy and smart delivery industry, will nonetheless provide smart solutions that might allow these economic outcasts to also benefit from China's growth, even in the remote countryside? Let us hope so. Because those who have been left behind in recent years are real and are estimated to be as numerous as the entire population of the United States. In 2018, they even coined a new name for themselves in street language: 'qiou', represented by a new character comprised from three existing characters, namely 穷 (poor), 丑 (ugly) and 土 (dirty): self-mockery to emphasise their unattractiveness in a society that increasingly associates their poverty with bad taste[86]. This is in stark contrast to the typical Chinese overdose of ambition and hope that I describe in this book, and which the Communist Party likes to promote as the ideal image of their nation.

For the past 30 years, China experts, sociologists and economists have all predicted that China is building an enormous bubble that will burst one day. But so far, I personally have seen no signs of this happening. On the contrary, what I have observed is a China that is systematically overtaking the West. In other words, it looks like the much anticipated time bomb might actually blow up in our own faces, rather than in those of the Chinese. Since 2011, the Chinese government has implemented an alternating approach to the financial imbalances that has seen it restrict lending one year (to prevent the bubble from growing further) only to encourage lending again the next (to give a further new stimulus to the economy). The high degree of interventionist control that the Chinese government has over the SOEs and the banks makes it possible to do this without the need to change overall fiscal or monetary policy. This situation is unique to China and it perhaps provides an alternative model that the West could follow in the event of a new world crisis.[87]

By nature, I am an optimist. I have always seen China's ambition, organisational skill and decision-making ability as a powerful antidote to the negativity of the prophets of doom. And that is what I still think today. This does not mean that the four problems outlined above are not real. They still represent a potential danger. It seems to me that the main risk is that this generation of Chinese citizens have not yet really known a deep recession or a serious credit crisis, and are therefore continuing to borrow more than is responsible or safe. That being said, for me the fourth time bomb is potentially the most dangerous, because it could destabilise the country's rock-solid social system. If millions of 'qiou' should ever unite to fight for social justice, Xi Jinping could find himself faced with a very difficult choice.

FINTECH BOOM

China's Fintech growth is simply breath-taking. In 2016, China was already making 47 percent of all the Fintech investments in the world and by 2020 this industry will amount to 65 billion euros, equivalent to the GDP of Luxemburg[88,89]. Once again, it was in the milestone year of 2013 that this boom started. Since then, online peer-to-peer loans, online investment management, online insurance and online transaction payments have all doubled or tripled each year, and this within the context of an investment climate in Fintech in China that kept increasing by 300 percent each year since 2013.

Fintech, as the name implies, has a 'Finance' component and a 'Technology' component. Chinese Fintech companies, such as Ant Financials (Alibaba), Lufax (Ping An) and JD Finance (JD.com) have flourished in a veritable rain forest of regulatory arbitrage and have managed to create their own Garden of Eden of financial products. With the growth of new legislation in the sector, the Chinese Fintech companies are now making the jump to the next level, which will see a technology and data-driven disruption of the existing financial markets.

It may seem strange that a country not known in the past for an innovative financial sector should now have so many new Fintech initiatives. Just as China was able to take the lead in 'new retail', in part because of the immaturity of its retail market, so again it is the outdated nature of the existing financial markets that are leading the largest financial institutions in the world to seek inspiration in the dynamic Chinese Fintech innovations. Fintech in China was able to advance with such speed primarily because Chinese regulatory authorities were prepared to adopt a 'wait and see' attitude, leaving sufficient room in regulatory frameworks for the Fintech companies to grow. The banks continue to provide the infrastructure and the necessary degree of conformity, while the Fintechs provide customers with easily accessible business models and high-quality services at lower costs.

Chinese banks prefer to lend to the state-run companies, who are covered by a state guarantee, rather than to private individuals. This helps explains why the Chinese save 47 percent of the GDP against just 4 percent in America and less than 10 percent in most Western countries[90]. In part this is due to higher rate of interest than in the West, but the main reasons are the ageing of the population and a generally less established social insurance and pension systems in China. In other words, the Chinese are putting money aside to cover their old age or in case they fall sick, with an extraordinarily high level of saving as a result.

At the same time, there is also very little transparency with regard to the creditworthiness of customers, due to a shortage of historical financial data. Today, almost 60 percent of the Chinese population remains financially 'invisible'. In addition, data, which forms the input for Big Data applications, is all too often unreliable in China. With this in mind, today there are Chinese companies like DataYes,[91] which are capable of extracting both quantitative and qualitative financial data from the internet via their AI algorithms. These work in the same manner as the algorithms that have been designed to distinguish real news from fake news. Data details and analysis of this kind were not generally available as recently as 2015. At that time, only the internet giants Alibaba, Tencent and JD.com were in possession of validated consumer data. However, in 2015 the National Bank of China (PBOC) gave permission to eight

Fintech companies to start providing credit rating services. These companies built their own creditworthiness platform in the same manner as the Sesame credit developed by Ant Financials (Smart Retail), with data collected via e-commerce, social media and mobile payments, supplemented with data from financial institutions and data platforms offering peer-to-peer loans between private individuals. With this goldmine of consumer data at their disposal, they soon created a 'lever effect' by using online-to-offline applications as a portal to offer financing, investment opportunities and insurance to their users.

The previously archaic nature of China's financing system has led to an explosion of Fintech companies in recent years, in part due to a shortage of financing options in comparison with the West. Today, 70 percent of all Chinese netizens make use of Fintech products, in contrast with 33 percent in America and 42 percent in England. The success of Fintech is above all the result of the 'long-tail' strategy, through which the Chinese internet ecosystems make large profits by offering unique, niche financial products in small quantities at lower fees to large numbers of customers. The biggest difference with the American or European Fintech companies, who are above all business-to-business players, is that Fintech in China is first and foremost a consumer market. In 2018, 78 percent of the growth in GDP was driven by consumers, in comparison with 27 percent in 2008.[92]

THE STATE

Economically, China is becoming increasingly more dependent on consumers and less dependent on the state. It is consumers who are stimulating the country's growth, admittedly partly fueled by new state debts, and now that most of them have been able to satisfy their basic economic needs, they want greater comfort. The most important group of Chinese consumers in today's markets were born during or after the 1980s. During the past forty years, this group of young people has grown into what might be called 'adolescent' or 'teenage' consumers: boisterous and full of energy, but still immature. Even within the patriarchal parenting style of the Chinese state, the 'teenage' consumer has been given plenty of space to explore and discover, which sometimes leads to excesses. Think, for example, of the corruption scandals, pollution and high-risk speculation that resulted from 'let be' governance. As the parent of such a teenager, you need to be smart — and this is what the Chinese state has been, certainly since the 1980s, by providing opportunities, support, leadership, inspiration and motivation to the majority of the Chinese people. But now that the Chinese consumer has grown to full adulthood, the government seems to be moving from a nurturing 'good father role' to a more disciplined 'strong father role'. The 'adolescents' have been allowed to play for long enough; the time has now come for them to take responsibility. China is about to enter a new era of rules, procedures and consequences. I predict that over the coming decade, 'compliance' will become the most important word in China.

Only a small percentage of private companies in China are able to get loans from a bank. In total, these companies receive just 25 percent of all bank loans, even though they are responsible for 60 percent of GDP, 70 percent of innovations, 80 percent of urban employment and 90 percent of new job creation. The situation for private individuals is even more restricted: just 9.6 percent of them are able to obtain bank loans. It is in this context, for example, that in 1999 the government set up a national system that requires employers, for example in Beijing, to pay a contribution of 12 percent on top of their employees gross payment into a 'housing fund', which stands as surety for them when they take out a loan to buy a house. The huge gulf between the demand for financing and its supply has led to the creation of thousands of shadow banks, which operate beyond the control of the bank regulator. Above all, it is the new rich, keen to secure ever higher rates of interest for their money, who fund these shadow institutions. Even though they operate outside the formal bank sector, they now represent a 10 trillion-dollar industry and have become the motor of the modern Chinese economy.

Understandably, the Chinese government is very concerned about the stability of its financial sector. As a result, it keeps a close watch on the shadow banks and smaller banks that give credit to SMEs via their funds, particularly if the companies in question have insufficient capital to cover their outstanding loans. If the economy should unexpectedly stagnate, so that millions of SMEs are suddenly unable to repay their loans, this would be a nightmare scenario for the government, given the huge proportions of these loans. This would lead to a rapid increase in unemployment, which in China currently officially stands at just 4.1 percent. It is to prevent this possibility that since 2018 the government has subjected companies to new procedures and actively monitors them to ensure proper implementation. In this respect, the Xi era is now characterised by a much higher degree of control and new forms of state intervention, such as greater Communist Party involvement in private companies, more checks to identify breaches of the new cyber-security laws protecting private data, scrutinizing foreign companies that dismiss employees on a large scale, and the integration of loss-making companies into state-run companies or their sale to foreign investors.

The Public-Private Partnership (PPP) mixed ownership model is the model of the future for China, with private companies being strongly encouraged to invest in state companies or to accept state investment and the appointment of Party directors in their own companies. At the same time, the banks are being guided to provide half of all their commercial loans to the private sector. This should all lead to more consolidations and more changes of ownership over the coming years. I foresee that both local and international companies will need to organise their China strategy in a more balanced manner, between an 'inside-China' and an 'outside-China' asset allocation model. This will be necessary to reduce the impact of increasingly uncertain and volatile trade tariffs, investment limitations, intellectual property right restrictions, state interference and an ever-stricter migration policy. Until now, most entrepreneurs in China have become successful by operating in the regulatory vacuum, an ever-shifting grey zone. Every new requirement that imposes more structure or introduces more regulatory obligations will no doubt be met with complaints about 'excessive' government control. It is usually the companies who have benefitted from the grey zone that are first to paint China in a negative light as a 'control state', and although there is obviously some truth in their claims, this is nevertheless more often than not a case of the pot calling the kettle black.[93]

MONEY IS TIME

China's traditional financial sector is notorious for its bad service and time-consuming bureaucratic procedures. The accountants of Chinese companies probably spend as much time in banks and tax offices as they do behind their desks. They have to wait for hours and hours in queues, with a ticket number in their hand. Having said that, my Chinese accountant, Lotus, never had to wait for long herself, because she paid people whose only job was to stand in these queues and sell their tickets to others who didn't want to wait. For us, this was much cheaper than paying her hourly rate, and we even got a VAT invoice into the bargain! For the rest of the time, Lotus was busy filling in forms or bicycling back and forth to our office to fetch some document that she had never needed before, but had now mysteriously become essential. In China before 2013, it was not a question of 'time is money'; it was more a case of 'money is time': No time, no money.

Running a business in China, you will often need to send your accountant to the bank with your company and financial stamps (a physical seal), because these stamps carry far more weight than the signature of the company boss. And because you will have lots of other things to more usefully employ your time, it is essential that you learn to trust your accountant. If you ever want to set up a company in China, my advice is to first find a good local accountant – and only then think about appointing a director to manage your operations. Pay your chief accountant well, and make sure that the Chinese director needs to sign off on all expenditures. If you want to do business in China, you will get much further by investing in a good and loyal accountant than you will ever get by trying to learn Chinese!

THE ANT THAT BECAME A GIANT

In Europe, every bank or insurance company wants to build its own ecosystem, while in China it is the internet giants working together with the banks and insurers who are building a collective ecosystem. Ant Financial, the largest Fintech unicorn in the world, is a good example of this. Valued at 150 billion dollars, it is the premier ecosystem for transactions in China, but works together with hundreds of different partners. In fact, Alibaba was already working with many Chinese banks as early as 2004 to guarantee safe transactions for the purchase of goods on Alibaba's platforms. By 2008, it was already possible via the China Construction Bank to conclude an AliPay loan or to pay all your utilities bills. 2009 saw a new partnership with the largest Chinese travel companies to use AliPay for all travel and holiday bookings. This process has continued to the present, as a result of which AliPay can now be used for every possible payment that a consumer can think of in his or her daily life: medical, gaming, food and drink, transport, credit, retail, education, social and government services, online services, etc.[94]

In 2010, 26 companies, including AliPay, were the first internet-based organisations to be given a transaction license by the Chinese Central Bank, and so Fintech in China was born. In 2012, licenses for investment funds were also issued, followed shortly thereafter by licenses for asset management. Since then, AliPay has been able to offer its customers twice the rate of interest available at the banks for any unused funds in their Alibaba accounts. In 2014, AliPay was finally granted a full online bank license under the name of MyBank, as a result of which Ant Financial was set up, into which AliPay and a number of other financial products were incorporated. In 2018, Ant Financial was able to raise funds amounting to 14 billion US Dollars to finance its international expansion plans.

In China, an ecosystem is more commonly built up around an area of expertise, not around an industry or sector. In the West, an ecosystem is often a network of partners, who help each other to become more competitive: the classic 'together we are strong' idea. In China, ecosystems often come into being through the actions of one of the data giants like Alibaba or Tencent, who innovate and co-create with partners in whom they also make financial investments. This kind of Chinese ecosystem investment and innovation process is more focused on customer comfort than on product innovation. As we have already seen, in this new 4.0 world it is above all important to be fast, not necessarily big. And to be fast, it is important to validate your expertise, not your position in the industry. The expertise of Alibaba is e-commerce; for Ant Financials it is transactions; for Ping An it is insurance; for Tencent it is communication; and so on. It is around these foci of expertise that the ecosystems build up integrated platforms and networks of partners. The internet giants invest huge sums of money in these partners, thereby creating both mutual dependence and mutual accountability. In this way, there is an efficient distribution of roles: the ecosystem managers provide the money as investors, while the partners become the creators within their own industry. Recently, I have noticed that the large Western companies have also been looking at ecosystems, but are constantly wrestling with the question of whether they should build their own or belong to someone else's. The problem in the West, as I see it, is that ecosystems are far too often seen as an opportunity to increase an existing business, rather than as an opportunity to create a new business, which is how they are viewed in China.

The Ant Financial Platform

Payments – AliPay:
AliPay is now a mobile portfolio of more than 600 million users and 110 million partners in 15 countries.

Asset management: Yu'e Bao and Ant Fortune
Yu'e Bao is a money market fund that invests surplus savings from the AliPay portfolio. It is the largest such fund in the world and at the end of 2017 managed a total of 233 billion dollars.

Insurance: Ant Insurance Service
Ant Insurance Service has almost 400 million users and is growing at an annual rate of 43 percent. This market place has already attracted more than 80 insurance companies, who together offer thousands of different products.

Credit scores: Zhima Credit

Zhima Credit calculates a credit score for users on the basis of other social networks and available payment histories. In 2017, it had 260 million users.

Consumer lending: Ant Fortune

Ant Fortune is a market place for other products of Ant Financials and third-party partners. In 2017, Ant Fortune had 330 million users. Ant Credit Pay is a consumer credit facility with 100 million users. Ant Cash Now makes it possible for users of AliPay to obtain quick loans, based on the risk profile of its users. In total, Ant Financial has already made loans amounting to more than 100 billion dollars.

DIGITAL PAYMENT

The world already knows that China is the most advanced country in terms of mobile payment systems. The figures are truly impressive; 75 percent of all online transactions are made by smartphone; more than 1.1 billion digital accounts have been opened in China, which is five times more than PayPal worldwide. In 2017, 30 trillion dollars of mobile transactions were carried out, which is 50 times more than in North America. More than 3.4 billion companies and people have opened a mobile payment account in order to buy or sell things.[95] Half of the urban population of China no longer take cash money with them when they leave their homes, since mobile payment is accepted everywhere for everything. China is set to become the first cashless society in the world. What's more, most Chinese welcome this development, because it is safer. You no longer risk being passed forged money, which used to circulate on a huge scale until recently, and if your smartphone is stolen, this doesn't give the thief access to your cash, which is not the case if your wallet is stolen. Even the beggars in major Chinese cities now have their own WePay and AliPay accounts, because otherwise they would not be able to survive — quite literally.

WePay from Tencent[96] and AliPay from Alibaba are the two largest mobile payment systems. The latter was launched back in 2004 as a PayPal type function for online e-commerce. By the time the 3G smartphone became more common in 2010 AliPay had already captured 60 percent of the market, with just 10 percent in the hands of TenPay (later on called WePay), with the remainder shared between 25 other providers, such as UnionPay.[97] But in 2014 something unexpected happened: Tencent launched digital 'red envelopes' (hongbao). This was a brilliant play on the Chinese custom which sees people exchange red envelopes containing money at Chinese New Year (the most important of all the Chinese festivals), much as people in the West exchange gifts at Christmas. Tencent decided to turn this tradition into a kind of online game. It was made possible to give money to a group of friends or members of your family in a way that suggested that the quicker and the smarter you acted, the bigger the share of the envelope you might get. This meant that hundreds of millions of people rapidly installed WePay so that they could receive money from their nearest and dearest. Jack Ma called this action: 'A Pearl Harbour attack on AliPay, beautiful and perfectly executed.' In 2017, the digital hongbao were good for 7 billion US Dollars of transactions. As a result, WePay enjoyed a new period of spectacular growth and today accounts for 39 percent of the market, with AliPay still ahead at 54 percent. Expressed another way, Alibaba and Tencent now share 93 percent of China's mobile payment market.[98]

ONLINE LENDING

Because the platforms within the Alibaba ecosystem and Tencent's WeChat are able to offer you everything you can ever dream of, it is hardly surprising that billions of dollars flow every minute through AliPay and WePay. As a corollary, China has also become the world leader in online lending. With the availability of new financial data sources, Fintech companies can now apply accurate models to evaluate the payment behaviour of customers, to better estimate if they will be able to repay their loans. For the financiers, this has opened up a whole new market of 600 million prospective customer, who were not previously thought to be creditworthy by traditional bank credit assessments.

The large-scale national social credit system that will be launched in 2020 (Smart Security) consists of two separate dimensions: a financial dimension and a social dimension. It is this first dimension in particular that can make a world of difference for the average Chinese citizen when it comes to obtaining loans to consume even more, which is crucial for China's continued economic growth. It was with this in mind that in 2015 the Chinese government gave licenses to eight companies, including Ant Financial, Tencent and Ping An, to explore the possibilities of setting up a credit system as part of a pilot project.[99] Two years later, however, Beijing decided not to give these eight companies a full license, and this was for three main reasons: none of the eight projects had succeeded in guaranteeing the privacy of the users; there was an over-collection of irrelevant data; and there were commercial conflicts of interest that hindered the sharing of data with each other and the government. This gives lie to the story often repeated in Western media that the Chinese government is only really interested in collaborating with the internet giants so that it can have access to all the available data about its citizens. This data — or so the story goes — will then be misused to turn China into a copy of the 'nosedive' episode from the Black Mirror series, in which people could rate each other for every interaction and therefore often tailored their behaviour with this in mind. Fortunately, this continues to be science fiction, even in a so-called 'control state' like China.

In reality, Big Data analyses of personal behaviour data can be a huge help in finding more customers for Fintech products via the large online ecosystems. Cross-selling with players from the physical world is a recent trend that looks set to continue. In this way, for example, an online travel company like Ctrip works together with online insurers (InsurTech) to provide travel insurance coverage, and also with Fintech companies to provide loan advances to customers during their journeys or to invest in their planned journeys for the future. This type of cross-selling is now in evidence in almost every consumer sector, including the car and leasing industry, healthcare, retail, food and beverage, social media, real estate and transportation.

In addition, the profusion of available data puts China in a unique position to offer more refined financial products through a better understanding of the price sensitivities and risk profiles of its potential customers. This makes the approval of loans much easier and much quicker, as well as facilitating the real time monitoring of creditworthiness, so that any changes can be detected early on, making it possible either to offer timely refinancing options or to refuse requests for future loans. Obviously, the most important aspect of any loan is the borrower's ability to repay it and here too the Chinese are developing ingenious solutions, particularly in the field of consumer credit. If you buy a laptop or smartphone on credit, it is possible that in future you will find it blocked and unusable if you fail to make your loan repayments. Of course, this is not so very different from what already happens if you buy software online, but we are less used to the idea, certainly in the West, of applying the same principle to hardware. Imagine, for example, that intelligent keys refuse to give you access to your own home, because you have not been able to pay the mortgage! You wouldn't hear the hotels complaining, but it remains open to question whether we can ever change our Western way of thinking about such things.

PEER-TO-PEER LENDING (P2P)

Suddenly, it seems as though China has become a lender's paradise. There are millions of wealthy people, all looking to earn more from their money than the 2.75 percent interest offered by the banks for three-year fixed deposits. With 73 million SMEs (small and medium enterprises) and even more private individuals all looking for small-scale credit, which the banks are not willing to give them, it is hardly surprising that since 2013 the P2P industry has witnessed explosive growth. P2P loans, also known as crowd loans, can promise the lenders a rate of interest between 8 and 12 percent. China's largest P2P loan company is PPDAI (拍拍贷), which in 2017 was launched on the New York Stock Exchange.[100] At its peak, China had no fewer than 5,890 peer-to-peer Fintech companies, generating monthly transactions worth 20 billion dollars. The P2P industry in China is bigger than in the rest of the world put together. It has 50 million users and outstanding loans amounting to more than 1 trillion dollars.[101]

When I was still in business in China, I was used to receiving calls almost every day from the sellers in Shanghai, asking me if I needed a loan. At times it was tempting to accept, especially if my customers were again late in paying what they owed me, but I managed to resist. Perhaps it was just as well. From 2016 onwards, things began to go wrong with China's P2P. It became clear that many of the P2P platforms were unreliable and the media uncovered a number of Ponzi schemes, in which companies fell under suspicion for paying huge bonuses when family and friends agreed to sign up for loans. The most well-known of these stories involved the highly regarded Ezubao (e租宝) company, which defrauded its almost 1 million investors of 7.6 billion dollars. The China Banking Regulatory Commission (CBRC) intervened to tackle the fraud problem, by obliging the P2P platforms and their shareholders to register with the local authorities and by introducing measures to guarantee the soundness of P2P products and provide greater transparency to consumers. There were also tighter controls on the number of new platforms, increased liquidation of failed platforms and heavy fines for lenders who failed to live up to their obligations. In the year leading up to June 2018, the number of outstanding P2P loans increased by 43 percent. But that is when the government decided to get tough. The next month 223 P2P companies were liquidated. 15 percent of the platforms were in trouble and 20 percent of the investors withdrew their funds in panic.[102] Hundreds of P2P owners tried to temporarily block their investors' withdrawals and in some cases even fled the country. By the end of 2018, only some 1,500 P2P companies had survived the government's culling and were still active. In reality, the P2P lending industry is still relatively small: it only represents 1 percent of all loans and constitutes just 9 percent of shadow bank loans. However, the events of 2018 gave the government the impetus to move in to regulate all aspects of the Fintech sector in China. In August 2018, thousands of cheated investors gathered in Beijing to protest, but they were given little sympathy and soon returned home disappointed.[103] The Chairman of the CBRC issued an official statement which said that: 'If the interest rate is above 6 percent, you should ask questions. If it is above 8 percent, that is a dangerous signal. If it is above 10 percent, you should expect to lose all your money.' Government statements don't come much clearer than that. For Beijing, this 'incident' with the P2Ps offered interesting insights into the possible risks of social unrest associated with non-compliant Fintech platforms in general, whilst at the same time sending out a clear signal that the best solution was a short, sharp shock to put things right. For the Fintech industry, the signal was equally clear: Chinese Fintech companies can no longer expect to continue expanding on the basis of legal loopholes in the regulatory provisions. If they want to grow in the future, it will need to be on the basis of an innovative 'tech' focus operating in a highly compliant manner.

THE NEW INSURER IS CHINESE

Ping An Insurance, the largest insurance company in the world, was founded in 1988. Until 2013, Ping An had a typical 'supermarket' approach, being active in many industries with many different products. In 2008, the company even took a 5 percent shareholding in the Belgian Fortis bank, which after the bank's dismantlement cost Ping An 2 billion dollars. After this foreign adventure, the company decided to focus exclusively on China. It made many new acquisitions and projects, the most daring of which was the Lufax project in 2012. Lufax started out as a P2P loan company, which brought together potential borrowers and lenders and took a commission on the deals, depending on the level of risk. Lufax is yet another example of a Chinese phoenix, which in just five years' time developed into a profitable company with 3,000 employees, an estimated value of 38 billion dollars and the largest online asset management platform in China.

For Ping An, Lufax is a lead generator, which attracts investors for its banking and insurance products. At the same time, it is also an information provider for the company's trading in financial assets. In this way, Lufax has helped Ping An to reach its current total of 500 million customers. Even so, Ping An's success is founded primarily on its innovative and ecosystem-driven strategy and its detailed analysis of the needs of its customers. It builds up its knowledge using four technologies — cognitive recognition, AI, blockchain and cloud computing — which it then applies in its five ecosystems: financial services, health, cars, houses and smart cities.[104] The strength of this kind of Chinese market leader is that they do all their innovation in-house, so that they can develop their own technology expertise without the need to rely on others. With an annual budget of 1.5 billion dollars for technology investment, Ping An has created eleven new digital platforms, which provide the company with great resilience.

In the magical year 2013, something very special happened in China: three top entrepreneurs, all named Ma, set up Zhong An (众安保险), the first fully online insurance company in China. The founders were Jack Ma (Alibaba), Pony Ma (Tencent) and Ma Mingzhe (Ping An). This was the first time that these three rivals invested together in a new company, one that in the future might easily become a fierce competitor for their existing companies. If nothing else, it shows the vision and the risk appetite of these three Chinese ecosystem gods.

In contrast to traditional insurance companies, where the sales team often represents 30 percent of a total workforce that can be as large as 10,000 employees, Zhong An employs just 5 percent of its personnel in sales. The biggest proportion of its staff complement (53.2 percent) is represented by its 1,536 engineers, who are responsible for technology developments.[105] The company sells its products via its 200 ecosystem partners, including Alibaba, Tencent, the online travel bureau Ctrip and the internet recruitment website Zhaopin. This revolutionary new internet partnership model has allowed them to eliminate the middlemen (insurance agents) of the traditional insurance companies. As a result, in just five years Zhong An has been able to turn the Chinese insurance industry on its head.[106] In 2018, they even launched (in collaboration with AXA) a Software-as-a-Service (SaaS) platform[107] for other insurers. This is an open data platform where these other insurers, with the permission of the customers concerned, can examine medical records or have access to claims data in real time, without the time-consuming need to request or collect the necessary details. Zhong An is a top Chinese phoenix of the New Normal. In theory, it is just a six-year old start-up, but in practice it has already been able to raise 2 billion dollars with the backing of the major internet companies and global investors, has listed on the Hong Kong Stock Exchange, has 500 million customers. With Softbank as a new investor in 2018, today it is getting ready to conquer the Japanese market.[108]

MICRO-AFFINITY

Zhong An is a classic example of how a digital newcomer can still find a place at the heart of what seemed to be an almost closed market, an existing red ocean populated by countless customers and insurers. Zhong An has succeeded in navigating its way successfully through this ocean, by catching lots of small fish in a net with a much smaller mesh than its rivals. The concept is actually quite a simple one: every traditional insurance policy is full of 'small print', which usually sets out what the policy does not cover. It is on these exceptions that Zhong An has chosen to focus: health policies that exclude cancer or diabetes, e-commerce risks such as product damage and returns, car insurance for young and inexperienced drivers, flight delays at airports, and even hooligan fights at football matches. Zhong An uses Big Data to identify these and other exceptional needs of its customers.

This trend is known as 'customer-centric micro-affinity', and it is part of the New Normal in China. 'Micro-affinity' is not new in the sector; as witnessed, for example, by the 1-euro train travel insurance policy. In the West, these types of policies were 'upsell' products with conditions and procedures that made it cumbersome and frustrating to submit a claim. Traditional insurers prefer to concentrate on professional liability insurance and standard products. Companies like Zhong An know that millennials are more concerned about things like breaking their smartphone screens or spilling coffee on their laptops. These companies respond to such concerns via automatic triggers linked to the purchase of phones, laptops or airline tickets, or product return guarantees for online sales. Zhong An uses IoT to refine the customer profile still further, so that it becomes possible for them to offer you cheaper vehicle insurance, because your car and/or phone have 'revealed' that you are a responsible young driver. At the same time, it also allows them to distinguish between false and genuine claims through the analysis of typical user profiles. If the traditional insurers fail to make the full transition to this new and more customer-oriented way of doing business, consumers will increasingly make the move to companies like Zhong An.

The advantages for the customer are clear: access to simple, affordable and relevant products that are available everywhere and anytime online and also provide a better claims experience. But there are also plenty of advantages for the insurer as well: lower fixed costs and faster claim processing in a scalable model with limitless distribution possibilities via a legion of internet partners. In short, it is a model offering better insights into the needs of more customers across more industries without any loss of customer retention. So, what are Western insurers waiting for?

THE FUTURE OF THE BANK

Banks often see the Fintech companies as their new competitors. The problem is not really the start-ups: they enjoy the confidence of neither the regulators nor the public, and so do not pose the real threat. In contrast, companies like Amazon, according to the Bain & Co. consultancy firm, may well be rivalling the world's largest banks in as little as five years' time.[109] This same phenomenon is already evident in China, but it is moving at an even faster pace. Why would Tencent or Alibaba want to become a partner of the Chinese banks? Why not simply become the biggest bank in China yourself? If competition is the impetus for innovation in China (the New Normal curve), why join forces with institutions that are cumbersome and outdated?

Of course, for the traditional Chinese banks there would be numerous advantages in this kind of partnership: access to much greater amounts of data, more customers, new knowledge, technology that matches the right customer to the right product, a Fintech culture that appeals to the new middle class, and the strong financial competence of companies like Ant Financial or Lufax. Bearing this in mind, the question of whether the banks would prefer to compete with or collaborate with the Fintech sector was soon answered. Since 2013, the banks have been engaged in a fierce struggle with each other, driven by demand from Chinese consumers, who want to experience the payment convenience of the digital transformation at their traditional bank. Banks that failed to make the change quickly enough began to lose customers in droves. As a result, they often paved the way unwillingly for the current Fintech revolution.

Alibaba has set the tone for working together with the banks. AliPay quickly arranged collaboration agreements with 19 national banks, and the other tech-giants soon followed their example. It needs to be remembered that Fintech still needs an important 'Fin' component and the Chinese banks certainly have this financial expertise, as well as personal relations with their customers via their network, strongly regulated compliance and controls and the trust of the government. This last point is important. The state still sees the banks as the regulators of the entire financial industry, and this is a potentially sensitive issue for the Chinese Fintech companies. As a result, the major Chinese tech-titans all sought to form partnerships with banks, seeing this as a means to continue growing themselves. Collaboration with the banks was a kind of 'insurance policy' for the Fintech companies, but also a way to expand their ecosystem. The concept of ecosystem partnering is so deeply rooted in China that there is generally a place for everyone, so that the real purpose of the ecosystem is not only to work with complementary partners to make more money, but to increase the total size of the ecosystem to its maximum possible extent, even if this means giving access to competitors. 1 + 1 is not always 2 in China and 1 - 1 can sometimes equal 3. This is the paradoxical sum of the Chinese ecosystem, which is making the financial sector in China smarter than anywhere else in the world.

What to Remember?

1. **The Fintech industry in China has grown exponentially since 2013**, primarily because the Chinese have more money than investment opportunities. In particular, the peer-to-peer model underwent a veritable explosion of not always healthy growth, until it was cut down to size by strict government measures in 2018. China is now concentrating on the 'Tech' aspect of Fintech and will increasingly inspire the financial world with its strong innovation focus.

2. **The Chinese financial miracle is partly created by state debt** that so far has made it possible for the economy to avoid crisis and continue growing; relying on loss-making and debt-ridden state-run companies that can dump products at cheap prices; built on a real estate bubble that is financed by new and more easily available Fintech loans; and by leaving behind a large part of the Chinese population that has not been able to benefit from the new prosperity. For the moment, the increasing powers appropriated by the government seem to be keeping this bubble under control, but it has certainly not disappeared.

3. **The Chinese government wants to make the entire Fintech sector 'compliant' as soon as possible** and its preference is to intensify the public-private partnership, so that this can serve as a model for the new Chinese economy. Chinese private companies continue to support further economic growth, but at the same time have become the victim of tighter state regulation and the limitations of the banking system. This has led to the development of shadow banks, which offer credit to millions of entrepreneurs.

4. **The Chinese insurance company and market leader Ping An is building a new insurance model for the world:** a system based on strong technological foundations in an ecosystem where the customer is central. The setting up of companies like Lufax and Zhong An are examples of how a market leader like Ping An continues to invest in its ecosystem, which has allowed it to cause further disruption with these two successful and innovative N-curve phoenixes.

5. **Alibaba has set the tone for Fintech in China through its collaboration with other financial institutions** and its focus on technology and data-driven innovation. AI, IoT and blockchain are three of the fundamental components of this new Chinese financial world. Together, the Chinese internet giants are investing billions in Fintech phoenixes, which are actively using these three technologies and absorbing them into their ecosystems, where they can continue to grow, even outside China. The banks in China need to be less worried than banks in the West, because the ecosystem and the Chinese government offer them both greater protection and more opportunities.

和谐号

<
A hundred high-speed trains stand ready to depart from Wuhan on the first day of the mass annual Chinese New Year migration in 2019.

5 SMART MOBILITY

CHINA SETS THE STANDARD: FROM 2013 TO 2030

As early as 2021, self-driving cars are expected to be seen on Chinese roads, allowing China to provide the world with a blueprint for **Smart Mobility**. Will people in the West all be driving Chinese cars in ten years' time or will Western car brands run on China's algorithms?

2013 2015 2017 2019 2021 2023 2025 2030

SMARTER CITIES

Cities in China are getting smarter much faster than ours in the West. There are currently around 1,000 smart city pilot projects in the world and no fewer than half of them are in China.[110] In comparison, 90 cities in Europe, 40 in America and 15 in Japan and South Korea are actively engaged with the development of a smart city programme. Global leaders are already emerging. Amsterdam leads the way in smart energy. Barcelona is already famed for its smart waterways and mobility. New Songdo in South Korea is setting the pace in smart housing. Although most of the cities in China started their smart projects later than elsewhere, their transformation is taking place at a faster pace, especially in the 'cluster cities' of the Yangtze Delta around Shanghai and the Pearl River Delta around Guangzhou. The driving force behind this process is the growth of urbanisation in China, which today has more than 100 cities with a population in excess of 1 million inhabitants and within just a few years will have 15 mega-cities with more 10 million people. When China opened its doors to the world in 1978, just 20 percent of the population lived in the cities. Forty years later, the urbanization ratio has risen to 60 percent and by 2050 it is expected to rise still further to 80 percent. During this same period, Western cities have only known a growth of 10 percent (and will reach 85 percent by 2050).[111]

This new and sudden reality has catapulted China from being a largely rural society into a strongly urbanised society, which creates many new challenges relating to quality of life. The most important of these challenges are **health, security, education, living comfort, the economy** and **mobility.**

In this chapter, I will look at smart mobility.

DISTANCE OR MOBILITY?

Smart mobility in my opinion is the most fascinating transition that China is currently experiencing. This revelation first became clear to me in mid-2016, when I returned from Shanghai to live in Belgium. The first weeks back in my own country were surprisingly confusing for me. I wanted to look up lots of different people to tell them the good news that I was back. But I soon discovered that nearly everyone was on holiday, and those that weren't said they could arrange to see me in four to eight weeks! I couldn't understand what was going on. I had been away for 20 years and when these same people had come to Shanghai, I had agreed to meet them almost immediately. In short, I made time for them. But now that I was back, it seemed they weren't prepared to make time for me. At first, I thought that people no longer regarded me as 'useful' to them here in Belgium, and I was disappointed in those who I had come to regard as friends. However, I quickly came to realise that people's agendas in Belgium are indeed blocked for weeks in advance. But even with this realisation, I was still puzzled. How on earth was it possible that I could get to see the founder of a top Chinese company with less than a week's notice, whereas it took me a month or more to see the manager of a run-of-the-mill Belgian company? Were people here in Europe really that busy? Or is it just that we worked so inefficiently that we no longer had any time to spare?

It soon became clear to me that in Belgium (and other developed countries) a person's professional life and private life are still kept almost completely separate from each other. In fact, in the West a kind of cult has grown up around the ideal of so-called 'work-life balance'. I had to learn a whole new vocabulary of expressions like 'unplug', 'digital detox', 'learn to say no' or 'leave work at work'. The most absurd thing of all was that attempting to find this balance often created more stress than it relieved! I was equally amazed when I heard the news that the French government had passed legislation in 2017 which forbade medium-sized and large companies from requiring employees to answer e-mails after office hours.[112] My first reaction was that 'China will have Europe for breakfast,' because in my experience work has always had a higher priority than private life for the Chinese. Perhaps today this is less the case among the younger Chinese, who now want to enjoy their free time. In this sense, China is perhaps evolving towards our Western norm, but the difference in priorities is still a very noticeable one. In our social relations in the West, we still keep our personal friends carefully segregated from our work colleagues. In fact, many people live a kind of double life: one with friends and one with colleagues. Very occasionally, colleagues may also become good friends, but seldom the other way around. Doing business amongst friends is largely frowned upon, because people don't want to risk losing these friends if something goes wrong with their joint business venture. In China, by contrast, you can only do business with your friends. If you are not good friends with someone, how can you trust them in business? Friendship comes first, then business.

It is for this reason that the Chinese feel morally obliged to see their business contacts at short notice, even if this means seeing them in their 'off-time'. In China, friends will always help each other with business matters, if they possibly can, whereas in the West we still feel slightly uncomfortable discussing business with our personal acquaintances. Spending that 'off-time' together is of great importance to Chinese staff and managers. They often work six days a week in the same office or factory, see each other in the evening for dinners and further business discussions and on Sundays it is not uncommon to spend a day out with the entire company staff. Everything and everyone is interconnected, and the improvements in mobility in recent years have made it even more feasible to make last-minute appointments. It sometimes seems as if Chinese businessmen and women are almost continually travelling to or from somewhere! Perhaps we should not be surprised. Many books have been already been written about the importance of face-to-face meetings for the Chinese. This has led to more optimal levels of mobility than in the West. While Europe and America are constantly trying to create new methods to make it possible to work from home or at distance (video conferencing, online collaboration tools, etc.), in China they are more concerned to find more efficient ways of physically getting from A to B. It is for this reason that I am convinced that China's approach to mobility is much better than ours: they want more meetings, whereas we want to do away with them.

A HIGHER GEAR

Since 2008, China has become a much smaller place. 20 years ago, if you took a train from Shanghai to Kunming, you were faced with an arduous journey of 2,266 kilometres that took 47 hours to complete. Today, the high-speed train does it in just 10.5 hours. The new trains travel three times faster than the old ones and stop at fewer stations along the way. In 1997, the average train speed in China was 43 kilometres per hour, with a maximum of 140 kph. The average traveling speed for the new high-speed trains (HST) is over 200 kilometres per hour and the maximum is around 350 kph.[113] In other words, on average China has become four times smaller through the development of the largest HST network in the world.

Over a short period of 10 years China invested 500 billion dollars to construct 26,000 kilometres of new track, as much as the rest of the world put together. There are plans to almost double this amount to 45,000 kilometres by 2030,[114] which means laying 9 kilometres of new track every day and building five new high-speed train stations each month.[115]

More than 4 million Chinese travel on one of the 4,000 high-speed trains on a daily basis,[116] 25 percent of whom are commuters between the satellite towns and the big urban conurbations, which are separated by distances of between 50 to 300 kilometres. For example, more than 200 high-speed trains travel between Beijing and Tianjin every day, while a high-speed train arrives in Shanghai every 90 seconds. This is not just a question of compressing distances. It is also a question of time: the frequency of these trains is extremely high. Even though the HST project is still currently a loss-maker, it has multiple benefits which are hard to quantify. For example, HST helps solve the problem caused by high property prices, which makes it virtually impossible for the majority of employees to live in the big cities where they work. In this sense, the vision of the Chinese government and planners is different from the American vision, where the federal government does not feel it has a role to play and seems to be waiting until private companies or Silicon Valley are able to successfully develop long-distance travel solutions, or safe self-driving cars. The European position is currently somewhere between the two.

The geography of China — with its surface area of 9.4 million square kilometres and more than 221 cities with a population in excess of half a million, separated by distances of between 200 and 900 kilometres — is unique in the world. It also makes it highly suited for an HST network of this kind. China has a population density of 145 people per square kilometre,[117] which is four times greater than America, but less than half the Belgian figure (375 people per km^2).[118] If, however, you take account of the fact that 94 percent of Chinese live on just 43 percent of the surface area, then the population densities of China and Belgium are broadly similar.[119] But the distances between the cities are not. Nor is the number of urban dwellers, which is 20 times greater in China, which also has 100 times more cities with over 1 million people. In other words, this creates a mobility landscape and planning in terms of distance and density that is between 20 and 100 times greater than that of Belgium.

In these circumstances, moving large numbers of people to new areas is a central goal of mobility planning. You often read in the Western media stories about how terrible it is that thousands of people need to leave their homes in China because a new dam is being constructed or a new HST route is being built. But if you remember the factor of the scale difference of between 20 and 100, the numbers compare favourably with, for example, the 1,300 people who were obliged to leave the village of Doel in Belgium to make possible the extension of the harbour in Antwerp. Being aware of the sheer size of China is essential for anyone who wishes to understand the mobility challenges faced by the country and, as a result, the decisions and huge investments that Chinese cities are making in this domain.

WITH OR WITHOUT A CAR

In the first weeks after my return to Belgium from Shanghai, I took the bus or the train to my appointments but was regularly late, because there were either delays or full strikes by transportation unions. To make matters worse, I couldn't trust the public transport routes, as many companies were hidden away in industrial estates, and taxis were difficult to find (and expensive). I quickly realised that I wasn't going to get anywhere on time without a car and so I decided to lease one. But that was not the end of my problems. The local police in Ghent had not yet called to check my residence, so I didn't have an identity card. This meant that I couldn't open a bank account, which I needed before I could start up my new company. I also needed a notary, but soon discovered they were all on holiday. As a result, until the summer was over I spent most of the time driving around in a rental car, although driving is an exaggeration: I was nearly always sitting in traffic jams. But this seemed to be the expected norm: every time I had an appointment, I received a message telling where I could park, since everyone automatically assumed that I would be coming by car. Sitting in traffic late for another meeting, I missed Shanghai a lot; imagine a city of 24 million people with the largest metro system in the world.[120] An underground train every

3 minutes, buses every 5 minutes (stopping whether you stick out your hand or not), 60,000 taxis charging just 50 dollarcents per kilometre, 400,000 Didi (Chinese Uber) drivers,[121] hundreds of shared bicycles on every street for 25 dollarcents per hour,[122] two airports and two high-speed train stations that open the gateway to the four corners of China. You can live and work perfectly in Shanghai without a car, a city that is 40 times bigger than Brussels, with more than two times the population of Belgium.

That being said, nowadays the Chinese all want a car. In China, there is currently just one car for every ten people, in comparison with one car for every two people in Europe, and one car for every American. In other words, there is a huge potential market. In fact, China is the largest automobile growth market in the world, accounting for more than 50 percent of total global growth.[123] Out of every three cars that are sold worldwide, one of them is manufactured and sold in China. The Chinese are now the most important global consumers of car brands, but because these consumers have recently become more refined and tech-savvy, the Western brands will need to reinvent themselves, if they wish to continue to satisfy their increasingly demanding Chinese clientele. In particular, Chinese consumers are more willing to accept the car of the future than their American or European counterparts. This car can be summarised by the acronym ACES: Autonomous, Connected, Electrical, Shared. It is clear to everyone that the whole world is moving in this direction. In fact, the ACES acronym was first made popular by the Center for Automotive Research in the United States. The main difference is that China has turned the ACES business model on its head, by taking consumers and mobility as the starting point, rather than how you drive from point A to point B.

The traditional car manufacturers see ACES as a technological evolution, less as a disruptive process. This means that younger companies that have not been immersed for decades in the traditional automotive industry perhaps have an advantage because they better understand the consumers of tomorrow. Over the past 30 years, China has not managed to develop and market a car to which local consumers feel emotionally attached. They also did not have the technical expertise to build the best vehicles. This expertise was to be found in Europe and Detroit. However, the ACES concept is no longer about building the best car, but is more concerned with space, time and services. For the car industry, this moment is comparable with the moment when Steve Jobs announced the launch of the iPhone with the words: 'Today Apple is going to reinvent the phone. The problem is that the usual suspects (read competitors) are not so smart and they're not so easy to use. What we want to do is make a leapfrog product that is way smarter than any mobile device has ever been, and super easy to use.' The new ACES car is the iPhone of the automobile market and Elon Musk is its greatest visionary. In the past, people often laughed at his ideas, but today every leading car brand, from Porsche and Mercedes to BMW and Jaguar, is trying to build a Tesla-killer. What's more, with new brands like NIO, Byton, WM and Kandi, China is also joining in the game: all these companies want to become the Chinese Tesla. And they may well succeed, because in my view China does indeed have all the 'aces' to make the transition to ACES faster and easier than in any other country.

AUTONOMOUS

One of the main reasons why the acceptance of autonomous cars will be much more difficult in the West is that we still regard the car as an emotional product, a symbol of freedom and status. In China, a car is simply a means of getting from one place to another. For the ordinary Chinese person, cars are much more expensive to buy in relation to their average salary, so that they focus more upon its functionality and sustainability than its impact on their personal prestige. For the wealthy Chinese class of buyers, there is much less difference with the West. For those with money, having your own chauffeur is still an important way to demonstrate your wealth and power. With this in mind, Volvo build their cars for the Chinese market with more leg room at the back, since this is where the most important person sits! All these factors mean that the mental shift to self-driving cars will be much easier for the Chinese than for us. In China, people see the switch to autonomous cars as a gain in status, time and space. In the West, we see that same switch as a loss of freedom and independence. This has been confirmed by numerous surveys, which show that we Westerners are not so keen to take our hands off the steering wheel.[124]

In China, autonomous cars are the perfect solution for consumers, companies, investors and the government. The first Chinese company to focus on this trend was Baidu, the Chinese Google. The biggest difference between their search algorithms and Google's approach is that Baidu attaches much more importance to the context of how words are used within text. This was made necessary by the more complex Chinese language.[125] It was hardly surprising that Baidu, the pioneer among the Chinese internet companies, was the first to venture into the landscape of Deep Learning. Deep Learning, which is an aspect of machine learning within the general domain of Artificial Intelligence, is also sometimes known as structured or hierarchical learning. This can be organised in a controlled manner, through which the algorithm learns on the basis of examples, or in an uncontrolled manner, as is more often the case with complex linguistic problems, when the algorithm is not provided with output examples. In the latter case, this involves exposing the many different layers of neural networks to the processing of huge quantities of words and sentences, comparable with the way human beings learn a language. This means that 'context' is well understood by Baidu and this is crucially important for the development of autonomous cars, because the way in which pedestrians and other vehicles move is just as complex as the way in which a word relates to the rest of a sentence.

Baidu acquired one of its most important assets in 2014, when it appointed Andrew Ng as the new head of Baidu's AI lab in Silicon Valley. Before that, Andrew Ng[126] worked for Google, where he set up the pioneering 'Google Brain' project. The million-dollar question is: why did Andrew Ng leave Google for Baidu? He later explained that the main reason was that Baidu had already built up good momentum in Deep Learning: with infrastructure, talent, product implementations, customized data centres, data availability and a strategy based on the investment of huge sums of money, fast decision-making and rapid iterations. In other words, Baidu created the ideal environment for Andrew Ng to push the boundaries of AI.[127] By 2015, Baidu's AI algorithms had already acquired a power of speech recognition that approached that of humans. This technology was later used in Baidu's 'DuerOS' conversation platform, which in turn was used to operate new consumer products such as Aladdin, the main rival for Amazon's Alexa or Google's Assistant.[128]

That same year, Baidu also launched its Apollo platform for autonomous driving, a platform that they later made open-source in 2017 as a stimulus for the autonomous car industry in general. More than 100 partners, including names like Nvidia, Ford and Daimler, now belong to Baidu's Apollo ecosystem, which makes it possible for them to build further on existing Baidu AI research. Robin Li, the founder Baidu, says his vision is to one day develop Apollo into the Android of autonomous vehicles. The Apollo platform has a simulator with mountains of data that can be used to test algorithms, as well as having the largest open databank of algorithms. In essence, Apollo wants to become the heart of the vehicle of tomorrow, leaving its other partners to build the other components and make them available in the open platform. In this way, Baidu plans to turn the automobile world upside down. Instead of the software developers supplying the car manufacturers, it is the car manufacturers who will become the suppliers, with the software developers now responsible for the ideas about how new models should be built. Traditional automobile brands and their suppliers are experts at building cars and their components, but they are less good at developing strong, consumer-driven software, algorithms and internet solutions. In contrast, technology companies are very good at all these things, but need physical 'atoms' in which to package their ideas. Just as Android offered the possibility for companies like Xiaomi or VIVO to suddenly become leaders in smartphones, even though they had never built a phone of their own, so Baidu hopes to play the same catalytic role in the autonomous car industry.[129] Given this ambition, it is hardly surprising that in June 2018 Baidu already launched its first Apollo-driven autonomous cars on China's roads, with mass production planned for 2019.

It is not just Baidu that is so enthusiastic about the prospect for autonomous cars; the whole country is under the spell. The Chinese government has set aggressive objectives, aiming for half of all new cars should be fully or partly self-driving by 2020. With this in mind, China has also built an 'AI City of Dreams', called Xiongan (雄安).[130] Xiongan is currently a small city 100 kilometres south of Beijing, but will soon be expanded to 20 times its original size, with an estimated population of 2.5 million people. This new city is a great example of how China works. If you want to build a country of smart cities, you first need a test city, and it is easier (and better) to build a new one, almost from scratch. This is the simple but powerful idea behind Xiongan. Baidu has an agreement with Xiongan to construct the entire vehicle infrastructure, starting with public service vehicles and buses.

Of course, Baidu does not have the autonomous car field to itself: the other tech-giants in China — Alibaba, Tencent, JD and Didi — also want a piece of the action. [131] Tencent has taken a share in Tesla, while Alibaba and Didi have done the same in Lyft. Although they have all entered the market later than Baidu, since 2018 they have been recruiting engineers on a massive scale and have obtained licences for on-road testing. JD, for example, is particularly interested in self-driving robot vehicles for deliveries.
This granting of licences for on-road testing is another important factor in explaining why I think China will win the worldwide race to introduce autonomous cars. Since May 1st 2018,

Beijing has given authority to all provincial and urban administrations to grant such licenses, which makes large-scale testing much more feasible.[132] In democratic countries, promising projects are often delayed or halted because of news reports that a self-driving Tesla or Uber vehicle has caused a traffic accident. Obviously, these incidents do need to be examined and discussed so they can be prevented, but in China — a land in which there are an estimated 700 traffic fatalities per day — this discussion is quickly concluded, so that further positive action can be taken with speed.[133] Priority is given to the 'big picture' rather than 'the full picture'. In the West, many politicians seem to prefer to accept the daily deaths on the road we are accustomed to by now, in preference to having to explain to the general public the possible additional victims caused by a technological change that sounds like many more years away in time. Some can still live with the anonymity of our tens or hundreds of daily road fatalities in our countries, but not with the emotions attached to a single death caused by a so-called 'emotionless' company. Of course, another benefit of broad-scale testing is that it provides masses of useful data. Ironically, this means that even if China is currently lagging behind in some aspects of self-driving technology, it will soon have much more relevant information than the West, which will allow it to make safer autonomous cars more quickly than its Western rivals.

CONNECTED

The fully autonomous car will be first and foremost a utilitarian vehicle, with much less emotional brand value than is currently the case today. The car of the future will be little more than a glorified 'waiting room' where we can do lots of different things while waiting to arrive at our destination: watch a film, read a book, work, arrange a meeting, have a date. The added value will no longer be found in the vehicle itself, but in the connectivity services it provides. The Chinese company that first grasped this idea is LeEco. In my mind its founder Jia Yueting[134] is the Chinese Steve Jobs. This visionary internet tycoon was determined to challenge companies like Apple, Netflix and Tesla. A self-made entrepreneur, after two successful start-ups he founded the LeShi company in 2004. His LeTV brand soon became the de facto streaming service for nearly every household in the country — the Chinese Netflix and YouTube of China. What set him apart from his Chinese rivals was his insistence on buying the intellectual property rights of the shows and film productions he broadcast, in much the same manner as Netflix or Apple. Later, in 2013, he moved into top-quality smartphones, which were comparable to Apple in quality but much cheaper. At the same time, he also developed a business model that converted the users of his phones into subscribers to his streaming service. What began with LeTV as a simple on-demand video site quickly developed into a 'smart' empire: the LeEco empire of connected hardware and software for use in smartphones, smart TVs, smart bikes and smart homes. Jia Yueting took the final step in 2014, when he announced his intention to build an electric car similar to the Model S by Tesla, which he called 'Faraday Future'.[135] Or to put it in Jia's own words: 'We refuse to be mediocre. We will be great or we will die.' Sadly, to date he has not been able to turn this dream into a reality, since the Chinese government froze his assets at the end of 2017, when his investors such as Evergrande got cold feet and stopped investing new funds in Faraday Future, which he needed to continue making his dream come true and pay the company's many debtors in China.

Jia Yueting's story is similar to the 'hero's journey' of Steve Jobs, Jeff Bezos or Elon Musk, who all had to overcome difficulties and major setbacks before achieving their ambition of creating their own vision of the future. Jia said in 2016: 'We consider the car to be a smartphone on four wheels; it is fundamentally not very different from a laptop or tablet. We hope to surpass Tesla and become the industry leader.' In effect, Jia wanted to build a car around consumer connectivity, rather than the other way around. And just as Jobs, Bezos or Musk were not always understood at first, so too the controversial and revolutionary ideas of Jia Yueting have regrettably led to his downfall — for now. But remember his name as I am sure he will be back on the scene one day soon.

I think Jia is right: the car of the future will be built around people and their needs, and not vice versa. The new business model will be about us, not about the vehicle. Another potential Chinese Tesla-killer is NIO, which aims to take up the connectivity story that Jia pioneered. NIO's fundamental objective is to acquire masses of consumer data, in the same manner as the video streaming subscription system of LeTV. NIO wants to be a company for users, not customers. And it aims to do this by providing connections through its various applications. Or in the words of its vice-president, Charlie Zhang: 'It is the amount of time that a consumer spends with your product that will predict your future. You have to make your customers addicted and you can only do that if you own their data. This, for instance, is why NIO has developed its very own voice assistant called Nomi, instead of collaborating with external partners like Amazon and its Alexa. He who owns the data owns the future.' In China, companies measure their success based on 'share of consumer time', not on 'share of wallet' as is the case elsewhere. In 2017, McKinsey conducted a survey into the brand sensitivity of vehicle consumers.[136] The results were as conclusive as they were astonishing: two out of three Chinese car users would immediately switch brands if a new model offered them more in-car connectivity, and would even be prepared to pay for this additional service. This is in stark contrast to Germany, where only one in every five drivers thinks the same.

NIO does not really want to build its own car factory, unlike Tesla and other manufacturers. If your main concern is applications (or so they reason), there is no point in turning the assembly of vehicles into your main activity. That being said, in 2018 NIO was 'forced' by the Chinese government to build a factory as a pre-condition for obtaining its sales license. Even so, it is NIO's 'back-to-front' thinking that the traditional car manufacturers have been unable to grasp. As a result, they are finding it hard to make the leap to a new business model where the consumer and not the car is central. I can hardly wait until NIO's new car 'Eve' is available.[137] The slogan of this concept car is: 'We give you time and space, an environment that adjusts itself to your needs and moods.' The car's digital assistant named 'Nomi' uses Artificial Intelligence to quickly identify the interests of passengers and uses this information to meet individual wishes and needs. Spaces are configured to connect, relax, explore or simply drive. Via augmented reality, it is possible to experience the environment in which you sit in different ways and to be connected with the network of other vehicles around you. The NIO Eve is certainly not the world's first futuristic concept car, but the fact that it is being developed in China again shows how China is taking the lead in shaping our future.

ELECTRICAL

Electric vehicles (EVs) and mobility are seen worldwide as a possible way to meet climate objectives. Chinese cities are notorious for their air pollution, which, according to the World Health Organisation, claims 1 million fatal victims each year.[138] Vehicles are unquestionably the biggest polluters in these cities, which helps to explain the Chinese government's decision to make the electrification of the automobile industry a priority. As a result, while Europe and America are still struggling to make the transition to hybrid models (PHEV), China wants to switch directly to fully electric models (BEV).[139]

Everyone knows that it is better to make the transition to electric vehicles as quickly as possible, but how can you motivate consumers to buy these more expensive cars, vans and lorries? In China, the government heavily subsidised the first years of EV production, so that the EV industry hit the ground running. At the same time, the government had a major ulterior motive, beyond the health of its people and the environment. EVs were seen as a possible way to break the nation's reliance on oil imports from the West and the Middle East. The rest of the world often complained that China's use of heavy state subsidies was unfair, but there is no disputing that they created the momentum that is necessary to make the transition to EV viable. The level of subsidies is now gradually being reduced, except for long range EV vehicles. This policy has helped to improve the quality of these vehicles, so that they now better respond to the needs of Chinese consumers. Consumers are also assisted by subsidies: the central and local authorities sometimes contribute as much as 10,000 dollars towards the purchase of an electric car. In Chinese cities like Shanghai, a car number plate for an ordinary car costs 13,000 US Dollars and new licenses are limited. For EV cars, number plates are often free and immediately available. Some cities even give the EVs special access to carpool lanes, free parking and other benefits.[140]

In China, a subsidy plan is based on three simple steps:

Step 1 is to encourage the producers. This helps to create lots of competition in the new market. The subsidies go primarily to local producers, so that it becomes possible to build up a new national industry, which will later attract foreign joint-venture investment. This creates an attractive market offer.

Step 2 makes it easy for consumers to make the switch. In addition to national subsidies for consumers, Beijing also encourages local administrations to compete with each other to offer the best purchasing stimuli to their citizens. This creates market demand and sets a (low) market price.

Step 3 involves the subsidy being carefully targeted at what is best for the consumer and for society as a whole. Since prices cannot be increased, this means that producers need to innovate in order to achieve the higher standards of quality that will continue to attract customers, leading to consolidation among the manufacturers. This creates better market balance.

One of the main problems with electric vehicles is, of course, their driving range. But if there is one thing that China is very good at it is the rapid development of efficient and effective infrastructure. And it is no different with EVs. China already has 500,000 battery-charging stations and plans to double that number by 2020. Today, Japan and China control more than 95 percent of the market for super-fast chargers and in mid-2018 they reached an agreement that sets a common standard for both countries. In all probability, these fast chargers from the Far East are likely to become the world standard in the not-too-distant future.[141]

In addition to charging stations, electric vehicles also need batteries. The country and/or organisation that can manufacture the most high-quality batteries will control the EV market. Lithium is currently a basic component for 99 percent of all electric-powered road transport. This lithium is mined primarily in Australia and South America, so it is not without good reason that Tesla has invested heavily in battery production in Australia. It is widely believed that the raw materials company Tianqi Lithium Guanfeng and other Chinese companies will soon have more than 50 percent of the world's reserves of lithium ore at their disposal.[142] In addition to lithium, cobalt and nickel are also necessary for EVs. Nickel is still reasonably plentiful, but cobalt resources are more limited and are found mainly in Congo, where the Chinese GEM already controls a third of the available supply. Estimates suggest that the world supply will last until well after 2035, but China does not want to be dependent on others and has therefore taken strategic action to secure a major interest in these key mines.[143]

Sony was the first company to introduce the lithium-ion battery in 1991, and until recently the Japanese were still the world leaders in this field. Not anymore: China is now responsible for almost 60 percent of the world production of these batteries, with Japan and Korea sharing most of the remainder between them.[144] Because of the huge demand for batteries for smartphones and vehicles, China has seen a massive growth in the number of battery manufacturers in recent years. There are now more than 200 of them, with CATL and BYD being the largest. BYD was founded in 1995 as a producer of rechargeable batteries and is today the owner of the biggest battery factory in the world. BYD stands for 'Build Your Dreams', and the company has certainly done full justice to its name. In 2008, Warren Buffet invested 230 million dollars in BYD, which immediately thrust what was then a modest maker of cell phone batteries into the international limelight.[145]

BYD's pitch to Buffet was that they wanted to build electric vehicles. I can still remember when BYD presented their first electric bus at the Busworld Exhibition in Belgium in 2011. They were regarded as something of a 'curiosity' at the exhibition and few people had much faith in this new player. Today, BYD is the largest EV constructor in the world, representing 20 percent of the Chinese market. With 220,000 employees, it is three times bigger than Tesla and sells 10 percent more EV cars than its American rival.[146] In addition, BYD also makes electric buses, as well as small vehicles, taxis and even monorails. 13 percent of the world EV market is in the BYD's hands, and the company has also become a global player with factories in Hungary and France.[147] But its real impact is closer to home, with its headquarters' city of Shenzhen once again leading the way. In 2017, the city's entire fleet of petrol-driven public buses — some 16,359 in total — was replaced by electric-powered buses, which is more than the total number of electric buses in use in the United States.[148] By the end of 2020, it is expected that all of Shenzhen's 17,000 taxis will also be running on electricity. Perhaps it is no surprise that a player like BYD has its roots in the Chinese city with the most progressive view of transport mobility in the entire country.

SHARED

Sharing is a natural part of the Chinese way of life. This goes back to Confucianism, which even today still dominates Chinese values: harmony, respect and generosity in a strongly ordered society. The Chinese people are community-oriented and are more focused on a collective identity than the more individualistic identity of Westerners. This collectivism stimulates inter-personal relationships and dependencies. As I wrote earlier in this book, people often refer to this as guanxi. This term literally means 'relations', but you can better translate it as your 'network of confidants'. Within this network a process of sharing continually takes place: a mutual exchange of favours (renqing), introductions, knowledge and experience within your own 'tribe'. In this way, the Chinese conduct a 'trade' in personal services, with payment more often than not being made with return services, rather than money. This is the main reason why consultancy services are so difficult to sell in China: giving advice is something that friends do freely.

In this way, in China the much-hyped 'sharing economy' is actually a continuation of an economic system that has been in existence for some 2,000 years and in which society as a whole forms the network. The simplest way to understand this is to observe the Chinese when they eat. In the West, everyone gets their own plate; in China, all the different dishes are shared with your fellow diners. And much the same thing can be seen in business organisation, where the management style is more focused on helping each other and sharing information. Companies often provide free services for their employees, ranging from small perks (shopping, a car, holidays, etc.) to truly important benefits (housing, schooling or even matchmaking). Sharing maintains harmony. If you also remember that during the first thirty years of communism under Mao Zedong everything in China was shared public property, it becomes easy to understand why the idea of a sharing economy sounds so natural to Chinese people. But you would be wrong to take this as a sign that the Chinese do not attach importance to private property and ownership. The very opposite is true. Chinese people are mad about brands and personal possessions, and they are willing to pay good money to acquire them. But if it becomes possible to 'temporarily' possess more by sharing within a community, they will often choose to do so. And the choice to share is not strange to them.

This all helps to explain why the sharing economy has taken off in such a big way in China, with an annual growth rate of 40 percent. By 2025 it is expected that some 20 percent of China's GDP will be derived from this economy.[149] In 2017, there were 60 new Chinese 'unicorns', 31 of which belong to the sharing economy.[150] In other words, sharing has become all the rage in China, a rage that is increasingly visible in every Chinese city. And the range of things you can use on a temporary basis is amazing: rooms, cars, bicycles, umbrellas, battery chargers, luxury watches, clothes, etc. If you can imagine something, in China people are probably already sharing it. The rise of this sharing economy, which is much further advanced than in the West, will give a different meaning to property, which means that ease of use will take priority above the brand name. In this way, the sharing economy perfectly matches the demands of modern Chinese consumers for greater comfort as part of an instant, simple, transparent and personalised process.

In the field of shared mobility, the Chinese Uber is Didi (short for Didi-Chuxing) and bike-sharing is already super-popular. Jean Liu, the CEO of Didi, is one of the most prominent female technology leaders in China. Armed with a degree in computer science from Harvard, her vision — which she expresses in perfect English — is both crystal-clear and inspirational. She intends to transform her company into a multinational that serves all personal transport needs. If you need a car, in the future she wants one to be available for you in less than a minute. Didi must also know what kind of car you prefer (self-driving, of course) and it must be able to take you quickly and easily to where you want to go. In Jean Liu's world, this means an urban road network without traffic lights and car parks, in cities that are increasingly green and clean. This is her dream, and it is one that she is systematically turning into a reality, in part thanks to people's understandable daily frustration with the traffic in Beijing and other Chinese cities. If you compare Didi with Uber or Lyft, the biggest difference is one of scale. Didi serves a base of 400 million customers in 400 cities with 25 million rides per day, and it harvests 70 terabytes of data daily — twice as much as all its competitors put together.[151]

Didi uses Artificial Intelligence to feed thousands of ride requests per minute into a platform called the 'Didi-brain'. This system is now able to predict 15 minutes in advance with an 85 percent probability where people will need cars, but Didi expects that in future reinforcement learning will make it possible to extend this advance period to an hour and, later, even to a day. At the moment, Didi employs 500 AI specialists, 100 of whom are experts working in Silicon Valley, where they carry out research into AI applications such as cyber-security, self-driving cars and the behaviour patterns of human drivers. Didi also has another lab focusing on virtual and added reality, with the intention of transforming car windows into interactive screens. Initially, these screens will be used to identify blind spots, but in the future it is hoped they can also be used for video calls, entertainment or even to check the menus of restaurants you are driving past. At the same time, AI also helps Didi to improve its levels of mobility and customer friendliness. In the city of Jinan in Shandong Province for example, Didi is helping the civic authorities to install smart traffic lights based on the masses of data transmitted each minute by thousands of Didi vehicles. A further AI algorithm is now able to arbitrate between the driver and the customer to decide which of the two was responsible when a ride is cancelled. This is in keeping with the new AI arbitration reality in China, which already sees algorithms being used widely in the judicial system to compare current legal disputes and decisions with past judgements and precedents.[152]

The battle in China between Didi and Uber once again proved the strength of Chinese companies in their home market[153]. Uber entered the Chinese market in 2013, immediately unleashing a price war with its local rival. By 2016, Uber had invested 2 billion dollars in its Chinese activities, but Didi had invested even more in response. In the end, Uber gave up the fight and sold its Chinese operations for 17.7 percent of the shares in Didi. Today, Didi is worth more than Uber,[154] so perhaps this was a smart move. Be that as it may, the lesson is clear: if there is a market in China, the local company will always be able to find money from somewhere to take on the foreign company in a price war.

Another good example of overinvestment in the sharing economy is the epic battle between Mobike and Ofo, the two largest bike-sharing companies in the world. In 2015, both companies launched a bike-share system that did not require fixed bike stations, a model that has been copied by Uber and many other companies worldwide. Instead their bikes were fitted with smart locks, which can be opened via an app by scanning a QR code. Their subsequent rivalry is illustrative of the way in which Chinese companies can rapidly grow to an enormous size. Mobike positioned itself as the company of high-quality bikes with sat-nav, bluetooth and a reservation system. Ofo differentiated itself as the company of lighter and cheaper bikes for people who want to pay less (for example, students).

Both companies ask for a security deposit from their users, which provides funds for the bike sharing companies to continue ordering and placing new bikes almost non-stop. In this way, each new user more or less pays for the cost of a new bike. The actual cost to use the bikes is ridiculously low: just 1 CNY (15 dollarcents) per hour. Obviously, it is impossible to make much money with such a low rental rate, but it does get you a lot of users, and their valuable data. To make this system work, you need the backing of major investors, as was the case with Amazon and Facebook, both of whom needed several years before they were able to monetize their users. But in China things move much faster. In just three years' time, Mobike and Ofo were each able to raise more than 1 billion dollars in five funding rounds from Series A to Series E. In Europe, it takes an average of five years to complete Series A and the average amount invested is just 4 million euros. This shows how and why China is unbeatable when it comes to investing in a promising new market. In this case, the competition was further stimulated by the rivalry between China's two largest ecosystems. Mobike was supported by Tencent and Ofo by Alibaba. In 2018, Mobike received 600 million dollars with Tencent as lead investor, while Ofo received 1.5 billion dollars, half of which came from Alibaba. A short time later, Mobike was sold for 2.7 billion dollars to Meituan-Dianping, the Chinese Yelp and Groupon equivalent, which is worth more than 53 billion dollars in its own right.[155] Between 2015 and 2017, Mobike and Ofo's 'winner-takes-all' strategy allowed them to jointly control 90 percent of the Chinese market, with more than 30 million bikes and 50 million daily users in 200 Chinese cities. These astounding figures illustrate how far and how fast things move in China. In Europe, it would be impossible to raise so much investment for a loss-making industry, just as it would be equally impossible to make so many new bikes and distribute them across the length and breadth of the continent (which is approximately the same size as China). People often say that everything in China move so quickly, but in fact things in China move at either an accelerated or a decelerated pace. If you want to understand China, you need to know if an investment project is currently in a period of acceleration or deceleration. Because China is always looking to press ahead, investment is primarily made in projects with acceleration potential, as a result of which lots of other projects are slowed down or even postponed. Most of the frustrations experienced by foreigners in China are because they find themselves in this second position: little wonder that they raise their eye-brows when people talk about 'China Speed'! The reality is that you can never — and I do mean never — be faster than the Chinese once they move into overdrive. Now that Mobike and Ofo have seen off all their rivals and carved up the market between them, they are finally in a position where they can raise their prices, allowing them to provide more long-term services and solutions, which will make it possible for them to pay back all those security deposits, should it ever be necessary. The real value lies in the data that the sharing economy yields. This data is worth its weight in gold for Tencent and Alibaba and other companies like Meituan-Dianping, who are then able to make even more personalised approaches to their customers via tailor-made promotions.

Data is also important to the Chinese government in its attempts to tackle the country's mobility problems. For example, Mobike is working closely with local governments to reach the target of 18 percent of all commuters travelling to and from work by pedal bike or e-bike by 2020.[156] It seems as if China wants to head back to the days of 'Nine Million Bicycles in Beijing', the 2005 hit song by Katie Melua. Everyone on a bike and everyone fit and healthy; a virtuous circle. To assist in this process, Mobike makes use of Artificial Intelligence and IoT to identify mobility improvements among its users. Thanks to Mobike, the amount of commuter traffic has been drastically reduced, the level of CO2 emissions in the cities has fallen by 4.4 million tons, and billions of kilocalories have been burnt.[157]

Of course, suddenly having millions of shared bicycles on the streets creates problems of a different kind, but the Chinese seem to deal with these things more easily than would probably be the case in the West. Government campaigns have been able to educate people to look after their bikes, whilst at the same time, thousands of randomly parked bikes have been confiscated by the police, leaving Mobike and Ofo no choice but to incentivize their users to 'park' them properly. The change in the situation between 2017 and 2018 is remarkable, with the overwhelming bike parking seen in 2017 scarcely visible just 12 months later. This is again typical of the Chinese approach: first deal with problem number one — mobility — before moving on to problem number two — managing the increased number of bicycles. In the West, we often fail to solve a problem because we are afraid of creating a new one in its place (Smart Security).

EXPORTING MOBILITY

Mobike and Ofo both went global at an early stage. However, at the end of 2018 Ofo experienced serious financial problems as a result of its overly aggressive pricing strategy, so that it was forced to give up its international ambitions. In contrast, Mobike is still active in more than 100 cities outside China. Even so, this foreign expansion is not without its challenges. Chinese companies soon discover that the rest of the world is more complex than their homeland: more stakeholders with differing opinions need to be taken into account, and there is much more suspicion of companies and brands. Another major problem is vandalism: in a city like Manchester, 10 percent of Mobike's 2,000 shared bicycles in the city are stolen or end up in the canal each month. This is one of the reasons why the company is now considering to postpone its plans for further European expansion. It would not surprise me if Mobike decides to cut its losses and concentrate exclusively on China. But it is ironic that many Westerners feel that the Chinese are 'robbing us', when we show so little respect for other people's property. Perhaps one reason why the sharing economy finds it harder to make breakthroughs in the West than in China is that we have 'danger zones', where basic standards of respect and control no longer apply.[158]

Another successful example of a Chinese mobility company that is ready to go global (and stay global) is Geely, one of the most famous car brands in China. The company was founded in 1986 as a manufacturer of cheap fridges, which made its founder, Li Shufu,[159] a fortune. In 2002, he decided to switch to cars, announcing his intention with the words: 'Is making a car so complicated that I can't do it myself? A car is just four wheels, a few sofas, plus a lid and an engine.'[160] As a mechanical engineer by training, he knew that making a car was not quite as simple as he made out, but this kind of comment is typically Chinese. If you have a complex problem, you first need to divide it up into smaller parts without losing sight of the whole. Then there is just one other thing you need: the courage to not be afraid of failing. Geely, like the Chinese car brand Great Wall, is a private company and, consequently, it did not enjoy much state support. In fact, central authorities in Beijing actively discouraged their success. But it was precisely this kind of hurdle that made Geely stronger: they did not have the luxury of government backing, on which the state-run companies and the joint ventures can rely. This made it much more difficult to build up their brand, which was one of the least respected in the Chinese automobile sector — and with some justification: until 2010, their cars were definitely sub-standard.

But that changed that same year, when Geely took over Volvo for 1.8 billion dollars plus debt. Volvo was owned by Ford Motors, which was going through a financial rough patch. As a result, in addition to Volvo, it was also forced to sell off Jaguar, Land Rover and Austin Martin.[161] At that time, Volvo was the largest takeover ever made by a private Chinese company, and the deal was viewed with deep mistrust by many people in the West. But Li Shufu soon showed that he had a bold vision, plenty of passion and deep respect for what he had acquired. He compared the Volvo brand to a tiger that needed to be set loose. The brand had a reputation for safety and innovation, and that is exactly what Geely needed to break through in the Chinese market. In 2010, there were just 200 researchers in the Swedish city of Gothenburg to help build the future of Volvo. Today, there are 3,000. This acquisition has certainly not done Volvo any harm. In fact, quite the reverse. Or as the Chinese say: 'Why kill the chicken that lays the golden eggs?'[162] In contrast to its former American owners, Geely knows exactly why it needs Volvo. Without the Volvo brand, Volvo designers, Volvo engineers and Volvo innovation, Geely can never become the Volvo of China, and that is its ambition. Perhaps for that reason, the management and workers of Volvo in Europe are better treated by Geely than they were ever treated by Ford. Li Shufu and Geely tend to watch developments from the sidelines, but give necessary support, funding and freedom to Swedish engineering genius, allowing it to launch the new 90 series onto the market. In addition, Volvo fully embraces ACES technology, since this is what China needs. In the meantime, Geely has bought up other brands like Lotus, the London EV Company (London Taxis) and Proton, as well as making strategic investments in Daimler and Volvo Trucks. Li Shufu is a man to watch in the years ahead.

As the Volvo story shows, Chinese takeovers should not always be seen as negative or dangerous. Because of the huge level of market demand in China, the glut of money available to Chinese companies, the vision of the Chinese state and the efficiency of Chinese factories and suppliers, Western brands acquired by Chinese companies can potentially turn into world leaders almost overnight, bringing jobs and renewed prosperity to their home regions. Of course, not all Chinese takeovers are good, but there are more dynamic business leaders like Li Shufu in China than people in the West are inclined to think. As Bob Dylan sings, "The Times They Are A-Changing", and it is these Chinese visionaries who will export China's ACES vehicles and smart mobility to the world.

What to Remember?

1 →

In China, developing smart cities is not a luxury, but a necessity for the population. China has more pilot projects than anywhere else in the world and wants to improve the quality of life for its citizens via better health, security, education, living standards, prosperity and mobility.

2 →

The high-speed train network has made China a much smaller and more efficient place. Chinese culture is based on personal relations, so that the Chinese have a natural desire to reduce the physical distance between people to a minimum, which acts as a stimulus to smarter mobility. However, the size of China makes any mobility problem between 20 and 100 times bigger than anywhere else, which underlies the need and determination of the Chinese government to tackle this problem.

3 →

The car brands refer to ACES as the transition to more autonomous, connected, electric and shared vehicles. **For the Chinese, ACES is no longer about building cars, but about offering their users space, time and services.** This is not a transition; it is a disruption.

Autonomous. In China, the mental shift needed to accept self-driving cars is a small one. Baidu has set up an open ecosystem with the aim of becoming the Android of ACES technology. The other internet giants are jumping on the bandwagon and the state is facilitating and speeding up the transition via subsidies, new regulations and even the development of a new smart city.

Connected. The new Chinese car companies now come from the internet industry. They see a car as something to be constructed around the connectivity of its user. The success of these new companies will depend on the time spectrum that people wish to spend in their vehicles. China is already building the car of the future.

Electrical. Electric vehicles are essential as part of the solution to air pollution, and for China reliance on imported oil. The state subsidises EV development in three steps by creating a market offer, market demand and market balance. The Chinese are constructing a huge infrastructure for EV cars and have already secured future access to the raw materials needed to produce batteries. Cities and the companies across China are taking the lead to realise the national EV transition.

Shared. The idea of a sharing economy is natural and traditional in China. Didi is the largest sharing platform in the world and via its AI implementations is set to become the innovation world leader in mobility. Shared cars and bicycles will help to make cities smarter and more mobile. The battle for new markets in the sharing economy is a fight to the death, where money continues to be pumped in until there is a clear winner. Only then will peace and calm return to the market.

4 → **The Chinese companies active in the mobility sector are multinationals.** Geely has provided these companies with the first blueprint of how to achieve successful win-win collaboration with the West with its successful acquisition of Volvo. ACES will more quickly become a part of the Chinese way of life and the Chinese Elon Musks will change the world's mobility from bases in their homeland.

SIASUN 新松

<
A technician adjusts a robot arm on the workfloor of an automated factory in Shenyang.

6

SMART MANUFACTURING

CHINA SETS THE STANDARD: FROM 2013 TO 2030

By 2023, most factories in China will have installed next generation robots, so that **Smart Manufacturing** will have its full impact from 2025 onwards. Is China truly evolving from 'Made in China' to 'Created in China'? Will China become the smart factory for the world or is the West destined to become the smart factory for China?

2013 2015 2017 2019 2021 2023 2025 2030

SMART FACTORY BOSSES

In 2007, I represented a European marketing communications agency in China. They had already helped top Japanese and Korean brands communicate effectively in the complex environment of Europe. The Chinese were now set to follow. I went in search of innovative companies with global ambitions. On one of these prospecting visits we flew to Shenzhen to talk with the IAG group (a producer of loudspeakers) and Hisense (a maker of televisions). Both had a strong interest in the European market and had invited us for discussions.

We arrived at the premises of IAG with high hopes. In those years, the company had acquired a number of other prestigious names in the audio world, such as Luxman and Quad, and had moved its factory to an outlying district of Shenzhen. We announced ourselves and a huge metal gate opened slowly in front of us. Once we were inside, we found ourselves in another world. It reminded me of a villain's hideout in a James Bond movie. We were welcomed by the owners (twin brothers), who drove up to us on a Segway. To our surprise, they led us through a luxurious oasis of peace and quiet, twenty hectares in extent, set around a lake in the rolling hills of Shenzhen. This company owned country club — for that is what it was — had three restaurants each one run by a foreign chef, a spa, tennis courts, bowling alley, swimming pool, fitness centre, a Filipino rock band, a cocktail bar and even a luxury hotel for guests like ourselves or for a few privileged members of the IAG staff, including the dozen or so audio-technicians from Europe and Japan. These experts, cosseted in their golden IAG cage, were encouraged to do and test out the most advanced innovations. The contrast with the factory next door could not have been greater. This was a place where more than 1,000 workers, each dressed in the same uniform and each wielding the same soldering iron, sat glued to their work stations day in, day out. This is an image of China that we know well, the image of sweatshops and harsh working conditions. And indeed, for many of the employees, most of them women, it was a hard existence to sit for long hours each day at the IAG production line. But this was a choice they had all made, a choice often motivated by a desire to earn more money for their children, their poor parents or to save to buy an apartment. In 2007, the minimum wage in Shenzhen was 110 dollars per month, although many factory workers could earn as much as 250 dollars per month. Back in the countryside, people often had to get by with as little as 1 dollar per day.[163] In the IAG compound, these two radically different worlds lived (quite literally) alongside each other and they needed each other. What they had in common was the loneliness of being separated from family and loved-ones.

What I learned that day is that Chinese factory owners understand how to best optimise cost and expertise. They buy or hire in the best foreign talent, treat them like royalty, and invite their new friends to innovate to their heart's content. They then use the cost-driven Chinese production model to produce the resulting innovations for the lowest possible cost, delivering a lower final retail price. This model is based on a process of consolidation: everything — research, design, technology, innovation and production — takes place within walking distance. At IAG, 95 percent of their components were locally designed and manufactured. Today, the IAG group is one of the top audio producers in the world.

Leaving IAG, we continued our journey to the Hisense plant in Guangzhou. This involved driving several hours through the well-known Dongguan district – sometimes known as 'the world's factory floor', where 75 percent of the workers are migrants from other Chinese provinces. After passing for what seemed like an age through an endless labyrinth of factory buildings, my Belgian colleague suddenly turned to me and said: 'Now I understand why they invented the atom bomb.' Totally shocked by such a comment, I asked him to explain. 'There is no other weapon that could be effective in such a densely packed place as this,' he replied. This terrible image has always remained with me whenever I think of the endless industrialised landscape of South China.

Arriving at Hisense, we were politely invited to give our sales presentation on the development of their new international website, complete with made-to-measure content management system capacities and a maintenance contract. We had prepared everything well, with attractive slides, catchy slogans and even a little bit of animation. Our sale price was set at 50,000 euros: it would be a large-scale project. After a pitch-perfect presentation, the Hisense managers told us that they were very impressed, but then asked if we could do it for 6,000 Euros! My colleague was furious. That kind of budget wouldn't even cover the preparatory work! After a number of similar experiences, the Belgian company decided not to pursue business in China. A few months later, I came across Hisense's brand-new international website online and I imagine it hadn't cost them any more than the 6,000 euros they had hoped. So how is this possible?

In China, there are always companies who are anxious to have important customers like Hisense as a reference, and so they tailor their price accordingly. This is what Hisense had expected of us. They would get an inexpensive, high-quality website and we would become the reference for future Chinese investors in Europe. This is a typically Chinese way of looking at things. Their vision of the future goes much further than ours, seeing every form of expansion as an opportunity. If, for example, you have a good idea as a Chinese start-up for the development of a voice-controlled speaker, you don't ask the bank for a loan or look for your own financial backers. In China, you go to a company like IAG. If they like your concept, they will help you to build your prototypes and make your first batch, and even invest money in your project. The only condition is that, if your concept takes off, you will stay with them for some time, so that the wheels of their factory continue to turn. This applies equally to many foreign hardware start-ups interested in getting off the ground. Instead of trawling through your home country for investors, just get on the first plane to Dongguan. It will save you lots of time, money and disappointment.

WHAT IS CHINA'S SECRET?

The key question is, of course, how China manages to produce things so cheaply?[164] The most natural answer is to assume that low wages are the main reason. The making of cuddly toys, for example, can be highly labour intensive, so that labour can account for as much as 75 percent of the total cost. This kind of work is not carried out by the 400 million new rich who now belong to the Chinese middle class, but by the half billion ordinary workers who still earn 150 euros per month or less. These are the people making the cheap products the world loves so much.

But if cheap labour is the only secret to success, why has the Chinese 'miracle' not been repeated in India or Indonesia? And how does the 'labour cost' argument apply to products where almost no manual labour is involved, such as the production of plastic toys such as the ever-popular fidget spinners? For these, all you need is a mould, heated plastic resin, an injection machine and an ejector mechanism. This type of self-contained system can operate 24 hours a day and requires little supervision. For this kind of product — in fact, for the majority of products manufactured in China — labour is less than 20 percent of the total cost. This does not mean that low wages are no longer a factor, but they are becoming a less important factor in explaining why we are buying more and more products from China. Goods made by cheap labour certainly still exist in China, but today the salaries of Chinese factory workers are double what they are in Vietnam and other neighbouring countries. It seems that 'bad practices' are not being eradicated, but simply transferred to the Southeast Asia, where sweatshop factories are often run by Chinese managers who have failed to adjust to the new way of doing things in their homeland.

In my analysis, what really makes China so cheap is the sheer scale of production. This is more a question of mental attitude than anything else: they 'think big' and so are able to profit from extremely large economies of scale. Chinese factories think first and foremost in terms of export. They buy in bulk and have several productions lines, with the aim of filling as many shipping containers as they possibly can. As a result, low margins are not a problem. All that counts is non-stop production and rapid growth.

The government has always supported local manufacturers in this nationally coordinated drive to turn China into an export powerhouse. Without a doubt, in the past this has sometimes resulted in dumping, when sale prices fell below the cost. Textiles, solar panels and electrical bicycles have been just three examples of this practice. However, now that China is playing a more prominent global role, it is increasingly learning to play by the accepted international rules. This is something that Europe, in particular, keeps a close eye on. The mistake that many people make today is to think that China still mainly engages in unfair competition through dumping. The truth of the matter is that most Chinese companies are simply cheaper, because they are much larger in terms of scale and much more efficient in terms of production. This is something we would do well to remember, now that more and more Chinese companies are making the move to our part of the world.

Because the Chinese government invests billions in infrastructure, cheap energy and automation to increase the country's levels of productivity, I predict that Chinese goods will continue to get cheaper and Chinese companies will become ever more competitive, despite steadily rising labor costs. Chinese factories also pay detailed attention to the selection and maintenance of their machinery and the training of their personnel. There are a number of areas where Chinese productivity still lags behind the West, but the gap is being closed with amazing speed. Both the government and the factory owners continue to pump money into the future. If we want to prepare ourselves to meet the increased Chinese competition that will soon be heading our way, we need to forget the image of Chinese sweatshops and think more in terms of an oriental version of the German car industry. This offers a much better picture of the true nature of the modern-day Chinese producer. The old sweatshops may still exist here and there, but it will be the countless new, highly-automated factories of China that will soon be selling products of outstanding quality to European and American consumers.

SHANZHAI

Chinese companies are famous — or rather notorious — for their ability to copy Western products via reverse engineering or disassembly, so that they can adjust them to the needs of the local Chinese market. This practice is known as shanzhai, a word that usually has a pejorative connotation, implying stealing and copying from others.

In fact, in Chinese 'shanzhai' literally means 'mountain village' and is a reference to outlaws who lived deep in the mountains to hide from the corrupt overlords of the day. You can see them as a kind of Chinese Robin Hood. The term is derived from a number of classics of Chinese literature, including Journey to the West and The Story of Shui Hu, works that have influenced Chinese thinking for centuries. In contrast with our Western view of the shanzhai as deceitful thieves, Chinese consumers see them as brave, generous, inspirational and intelligent.

Back in the 90s, these modern 'bandits' were originally the smartest Chinese engineers who were employed by the best foreign companies in China. They worked very hard to make a difference for their employers and often suggested improvements to Western ideas, so that products of various kinds would better match the specific needs of the Chinese market: more cost-driven, a wider spectrum of products and more functionalities. Chinese businessmen often see opportunities in the long tail, selling specific solutions to various niche markets, while Western brands prefer standard products that fit and scale to a wide range of customers. When these suggestions were rejected (as was often the case), some of them decided out of sheer frustration to become shanzhai. They started their own companies and 'stole' ideas and concepts and designs from the wealthy West, so that they could sell cheaper products that were more appropriate for poor Chinese consumers with lower buying power.

Because the shanzhai always had a negative connotation, little attention was paid to the underlying context that led to the development of these companies and the manner in which they evolved over time to often become more efficient and innovative than the originals they copied. This had little to do with the protectionism of the Chinese market, as is so often claimed. The real reason why the shanzhai became the most important innovators in China is that they took the needs of the customer, not the needs of the company, as their starting-point. They understood what consumers wanted and went in search of the components, experts and designs that would allow them to provide it. As a result, they became the start-ups that made all the fun gadgets and smart consumer devices in the world.

Of course, it is true that in past decades China has demanded significant technology transfers in return for access to the huge Chinese market. This is certainly the case in sectors like the automotive industry, power plants and aircraft, which creates a dilemma for the Western companies active in these sensitive sectors. If they fail to share their technology, they risk missing out on the fastest growing market in the world. But if they decided to share, there is a risk that they will give rise to hungry Chinese companies as local or even global competitors. Of course, no-one 'obliges' these companies to enter the Chinese market, but most Western CEO's eventually conclude that the risk of not selling in China is far greater than the risk of a few new market rivals. The reasoning of these Western companies has been based on the belief that they will be able to maintain their technological and innovation advantage, with the automotive industry as a case in point. Unfortunately, this was often a flawed assumption and many Westerners have been caught off guard by the pace and the inventiveness with which the Chinese improved. To compete in the future, we need to focus on the speed of innovation, and not exclusively on the so-called 'strangle hold' of tech-transfer. In fact, the Chinese government is even considering making the forced transfer of Western technology illegal from now onwards.[165] It is the high tempo of Chinese change — and not protectionism — that represents the West's greatest challenge, especially now that China is gradually opening its market. If we want to prepare ourselves for 'the day after tomorrow', we need to look at China openly and honestly, assessing the country on the basis of its capacities, ambitions and opportunities, and not on the basis of its perceived past limitations.

The secret of how modern Chinese companies are able to move faster than many of their Western counterparts is inextricably linked to their ability to innovate at high speed. They will certainly attempt to reproduce this success model as they increasingly expand into Western markets. It is a model based on a quick succession of micro-innovations that add value to the daily lives of millions of people. So what can we learn from this Chinese micro-style?

MICRO-COLLABORATION

Since the 1980s, Chinese companies have been brazenly imitating their Western counterparts. This is not something that we in the West like very much, because we want to protect our unique creations. In China, however, the process of creation is much less linked to 'ego'. Designers know that their designs will be copied and improved, before often being re-shared, either directly or indirectly, with their initial creators. In other words, China has long been a centre of open innovation, although this is not what we like to call the practice. We prefer to call it theft.

During the 20th century, there were fewer innovators worldwide and the process of innovation was much more expensive to realize than it is today. Legislation protected the heavy investments, which were mostly made by Western companies. Today, the world is networked. Companies need to change gears more quickly and start-up costs are much lower. Consumers now expect a new smartphone model every three months, whereas it still takes three years to complete a patent application. Speed has become the new protection for new creations and working at speed is something that the Chinese are accustomed to doing. What's more, people in China do not find it a problem to exchange ideas and innovations. In this way, they form micro-collaboration networks of experts, who help each other to put together all the pieces of the puzzle. Companies like Huawei or ZTE have been doing this for decades and are now bringing this same high-speed collaborative product innovation to Europe.

MICRO-INNOVATION

Two key factors encouraging the Chinese to collaborate are the intense level of competition on the Chinese market and the impatience of Chinese consumers. These consumers want quality products like we have in the West, but at much lower prices. If a company like Lenovo is unable to do this, Xiaomi will do it in their place. Xiaomi, the Apple of China, is proud of the fact that as early as 2013 it was already asking for the active input of its consumers for the product development of their first smartphones. There was a non-stop inward flow of new ideas and suggestions from the Xiaomi chatrooms. These ideas helped to reduce development and marketing costs, benefits that were also passed on to the consumers. China is a 'winner-takes-all' market. If you want to survive, you need to become market leader at lightning speed and then hold on to that position. This has made the Chinese producers masters of the art of reducing the cost of their components continuously, whilst simultaneously increasing quality.

This is possible in China because of the country's micro-innovation model, where fast incremental improvements are more important than the kind of disruptive innovations in which Google specialises. In this way, the Chinese integrate the VUCA (Volatile, Uncertain, Complex and Ambiguous) market environment into the company. In the West, we prefer to do the opposite, attempting to keep the company as stable as possible because we fear the potential impact of change. As a result, Western companies are more concerned with conceptual value creation, and less with cost price and speed. We take our time to do things thoroughly and properly, believing this is the way to remain relevant. But now that Chinese companies are aggressively moving into Europe and America, they will no longer allow us the luxury of this time. Just ask Ericsson, Nokia or Siemens.

MICRO-ENTERPRISE

The biggest difference between a start-up and a corporate company is the flexibility and speed of execution of the former. The founder makes a decision, the developers move into action and the sales team hits the road the same week. Chinese technology companies act as a kind of beehive of start-ups, with a wafer-thin middle management level. The reasoning behind this method is simple: every manager is expected to quickly produce a direct result for the company and create value for the consumer. A director of Huawei in Europe once told me that the company's country managers need to achieve an annual growth rate of 20 percent, otherwise they will be replaced. When the state-run white goods manufacturer Hai'er was privatised, 10,000 middle managers were sacked by the new owner and self-made entrepreneur Zhang Ruimin.

The pressure on employees in large Chinese private corporations is huge, comparable with working for a struggling start-up in the West. This pressure has been reduced somewhat since the introduction of new legislation in 2014 that gave Chinese workers more rights and protections, but the habit of innovating in small units with minimal middle management remains typically Chinese. You can compare it to some extent with Google's cross-functional organisation structure, but with the retention of a 'big boss' hierarchy. For example, Tencent has more than 500 product groups, which are set up as separate divisions with their own resources. If a division is successful, it is allocated more money. In this way, WeChat has become Tencent's biggest success, but it only accounts for 5 percent of the total Tencent workforce.[166] In other words, there are half a million WeChat users for each WeChat worker: now that really is what I call 'lean and mean'! Using this strategy, Tencent succeeded in 2010 in growing two semi-comparable products — QQ and WeChat — in parallel, so that they both passed the landmark of 1 billion monthly active users. In the West, these divisions would either have cannibalised each other or been forced to merge. In China, teams do not compete internally for more resources, but externally for more customers, in part by being able to offer the best product.

MICRO-SURGERY

What we all want to know, of course, is whether or not the Chinese giants like Alibaba, Tencent, Lenovo, Huawei and Geely are going to conquer the world, and if so, when. After 30 years of development, some of these brands are now ready to make the breakthrough in Europe and America. Even so, it is not from the big players that we can expect the real tsunami of innovation, but from the legions of younger technology companies: companies like DJI with their drones, Mobike with bike-sharing, NIO (who wants to beat Tesla), UBTech with robots, or Toutiao and CloudWalk with their intelligent apps. It may take five or ten years before this tsunami finally breaks in full force on our shores, but it is already building up its potential energy out in the red ocean inside China.

These new high-tech companies are very different from their predecessors and from the other more local companies that have not taken the plunge in foreign markets. Many of the founders of this new wave of Chinese companies were trained in the West, have acquired valuable management experience at Alibaba, Baidu or Uber China, and are building up a team of experts around the world. They call themselves 'global start-ups' and they are relying on Artificial Intelligence to sweep away their competitors worldwide. They will not do this with much fanfare, unlike Alibaba or Huawei, but with stealth and almost surgical precision, one market at a time. They are not so very different from the Silicon Valley whiz kids, but these phoenix companies have the added advantage of being able to apply the successful China model of their predecessors: **the development of micro-collaboration, micro-innovation and micro-enterprise.**

THE SHENZHEN MIRACLE

Once a small town of 30,000 inhabitants close to the border with Hong Kong, in just 40 years Shenzhen has been transformed into a metropolis of more than 12 million people. This was made possible thanks to Deng Xiaoping's decision in 1978 to declare Shenzhen the first economic zone open for international trade. The worldwide growth of personal computers in the 1990s gave a significant early boost to business in Shenzhen. Moore's Law ensured that the speed of processors would double every 18 months, so that worldwide there was not much interest in innovation in hardware. As a result, computers rapidly became a commodity and Shenzhen was the cheapest place to make them. Worldwide demand turned Shenzhen into a centre for hardware experts (design and manufacturing) in a world that was primarily concerned with software. Today every smartphone is a super-computer, so there is a search on for new applications that move beyond the cell phone, laptop and tablet. This means hardware innovation is suddenly back in fashion. People want smart, connected devices and are beginning to realise that Shenzhen has evolved into the world's unrivalled, incredibly interlinked and hyper flexible hardware design and manufacturing ecosystem. In its haste to focus on software, Silicon Valley forgot to maintain hardware developers, preferring to outsource this role to China. This is now what makes Shenzhen so unique, certainly in our present-day world of IoT, smart houses, smart cars and smart cities. It is precisely these skills that make China in general, and the Pearl River Delta Region and Shenzhen in particular so attractive for investors in the new reality of connected appliances.

It is no accident that HAX, the most successful hardware accelerator in the world, is based in Shenzhen. HAX describes Shenzhen's ecosystem with four S's: the **S**peed, **S**avings, **S**cale and **S**kills of Shenzhen.[167]

1. As far as **speed** is concerned, thanks to the efficient electronic supply chain in the Shenzhen region, that is constantly fed by huge demand from the world's leading brands, you can build things there in a week that would take at least a month outside of China. Everything is instantly available. If you can't find the component you need in Shenzhen, you probably won't find it anywhere in the world.
2. China's production model, as previously described above, means that it is possible to reduce development, integration and prototype costs by more than half, resulting in huge **savings**. In other words, taken together speed and savings yield an eight-fold improvement in performance.
3. At the same time, there are also massive economies of **scale**. In Shenzhen and the surrounding province of Guangdong there are literally thousands of factories ready and able to build almost anything you can think of. And it makes no difference if you want a prototype of a single unit or a production run of a million units: any order size is possible. If you look back to how Shenzhen developed in the 1980s, it is clear to see that many of China's most adventurous and talented souls moved there. Even in 2017, just 32.3 percent of the local population was registered as citizens of Shenzhen.[168] The remaining two-thirds are migrants, including many of the best and brightest people in the country. In other words, this is a place where people are not afraid to try something new. If you are looking for the 'pioneer users' to test out and buy your prototypes, you will find them in Shenzhen.
4. Finally, the range of **skills** possessed by the workforce in Shenzhen is exceptional. Tim Cook, the CEO of Apple expressed it in the following terms:[169] 'The number one reason why we like to be in China is the people. The Chinese have extraordinary skills. [...] China has moved into very advanced manufacturing, so that in China you can find the intersection between craftsmanship, sophisticated robotics and the computer science world. That intersection, which is very rare to find anywhere, is very important to our business, because of the precision and level of quality we need. [...] Our products require really advanced tooling and the tooling skill is very deep here. In the US you could have a meeting of tooling engineers and I'm not sure we could fill the room. In China you could fill several football fields. [...] Vocational expertise is very, very deep here, and I give the education system a lot of credit for continuing to push on that, even when others were de-emphasizing vocational. Now I think many countries in the world have woken up and said that this is a key thing, and that we've got to correct that. But China called it right from the beginning.'

PROTECTION OF INTELLECTUAL PROPERTY RIGHTS

China, with Shenzhen as an epicentre, is the largest manufacturing zone in the world. What impact does this have on the protection of intellectual property rights (IPR)? Notwithstanding the shanzhai phenomenon and the many past examples of Chinese patent infringements, it is fair to say that from a legal framework perspective at least, China no longer has any serious systemic IPR problems. After China joined the World Trade Organisation in 2001, Beijing felt obliged to put its regulatory house in order. And although it would be wrong to say that all the problems have disappeared, many Chinese lawyers have confirmed to me that laws exist so that you can now protect and enforce your IPR in China in much the same way as in the West. In fact, the current IPR legislation is probably the most comprehensive aspect of all Chinese legislation. Partly as a result, the country is currently the largest applicant for patents in the world, with 95 percent of legal cases involving IPR now being between Chinese companies. This growing domestic interest in protecting IPR is one of the reasons why the legislation is so complete, but this also works to the benefit of foreign companies: like their Chinese counterparts, they win roughly 80 percent of the patent cases that go to court.[170] Today, the IPR problem in China is first and foremost a market problem. Competition in Chinese markets is so fierce that many companies continue to take irrational, and illegal actions to gain an advantage over their rivals. In other words, the problem has not gone away and it remains difficult to track down offenders, and even when you do find them, prosecuting them is not always worth the money it costs. However, a robust legal framework exists and China's ability to provide protections is improving. In fact, in today's China IPR has become an issue for Chinese companies who protect their ideas by using a veritable army of lawyers. Many of these lawyers are even paid on a commission basis, based on how many copy-cats and counterfeiters they can track down and the amount of penalties they can force them to pay.

On the other side of the equation, China is the prime-mover of a new open-source hardware movement, once again centred in Shenzhen. The open-source hardware idea is much closer to the DNA of Chinese micro-collaboration, whereby each new innovation is shared and improved. In the West, this kind of open-source project is often attached to a 'hackathon' event organised by a company or organisation, in which people take part as a hobby or simply to pass the time. Sometimes the ideas generated are good, but often the company has no real understanding of how to make money from them. Things are very different in China. The Chinese see open source as the most natural way to get something built quickly. At the same time, the patent system allows the leading global companies and their lawyers to hang on to their market position, even if they are making nothing fundamentally new. The fact that a global leader like Apple or Samsung can protect a very slight modification on a patent or protect a design which has been used in other environments before is something that puzzles the innovators in Shenzhen. Modern Chinese micro-enterprises prefer to operate within a tightly networked ecosystem of innovation exchange. While business leaders in the West are still more concerned about their property rights and patents, the Chinese are already well on their way to creating a new type of shared economy of ownership. In this respect, perhaps China offers an alternative model for the international future of intellectual property, the fundamental asset underpinning many established Western companies.

No matter how China evolves in the future — whether it follows the open-source route or the more traditional pattern of patenting and protection — there is no longer any reason not to come to China out of a general fear of having your intellectual property 'stolen'. Improved protections do exist, and the risk of failing to take part in the world's fastest growing market is far greater than the risk of being copied, particularly now that China is starting to create its own standards that will allow it to break through many of the monopolies created by Western patents in the past. Huawei's most recent request to the US carrier Verizon to pay 1 billion USD in licensing fees for using its patents is a sign of a future waiting for many industries.

ACTIVATE POOR ENTREPRENEURS

These days high-impact innovations are more likely to come from smaller entrepreneurs and companies, so it makes good economic sense to support this group. But building hardware is hard and gaining access to leading edge technologies and production facilities remains largely the preserve of the large corporations and their OEM partners, with their massive capital and negotiating power. However, China is attempting to break this 'chicken-and-egg' problem.

At the very bottom of the global supply chain, hundreds of millions of desperately poor entrepreneurs live in the Southern hemisphere of the globe. For decades, the rich West, despite the very best of intentions, has been unable to make a real difference with the poorest of the poor. But I believe a new era of possibility is opening. Today we are living in a truly connected world, so that the poor now have the option to use the internet platforms and technologies from China to lift themselves out of poverty. I am not referring to the One-Belt-One-Road (BRI) project[171] or the massive Chinese investment to increase Chinese influence in the underprivileged regions. No, I am referring to a different kind of infrastructure, which is giving the global poor all the building blocks they need to solve their own problems. China provides them with the cheapest smartphones for their communication, free applications for their creations, open-source hardware to build things, experts to provide necessary training, factories to produce and business models to sell. In Guangzhou, there is already a thriving African and Middle Eastern community, a new generation of entrepreneurs itching to make a name for themselves. They represent a largely invisible aspect of the new 'Made in China'. I believe this 'left behind' segment of the world's population will burst into life thanks to China. Poor entrepreneurs are highly motivated to solve the 'real' life problems facing large parts of the world, and not the many 'luxury' problems of the West, where most of the focus of creativity is focused today. Instead of spending time in your home country writing a business plan or devising fancy sales presentations, the normal reflex of every new hardware start-up or entrepreneur should therefore be to get on the next plane to South China. If you have very little starting capital, that plane ticket is almost certainly the best investment you can make.

IngDan is one of the finest examples of this kind of motor for change. The company orchestrates an open ecosystem available to entrepreneurs all over the world. The company helps these entrepreneurs, rich or poor, access a supply chain of over 8,000 electronics production factories. IngDan is able to do this because of their mother company, Cogobuy, which is the largest e-commerce platform in China for the purchase of imported electronic components. The company's founder, Jeffrey Kang, the Jack Ma of electronics, wants the IngDan online platform to connect entrepreneurs from all around the globe with Chinese factories and Chinese innovation. His dream is to turn IngDan into the largest Internet-of-Things (IoT) sharing platform and community in the world. With more than 30,000 projects currently up and running, he is already well on his way. He prefers to describe the platform as AIoT-based (a combination of AI and IoT), because he believes that IoT cannot function optimally without AI to turn all the IoT nodes into intelligent machines. If you walk through the IngDan showroom in Shenzhen, you can see literally hundreds of prototypes for products that all have one thing in common: they improve people's lives.

SMARTER MACHINES

In the West, people often talk about 'Industry 4.0', which will make production more efficient, cheaper, more profitable and improve delivery to customers. This is 'factory-to-customer' thinking. In China, they do things the other way around: customer-to-factory. Chinese business leaders think that the demand must come from the customer. Thanks to Artificial Intelligence it is now possible to better assess and estimate customer needs, so that factories can be further optimised. In 2016, for example, when the bike-sharing market suddenly took off, hundreds of Chinese factories began to make bicycles for a market they did not know. But they followed market trends closely and took bold and prompt investment decisions that allowed them to surf on the bike-sharing wave. Two years later collectively these companies manufactured over 30 million new two-wheelers. In the West, similar factories could never have achieved this rate of output at the same speed, and many potential suppliers would have continued to make ever-better aluminium window frames, instead of converting to meet a new 'hot' demand. In Chinese factories, AI, Big Data and Cloud computing are used on a massive scale, not only to improve traditional production processes, but also to respond to the market demand on 'the day after tomorrow'. This is called the ABC of smart manufacturing.

China is now making the leap from smart optimisation to smart automation. This process enjoys the strong support from the Chinese government, which wants the country's companies to move to higher-value manufacturing and also prepare for a smaller workforce in the future as China rapidly ages. In the field of robotics, for example, China wants to become the world's number one robot powerhouse and is aiming at 40 percent of worldwide robot sales in 2019. Another reason for concentrating on robot automation is the increasing level of wages in China, which have doubled in the past ten years. In 2017 alone, Foxconn, which produces nearly all the world's iPhones in China, replaced more than 60,000 workers with robots. Of course, several crises around working conditions due to Foxconn employees committing suicide as said because of work stress, could also have played a factor in this decision. In that same year, 2017, China had 78 robots per 10,000 workers, in comparison with 167 robots in North America. Beijing wishes to double the Chinese total to 150 robots per 10,000 workers by 2020, which will move it into the world top ten on a relative basis.[172]

In 2016, the Chinese household appliances manufacturer Midea purchased the German robot maker KUKA for 5 billion dollars. This was a turning point moment for the Chinese manufacturing industry. The acquisition is a way for China to upgrade both its global image and its capabilities. 'Manu-facturing' (which in Latin literally means 'made by hand'), will eventually die out in modern Chinese factories, which would be freed from their mostly undeserved reputation as being little better than sweat-shops. In this way, China is evolving from 'Made in China' to 'Created in China'. Automation and robots are critical to this plan. The acquisition of KUKA and other similar companies from the West will allow China to truly evolve into an Industry 4.0 country. This is urgently necessary to be able to satisfy the increasing demand of the new middle class for better quality products. KUKA's takeover by Midea was a blueprint for other Chinese brands and has emboldened them to do the same. As in the case of Geely's approach to Volvo, maintaining the local management, local decision-making powers and the local workforce are all characteristics of Midea's management of its new crown jewel. China wants to build 1 million robots by 2025 and Midea is targeting a 50 percent market share.[173] In collaboration with Huawei, Midea wants to build a new standard for smart factories. And with 36 percent of the world growth in the robot market already generated in China, who is to say that they won't succeed.[174] Leading Western technology companies need to take notice of the automation 'gauntlet' being thrown down by China.

On the German side, the KUKA takeover caused an outbreak of near-panic, as they saw one of their most innovative companies being 'carried off' to China. For Angela Merkel, the deal was a wake-up call. In response, the German government intends to screen any investment from outside the European Union involving more than a 25 percent stakeholding.[175] Chinese acquisitions are now high on the political agenda in many European countries. China needs acquisitions of this kind to achieve the leap forward it wants to make, and it certainly has the money to pay for them. So, what will be next moves in this chess game?

MADE IN CHINA 2025

The acquisition of KUKA was the last straw for many in Europe, but I believe it was merely a foretaste of what we can expect based on the 'Made in China 2025' (中国制造 2025) national plan, which China has been developing since 2011. Premier Li Keqiang formally launched this strategic plan in 2015. It is based on the German model for industry 4.0, with the intention of allowing Chinese industry to climb higher up the value chain. In theory, the plan is designed to inject more innovation into Chinese manufacturing, so that quality can take precedence over quantity. But in practice the plan goes much further, with goals around a reduced ecological footprint, an improved industrial structure and the further stimulation of top talent. The unspoken objective of Made in China 2025 is to complete a transition that will make the country less dependent on the West. Today, this dependence is China's Achilles' heel. As long as China continues to rely on the massive importation of Western technology, the government is not confident that the nation will be able to take the next step towards world innovation leadership, the real ultimate goal. China wishes to avoid at all costs falling into the dreaded 'middle-income trap'. This is a real risk for the country if the expanding middle class continues to expect higher incomes and a better standard of living, but China's internal growth is insufficient to turn these aspirations into reality. This might lead to social instability, which is something that Beijing will do everything it can to prevent. Consequently, for China it is imperative that it becomes a world leader in innovation, so that it can create the higher income levels that its middle class demands. And given President Trump's actions to block China's access to high technology, the strategy of ensuring China's greater independence from the West has become even more imperative. In fact, this is no longer just a strategy; it is a national mission.

The Made in China 2025 plan identifies ten sectors (see box) in which China wants to be among the world leaders by 2030. It is no coincidence that these are mainly sectors where Europe and America currently regard themselves as world leaders. In Washington, the formal announcement of Made in China 2025 exploded like a bomb: it made 'official' what until then had been China's unstated intentions to undermine the West's economic and technological dominance. Faced with America's heated reaction, in 2018 Beijing tempered its public communications about the plan since suspicion from America and Europe could hinder the international acquisitions, on which the plan's realisation in part depends. But notwithstanding this softer diplomatic tone, China's innovation ambitions remain unaltered.

Made in China 2025 sectors: 1) new advanced information technology; 2) automated machines and robots; 3) space and aviation; 4) maritime shipping and equipment; 5) modern train transport; 6) new energy vehicles; 7) power plants; 8) agricultural machinery; 9) new materials; 10) biomedicine and advanced medical products.

THE ACCEPTANCE PROCESS

Should we all be concerned by China's ambition to become the leader in world innovation? Many politicians in the West argue that we need stronger protectionist measures against China. But building high dams against Chinese investment may simply isolate the West from innovation developments occurring in the dynamic Chinese market, and most likely cause us to miss economic opportunities, and potentially even tip us into a deep economic depression. The higher we build the dam, the more opportunities we will miss and the longer our recovery will take.

Indeed, Europe is already losing its economic position to China and is only now slowly coming to terms with the implications. In 2018, the GDP of China was 13.2 trillion dollars, which for the first time was higher than the combined GDP of the 19 member states of the Eurozone at 12.9 trillion dollars.[176] In the near future, our economic dominance will be lost forever and will pass to China, plunging the West into the five typical phases of the grieving process: denial, anger, bargaining, depression and, finally, acceptance.

1. We have seen China's rise as a world power for some time, but convinced ourselves that we could remain more creative, more innovative and more strategically aware. We depicted China as a cheap 'copycat' land and denied that it posed a real threat. This denial was the first phase of our grieving and acceptance process.
2. The announcement of the Made in China 2025 plan in 2015 was a wake-up call for the world. The resulting anger was the second phase in the grieving process. People were now aware that the Chinese want to buy our top companies, and were furious when such takeovers happened.
3. Since 2018, we have been fully aware that China is taking steps to buy up our best technology. This is the third phase of our grieving process: bargaining. Now we are prepared to do anything to prevent the situation becoming irreversible. We support Western protectionism; we call in the help of the state security services; we allow President Trump to orchestrate a trade war, which I believe is a direct response to Made in China 2025 and not to the difference in the balance of trade, that he would like to have us believe. Americans are actually buying masses of Chinese products on credit using money that they have partially borrowed from China. Fake news? Perhaps. But because the West now systematically screens Chinese acquisitions, we can use this mechanism as a way to bargain with China, instead of just automatically blocking Chinese innovation plans. By building dams against these plans, we may be able to slow the Chinese down, as we see with the blocking of the US microchips sale to Huawei, but will never be able to completely stop them because the Chinese innovation train has already left the station. The illusion that it will still take China many more years to achieve parity in the ten Made in China 2025 sectors is nothing more than self-deception.
4. The next phase is depression, which will arrive some time before 2025, once China loses interest in our tech companies because it has already achieved parity in many areas. This is the moment when Europe and America will finally recognise their mutual dependence on China. A first sign is the American offensive against the 5G technology developed by Huawei, which can cause great problems for many Western telecom operators. Who should we trust? What should we do?

5. Shortly thereafter, we will reach the final phase of full acceptance. This is the moment when the West will be economically dependent on China. My crystal ball says this will happen around 2030.

This scenario often reminds me of the story of Kodak, who refused to accept that the digital world was coming, believing that 'real' professional photographers would always want a reflex camera. Kodak failed to understand that ordinary consumers had become the photographers of a new age, who via selfies now wanted to place themselves in the limelight and be able to instantly share their experiences, rather than just taking nice snapshots of families, friends and holidays for a family album sitting on a shelf.

Instead of trying to block China's progress, it might be smarter simply to assume that within 20 years China will be the most innovative country in the world, populated with the world's the most sophisticated consumers. These consumers will stimulate fierce competition among local companies to create the most innovative solutions to serve their needs. Would it not be better to try and imagine this possible state of affairs in 'the day after tomorrow' and then think through what steps we can best take today to adjust to this possibility?

If we can do this, it might be possible to take advantage of the current Chinese hunger for our technology and expertise to gain much better access to China's huge markets, innovations, money and influence. In this alternative scenario, we would be wise to conduct hard negotiations with China to achieve some kind of political and economic equilibrium. In other words, make friends of the Chinese rather than enemies; build bridges, not dams.

Of course, no one can really know what the future will bring. But we can look with clear eyes at the past. We can see that China has realised nearly all of its evolving ambitions over the past 40 years, in the process generating 30 percent of world economic growth, creating the largest consumer market in the world, becoming the world's factory, developing some of the world's most valuable companies, and providing its own people with prosperity and a national infrastructure that is second to none.

I do not believe that the Chinese innovation train will 'break down' anytime soon. It will stay on track, not simply because of Made in China 2025 or the widespread automation of factories, and not even because of foreign acquisitions like KUKA. No, the Chinese innovation train will continue to speed forward because Chinese consumers desire the same or better quality than we have in the West. Chinese companies need to make better products, and so to survive they are compelled to upgrade their research and their factories. State planning certainly helps in this process, but it is not the prime-mover. The prime-mover is the market.

What to Remember?

1 → **China's secret for cost-efficient production rests in the ability of factory owners and the government to think and plan big,** allied to extreme differentiation in the cost and expertise levels. The shanzhai phenomenon has taught China how to innovate at speed.

2 → **The Chinese think big, but their method of innovation is small-scale.** The Chinese collaborate in small groups and aim to develop micro-innovations faster than their competitors. Chinese companies grow like an embryo that constantly re-divides its cells. China's new innovators have global ambitions, but aim to achieve them in a fast succession of small steps.

3 → **It is the four S's of Shenzhen that make China the smartest producer in the world: Speed, Saving, Scale and Skills.** In particular, the skills of the Chinese workforce are the real economic strength of China. The open-source thinking of these experts challenges the Western concept of intellectual property ownership, while Chinese legislation has now enshrined this concept in law and China's IPR protections are improving.

4 → **The Chinese product ecosystem is ready to help every entrepreneur in the world to disrupt the dominance of the large companies.** China is evolving from a factory to an open platform, from stealing technology to sharing it, from cheap to smart components with AIoT, from 'Made in China' to 'Created in China'.

5 → **With the Made in China 2025 plan, the Chinese government aims to transform the country into a world leader in innovation.** At any cost, China wants to upgrade its industry in ten key sectors, based on foreign acquisitions and the expansion of its own expertise. The West is currently going through an acceptance process to adjust to these new Chinese ambitions, but we still think too much about tomorrow and not enough about 'the day after tomorrow'.

SECOND INTERNATIONAL SUMMIT
27-29 November
Lee Shau Kee
Centennial
The University of
The Academy of Sciences of Hong Kong 港科院
THE ROYAL SOCIETY
NATIONAL ACADEMY OF
Supported by:
UNIVERSITY OF HONG KONG
Technology
SECOND INTERNATIONAL SUMMIT ON
HUMAN GENOME EDITING
Convened by
The Academy of Sciences of Hong Kong 港科院
THE ROYAL SOCIETY
NATIONAL ACADEMY OF SCIENCES
NATIONAL ACADEMY OF MEDICINE

<
In Hong Kong, Chinese biologist He Jiankui proudly defends his controversial achievement as the first researcher to alter the genes of a twin embryo.

7

SMART HEALTH

CHINA SETS THE STANDARD: FROM 2013 TO 2030

By 2025, I also predict that healthcare in China will have been so radically transformed that it will no longer be recognisable in its present form, with a new form of **Smart Health** being available for most Chinese citizens. Can China's transformation in this field perhaps help to solve the problems of employment and service provision in our Western health sector?

2013 2015 2017 2019 2021 2023 2025 2030

HOSPITALS

My wife is an artist.[177] Her art serves as a mirror to reflect human life and the existential questions that go hand in hand with the natural process of the human body. She is fascinated by the human condition in all its different stages: birth, illness, cure, death. Her work is strongly autobiographical and hospitals play a central role. During the time of our stay in Shanghai we had to visit hospitals rather more frequently than we would have liked. Often for minor ailments, but sometimes for tests, operations and admissions. Like most Westerners, at first we only trusted the city's international hospitals. But one time after we received a massive bill, we decided that next time we would give the local hospitals a try. It soon became clear that the local doctors were every bit as good as their foreign counterparts. If fact, we frequently found them better, because they were quicker to recognize symptoms, probably because they had more practical experience in treating a large number of patients each day.

If you approach a public hospital in China early in the morning, you will already see a long queue of people waiting to get in. They have often spent the entire night there, so that they can be the first to see a specialist. Even if you arrive at four o'clock in the morning there will be 50 people ahead of you. All you can do is wait. If you have money, you can risk buying a ticket from one of the people — scalpers — higher up the queue. But not everyone can afford this luxury. The majority of patients come from outside the city, from smaller towns and villages where there is often a shortage of competent doctors. In fact, China only has one general practitioner for every 6,666 people, whereas the international norm is around one doctor per 1,500 people.[178] In 2017, there were 8.18 billion registered medical visits in China, a total that exceeds the number of people on our planet.[179] Just 7.7 percent of Chinese hospitals have an AAA-rating, but they deal with more than half of all the out-patient visits.[180] The biggest problem is the salary of China's 210,000 local general practitioners:[181] they earn less than half what a hospital specialist earns. The Chinese have little faith in these underpaid local doctors and so head off en-masse to see specialists in the big city hospitals, sometimes even if they only have a cold or a headache.

In September 2014, I contracted a serious pneumonia. I went directly to the emergency room at a local hospital in Shanghai, because I didn't want to infect the rest of the queue with my coughing. After just two minutes, the specialist sent me to the radiography department. They took an x-ray of my lungs and within 30 minutes I knew exactly what the problem was, and also the proposed remedy: I was told that I would need to be on an IV drip for two hours a day for the next three weeks. This was one of my most surreal experiences in China. Each day I sat in a ward jam-packed with 200 other patients who needed IV infusions of glucose water or blood plasma. For me, this was the worst possible breeding ground for germs I had ever seen. But for the Chinese it was normal. And after three weeks, I had made lots of new friends. Because I was still weak, there was nothing much I could do while I was sitting there, so I began to watch the nursing staff going about their daily routine. A team of just five nurses were so attuned to each other that without words they were able to insert hundreds of IV needles into hundreds of arms each hour, for a full eight hours every day and without a single mistake. My respect for these nurses grew every day. It was here that I truly came to understand what Chinese working efficiency really means: in this case, a clever system of codes, hierarchy, sign language, shortcuts and, above all, speed. It reminded me of the way stockbrokers in the West work on the stock exchange floor, although for much bigger salaries than the paltry 330 US Dollars per month paid to these turbo-charged nurses.

Before 2013, it was common for doctor-specialists to receive kickbacks from their patients and the pharmaceutical companies. GlaxoSmithKline once had to pay 489 million US Dollars in fines because of such practices. In 2014, Xi Jinping decided to adopt a hard approach to this kind of corruption, but it is difficult to eradicate 30 years of deeply entrenched illegality overnight. As a result, the Chinese health sector continues to be coloured by various shades of grey. Surgeons can still legally earn extra payments based on the success of their operations, which offers little financial stimulus to experienced doctors to train new young surgeons. Moreover, they are also quickly made liable for any complications that may arise, even if these operations are carried out by trainees under their supervision. The net result is that most operations in China are carried out by the experienced surgeons, which again serves as a discouragement for young new recruits. Less than 5 percent of practicing surgeons in China are currently younger than 43 years of age.[182] A specialist in a typical city hospital sees an average of 100 and sometimes as many as 200 patients each day. That means just five minutes per patient. Five minutes to understand the problem, reach a diagnosis and prescribe a cure. What's more, there is very little privacy when you visit a Chinese doctor. With so many people waiting to get in, the door to his or her office is seldom closed. My wife and I had to learn how to put our Western sensibilities to one side and were eventually able to discuss our most intimate problems in the presence of total strangers. After a time, we were no longer bothered by this, and nor are the Chinese. Inevitably, a specialist who sees more than 20,000 patients a year knows almost none of them personally. This lack of a personal relationship means that patients seldom confide much in their doctors and so do not really expect to have confidential discussions with them. The only things they trust, in part, at least, are the doctors' diplomas and experience. It is hard to imagine a bigger contrast with the West, where a general practitioner will often spend up to half an hour talking to a patient in complete confidence.

TRUST IN AI TECHNOLOGY

Given this background, it is hardly surprising that the average Chinese citizen is more inclined to trust technology than a doctor or the healthcare system. Let's take cancer detection as an example. According to IBM, thanks to AI processing of hundreds of thousands of cancer images, their Watson machine is capable of offering new insights into the diagnosis and treatment of the disease. Almost every Chinese man and woman would almost certainly trust this machine in preference to the oncologist at their local hospital. A few years ago, the Watson AI was being seriously hyped, primarily because people remembered how IBM's AI computer had beaten two top champions at the Jeopardy game show on television. And we are now asked to believe that the IBM machine is also smarter than humans at tracking down cancer. Of course, the reality is not so straightforward. In particular, IBM had two growing pains to deal with.[183] First, the machine was primarily trained by top American oncologists, with all the human preconceptions that doctors in any country have, so that instead of creating a cognitive AI application, as they claimed, they really ended up with a 'self-reinforcing' super-computer. The second problem is that Watson did not have access to a sufficient number of patient notes from American hospitals. This is much less of a problem in China. That being said, at the end of the day it doesn't really matter how good the IBM Watson is at identifying and making recommendations for cancer treatments, as long as it helps our doctors to recognize the patterns and choose the possible treatments. Today IBM Watson is already available in 68 hospitals in China, where oncology departments regard it as a state-of-the-art diagnostic tool.

In June 2018, there was another similar breakthrough when 'BioMind', an AI-doctor machine developed in China and Singapore won a competition against a panel of doctors and specialists. The human medical experts took 30 minutes to achieve a 66 percent accuracy rate in the recognition of brain tumours; BioMind achieved 87 percent accuracy in just 15 minutes.[184]

That AI will one day revolutionise the medical world is beyond question, but today we are only just at the start of that journey. However, it is a journey that China is likely to make quicker than other countries, for three reasons: its needs are greater, the government recognizes the urgency of the need, and there are huge amounts of relevant data available. In 2018, 9.6 million people died of cancer worldwide, 2 million of them were Chinese. In China, someone dies of cancer every four minutes.[185] According to Ni Hao, the founder of the leading AI unicorn Yitu (Smart Security), China has already made much more progress than the US in the field of AI supported diagnoses. Why? Because the shortage of doctors in China compels the use of technology to help patients and because doctors in the West are on average 100 times more expensive, so that there are very few Western AI start-ups who can afford to pay for a medical team. Yitu has recruited a part-time group of 400 doctors, who help the company 10 hours per week to label data, while 20 percent of their full-time workforce also have a medical diploma. At the same time, Yitu collaborates with a hospital in Chengdu, a city in Southwest China, which has provided them with a database of 280,000 lung cancer studies. The result is a new AI-algorithm that can make a lung cancer diagnosis with good accuracy in a matter of seconds.

As you might expect, the major data players are also keen to get involved. Tencent is working with 100 Chinese AAA-rated hospitals and has launched an open AI platform known as AIMIS (miying), which deals with 700 different illnesses (covering 90 percent of all ambulatory illnesses), based on a combination of image processing and AI analyses. The training of the platform involves various AI processes: neuro-linguistic programming (NLP) and deep learning to understand the medical literature and the patient records, followed by the use of diagnosis algorithms and, finally, optimisation by human doctors. Baidu has also made its AI technology platform open source to help pathologists to unlock the secrets of breast cancer. Alibaba has created its own smart health platform with a blockchain application that allows data to be exchanged between hospitals. In other words, the BAT companies seem keen to jump on the AI diagnosis bandwagon. However, as is so often the case in China, the relevant legislation is lagging far behind, so that for the time being the available tools play only a supportive role for human doctors and nurses, although their generally open and free nature means that they are being consulted with an exponentially increasing frequency. When the CFDA[186] (Chinese Food and Drug Administration) regulations are finally in place, no later than 2030, the health industry in the West will probably look surprised and ask how it was possible for China to overtake us. But the trend is already there, plain for all to see.

THE WORLD'S MEDICAL FACTORY

During my search for Chinese technology companies with European market ambitions, in 2007 I visited the listed company Mindray, which was founded back in 1991. Even back then, Mindray already had 50 or so products dealing with patient monitoring, in-vitro diagnostics and medical image processing, which had been sold to 37,500 hospitals and clinics. With 12 international offices, 5,500 employees and a turnover of 300 million dollars, they were a strong prospect for our company.[187] In those days, the market for medical equipment, particularly the high end, was firmly in the hands of Western companies like Medtronic, Johnson & Johnson, G.E., Philips and Siemens. Chinese producers concentrated on the middle and lower-end segments, where prices were much lower. By 2015, however, China was ready to try and move its local companies up into the top division of medical suppliers. With this in mind, the 'Made in China 2025' plan identifies medical equipment as one of the ten sectors in which China would aim to become a world leader with government support.

The Made in China 2025 strategy contains a strong protectionist element, with 70 percent of the domestic market ear-marked for local manufacturers, an aspect that has come under heavy fire from Europe and President Trump. Even so, it should be clear to anyone that a company like Mindray can no longer be regarded as a copycat: 30 percent of its employees are engineers and 10 percent of its net turnover is pumped into R&D. As a result, Mindray is now able to position itself as a serious rival to Western brands.[188] Of course, this is still a long way from world leadership, but Mindray and other Chinese companies, such as United Imaging, have already captured more than 10 percent of the lucrative high-end market in their homeland: no mean achievement in direct competition with other world players in the world's second largest market with a growth rate of 20 percent per year.[189]

DIGITAL HEALTH

According to McKinsey, the impact of digital technology on the Chinese health sector could grow up to 45 percent of the total medical expenditure by 2030.[190] China already has a huge profusion of mobile medical applications, but the real breakthroughs are in the making. Most patients use the apps primarily to make appointments in hospitals, which can sometimes save them up to two days' time. The reason for this slow adoption is that the large majority of Chinese patients, such as the elderly and migrant workers, traditionally still prefer to rely on the recommendations of family and friends to visit a specific doctor or hospital. However, the rich and the young urban middle class are now starting to reverse this trend, and because there are so many of them, China will soon become the world's biggest user of medical apps. In order to mobilise the entire population to use Online-to-Offline (O2O) medical apps, I predict that in the years ahead it will be the big players who first and foremost will lead the way. Companies like Tencent, Ping An and Alibaba. Alibaba, for example, has already become the largest e-commerce site for medicines in the world. Once again, these companies have the users, the data, a network of online apps and the necessary funding to cover the entire nation, as well as having good relations with the government, the pharmaceutical industry, the hospitals and the doctors. No start-up can match this set of advantages, so the best advice for them is to find a good place for themselves in one of these larger ecosystems.

In 2014, Tencent launched its WeChat Intelligent Healthcare app to allow patients to book appointments, make medical payments and use other health services, such as online consultations, via WeChat. More than 38,000 Chinese hospitals now have a WeChat account to offer their services[191] and 110 million Chinese citizens have already made use of the app. Since 2014, Tencent has also invested some 3 billion dollars in at least 40 MedTech start-ups, 40 percent of which are involved in the development of O2O apps, like WeDoctor. WeDoctor was already a pioneer in the market back in 2010 and now provides functions that include diagnoses, appointments, and the purchase of medicines and insurance, all linked to a network of 2,700 hospitals, 22,000 doctors, 15,000 pharmacies and 27 million users. Tencent also has DoctorWork, a kind of WeWork co-working sharing economy model, but for patients who want to monitor their health across different locations. Admittedly, this is more a product for wealthy consumers, but Tencent has rolled out other initiatives that better fit within the growing trend for social e-commerce. In this context, WeSure is an insurance app (backed by 20 leading insurance companies, including Ping An) that allows family and friends to recommend insurance to each other via WeChat in a highly personalised and original manner. [192]

The real challenge facing the digital medical industry is that every patient really wants to visit a good doctor, but this is not always possible. In fact, according to Ping An, it is physically impossible, certainly as far as the traditional hospital sector is concerned. It was for this reason that in 2015 the company launched the appropriately named Good Doctor app.[193] Good Doctor claims to be the most advanced AI medical application in China. It prevents doctors from making the wrong diagnosis, helps to simplify their workflow and matches their needs to those of their patients. The average consultation time of all online patients using Good Doctor is 26 seconds and the patients receive medicines delivered to their home within the hour. Since the purpose of most of these online consultations is to obtain a doctor's note, perhaps this low average consultation time should not come as a surprise. Even so, Good Doctor conducts 500,000 internet consultations each day for 228 million users, with the assistance of 1,000 internal and 50,000 external doctors spread over 5,000 hospitals and clinics. The next step involves plans to link Good Doctor with the Internet-of-Things, so that the smart IoT devices of patients (such as blood pressure or heart monitors) can be directly connected to the app, with the aim of offering even better health management and illness prevention. In a country where AIoT (AI + IoT) is set to become the New Normal, China again seems ready to take the lead in MedTech applications. As a sign of what is to come, in May 2018 Good Doctor was launched on the stock market and immediately became the world's most valuable internet healthtech company, with a valuation of 5 billion dollars.[194]

TRADITIONAL THINKING

If we think of China, big numbers are usually involved. Numbers of hospitals, doctors, patients, etc. If we want to try and understand these numbers, we speak in terms of averages, demographics and statistics, because these can show us how great a problem and how big its impact in China really is. But in healthcare, patients are not interested in averages. A patient is either sick or well; cured or suffering, living or dead. Healthcare is about individuals, and in China they have been concerned with this aspect of medical treatment for millennia, in fact longer than the West. Western healthcare is much more focused on the curing of an average number of patients, so that each person with the same illness gets the same diagnosis, medication, surgery, etc. Our medical system, both in theory and in practice, is based on empiricism: Western doctors believe in validating a treatment method following testing, measurement and the application of reason, confirmed by independent observers. In contrast, traditional Chinese medicine (TCM), like other forms of alternative medicine, not only takes account of the empirical, but also makes use of theories and concepts that have not yet been confirmed by the scientific world. TCM has existed for the past 2,500 years and even today is deeply rooted in Chinese culture, with its use of herbs, acupuncture, massages, diets and qigong exercises.

Western medicine is deductive: facts are deduced from other facts. Chinese medicine is inductive: generalities are extrapolated from specific trends. In Western hospitals, patients visit doctors because they have specific symptoms and wish to receive a diagnosis of their illness. In other words, we begin with the causes to determine the effects. In China, it is the other way around: doctors start from a patients' overall health picture, and then work back to discover the possible causes of illness: stress, sleeping badly, not drinking enough, drinking too much, etc. The advantage of this method is that it is more flexible and can embrace more than one hypothesis simultaneously; the disadvantage is that its methodology can be subjective. The difference between our Western deductive thinking and Chinese inductive thinking is perhaps the main reason why we so often misunderstand each other. In our Western communication style, we present an important fact or question to others with supporting arguments for the purpose of confirming or refuting something.[195] We say that it must be A, because of B, C and D. In their communication, the Chinese first present the most important arguments, before drawing a conclusion from them. They say that because of A, B and C, it must be D. While we usually start our message with information (or the stating of an objective), the Chinese build up a story in which the information only comes at the end. This is inherent in the sentence structure of the Chinese language, which represents a much more spiral form of discourse than the linear discourse of the West. Chinese inductive thinking leads from the specific to the general; from the concrete to the abstract. Our Western deductive thinking does exactly the opposite. This leads many Westerners to observe that the Chinese are unclear in their communication, lack creativity and engender little trust, and that —and they tend towards pragmatism, caution and conservatism. These are superficial and flawed observations. It is true that most Chinese prefer to get the facts straight before coming to conclusions or taking creative action, whereas we prefer to have an immediate objective in sight: develop a company, do business together, find a partner, enter a market, etc. In contrast, the Chinese do not want to risk losing face by making a wrong initial assumption. Or as the philosopher Lao Tze once put it: 'The man who is wise, does not speak.' That being said, it is a myth that you need to have a lot of patience with the Chinese. You just need to learn to gather your facts more quickly and you can certainly chase them up to find those facts for you, because that is part of their own culture and mindset.

CHINA'S CODE FOR SUCCESS

Western deductive thinking separates sickness and health, whereas TCM regards health as being in a balanced state and sickness as being in an unbalanced state. Western medicine looks for signs of sickness, whereas Chinese medicine looks at the person and his environment as a whole. Chinese medicine better understands that every person is unique and takes a long term-approach, contrasted with the Western approach of more uniform medication and treatments. If Western medicine talks about 'being unique', this is usually a reference to genomics, the study of genomes, which are the sets of genes possessed by cells and organisms. A gene is a piece of DNA code that determines how you look, how your body works and how you are as a person. Your genome is your complete genetic code. You can compare a genome with a programming language, with DNA as its code. A genome is therefore the entire sequence of DNA letters that together form your genes. A complete genome analysis therefore maps out your complete genetic code. Following millions of years of evolution and change, a certain type of genome has developed for every plant and animal, including human beings. In 1988, the international Human Genome Project (HGP)[196, 197] was launched, with the intention of locating and identifying for the very first time all the base pairs of genes in the human organism. At the time, it was described as the 'Apollo moon landing project' for the medical-academic world. Francis Collins, the director of the NHGRI, a human genome institute in the United States, compared the entire human genome with three books: a history book to study mankind; a detailed manual to explain the build-up of every human cell; and a medical textbook to give doctors and other carers new insights into the treatment, prevention and cure of sickness and disease.

The HGP sequencing research was conducted over a period of 15 years in different academic institutions in the US, the UK, Japan, France, Germany and China. In China, this was done at the Beijing Genomics Institute (BGI). When the HGP project was completed in 2003, by which time some 20,500 genomes had been mapped, BGI consequently lost its funding. However, the institute survived by offering its genome sequencing services to commercial clients and, in the meantime, managing to reduce the cost for the sequencing of an entire human genome dramatically from 40 million dollars to just 600 dollars. In 2010, BGI turned China into a genome superpower when it purchased 128 of the world's most sophisticated machines from the American Illumina company for an estimated 1.58 billion US Dollars. Since that move, the Chinese have been able to collect a quarter of all the world's genome data.[198]

In 2013, BGI also bought out Illumina's biggest competitor, Complete Genomics, also an American company. This enabled BGI to evolve from a service provider to a producer of machines in its own right, with the promise to reduce the cost of sequencing still further to under 100 dollars, a promise they intend to keep due to their most recent software innovations. The battle between the Chinese and American innovation leaders is no longer just a technology battle, but also one of paradoxical objectives. To innovate, you need to make profit; but that profit is coming increasingly from China. Illumina has become dependent on BGI as a customer, a company that is also its competitor. The more machines Illumina sells to BGI, the more profit BGI makes from its sequencing, which allows it to invest in innovation to make new machines that can be used to take market share from Illumina. The weakness of many Western market leaders is that they are focused on being a supplier and do not want to enter into direct competition with their customers. The Chinese think much less in terms of the supplier-customer context, preferring instead to concentrate on market demand and ecosystems. Why not become your own customer? And if someone else has a better machine, just buy it from them, not internally. In this way, you create greater urgency to make sure that you continue to build the best machines, and that is what turns you into an innovation leader. This being said, I am convinced that in domains that make it possible for human beings to live longer and more healthily the current competitive battle between America and China will ultimate benefit mankind as a whole. In the West, we need to stay awake, and in that sense perhaps the competition from China is something we really need.

IS THIS RESPONSIBLE?

At the end of 2018, the Chinese scientist He Jiankui claimed publicly that he had created the first genetically modified baby, by changing the genes of a healthy embryo without hereditary defects to give it greater protection against HIV. The story made headlines around the world, because it raised critical ethical questions in a darker area of medical science: should we be allowed to alter human DNA, something which could have untold consequences for future generations? He Jiankui was compared with Dr. Frankenstein. The de-activation of a single gene with the CRISPR-CAS9 method had been carried out previously, but always in a controlled environment to treat an imminently fatal illness. China, in the person of He Jiankui, had now crossed a new boundary. China was already one of the few countries in the world where CRISPR tests are carried out on people, mainly cancer patients, but that does not mean that He Jiankui's experiment was legal. In fact, the Chinese government was quick to condemn it as 100 percent illegal and a serious breach of the basic ethical rules of the scientific community.

Describing the incident as 'shocking' and 'unacceptable,' Beijing immediately halted the activities of He's research team. Even so, everyone knew that this was a Pandora's box that would one day inevitably be opened. It could have happened anywhere in the world, but the fact that it happened in China surprised no-one. In fact, it may well be a cloud with a silver lining. It made clear that Chinese legislation is lagging far behind the pace of scientific progress in an industry where China has ambitions to become world leader. That this experiment could be carried out in secret indicates a dangerous lack of transparency in the Chinese scientific community. He Jiankui will not escape his punishment. More importantly for the rest of the world, we can expect that China will be more willing to enter into the global ethical debate on such matters. In a technological future of AI, robots and genetics, where mankind must make crucial new choices, we can only hope that there will be increased openness and dialogue between the world's scientific superpowers. And the signs are promising. At the start of 2019, Pony Ma, CEO of Tencent, and Robin Li, CEO of Baidu, proposed a set of ethical rules to the Chinese government. The discussion to allow human values to take precedence over technology and the desire to better manage the relationship between man and machine are both now firmly on the agenda in China.[199]

CHINA'S VISIONARIES

Wang Jun was one of the initial researchers and a founder of BGI in 1999. He was the company's CEO from 2008 onwards, but resigned in 2015 to set up iCarbonX. At first, no-one could understand why he wanted to leave the BGI mother ship, but he soon provided his explanation. He said that he had founded the new company because he wanted to change the focus of sequencing to multi-omics, making use of Big Data and Artificial Intelligence to allow us to better understand life. The study of omics investigates the fields of biological science that end with the suffix '-omic', like genomics, proteomics (proteins) or metabolomics (metabolism). A biological multi-omics study seeks to translate, collectively identify and quantify the structure, function and dynamics of a living organism. Put simply, iCarbonX wants to take things a step further than pure genomics. For example, pure genomics can explain why a child has a birth defect or what dosage of a medicine is ideal for treating someone with cancer. However, what genomics cannot explain (because genomes are formed over multiple generations) is why 11 percent of the Chinese population now has diabetes in comparison with just 0.67 percent 30 years ago. Changes in patterns of sickness in the short term are caused by other factors: diet, lifestyle, stress, environment, etc. These are external factors to which every genome and every person reacts differently.

According to Wang Jun,[200] life is a journey and the genome is just the first step. The important question is whether it is possible to map all the external factors that affect us, so that in turn it becomes possible to create a more accurate digital profile of life. With this in mind, iCarbonX not only builds up a DNA profile, but also an omics profile, that looks at proteins, antibodies, metabolism, bacteria, viruses, etc. These profiles are then combined with medical records and life habits to create a complete digital profile, which is valid at that particular moment in time. Gathering data for the external factors requires the use of smart devices with sensors, such as smartphones, smart watches, smart fridges and, above all, smart toilets to analyse our daily waste, so that all relevant data can be captured each day. What if all this data from thousands or even millions of people, who all live their lives in different ways, could be aggregated? Would Artificial Intelligence be able to use this Big Data to work out a digital profile for humanity? An internet of life? A medically up-to-date curriculum vitae? The availability of such a digital status check would allow each of us at every moment in our lives to make smarter choices, because the data will tell us the most likely outcome of those choices in the short and long term. I am talking here about everyday choices, like smoking, drinking coffee or playing sport. Choices that would no longer need to be made on the basis of what is generally known to be better or worse for your body, but choices that have a specific and different impact on every individual. In other words, choices about life, your unique life. Wang Jun is a dreamer. ICarbonX is a project of the kind that Google refers to as 'moonshot innovations': super-ambitious research that aims to solve a major societal problem through radical solutions using ground-breaking technology. I see no real difference between the hundreds of Wang Jun's in China and the GoogleX or SpaceX projects in the United States, although the latter are well known, and the former are not.

DATA PRIVACY

ICarbonX wants to become the Amazon of digital healthcare and is well on the way to achieving its goal. It is the fastest growing unicorn (phoenix) in the world, that after just six months, was already worth more than 1 billion US Dollars, thanks to a major investment by Tencent. The Chinese like to take risks. In order to provide personal healthcare and predictions, you need masses of data that can be processed by Artificial Intelligence. In this respect, China is in a unique position, not only because 1.4 billion people live there, but also because the Chinese people share their data more easily than people in the West, while the government also adopts a positive stance towards the harvesting of DNA information.[201] When you visit the iCarbonX headquarters in Shenzhen, you enter on the ground floor into what is effectively a kind of clinic. This clinic is a prototype of different rooms equipped with smart devices and wearables, where material and data can be collected. In addition to AI software, ICarbonX also builds clinical spaces and hardware for many hospitals, so that the patient's most important omics data can be collected during each doctor's visit with a minimum of fuss. According to iCarbonX, this data remains at all times the full property of the patient, not of the company or the hospital. It is false to think that the Chinese are not sensitive about their personal data and that Chinese companies are allowed to deal with that data in a cavalier fashion, because there is no data protection legislation to prevent them. Those days are fading away.

As we have mentioned several times, it is certainly true that to date Chinese consumers have been less wary about sharing their data with the government and the large companies. But this does not mean that they have an indifferent attitude towards those who are responsible for managing their data. In the spring of 2018, Facebook was hauled before a hearing in the US Senate to explain its role in the Cambridge Analytica data privacy scandal.[202] This hearing was followed closely in China, not only by the government and the data harvesters, but also by millions of ordinary Chinese netizens. Since then, nearly all the Chinese tech companies have become much more careful when it comes to privacy, often more so than in the West, because in China a public investigation of the Facebook kind could mean the end of the company.[203] In Washington, Mark Zuckerberg was able to wriggle his way out of a tight corner by offering his apologies and making a few bland promises to a committee of digitally illiterate politicians. In Beijing, a Chinese Zuckerberg would not get away with things so lightly.

The Chinese technology world, certainly in the biotech sector, awoke to this area of risk in 2018. Around that time the Chinese government introduced new national guidelines for the protection of personal data,[204] which stipulated how the permission of consumers should be obtained and how personal data should be collected, stored and shared. In essence, these guidelines are comparable with the GDPR[205] legislation in Europe. This is a major worry in particular for the companies that have invested everything in AI in recent years and for whom the collection of large amounts of data is an essential prerequisite to their business models. If they fail to deal with this data properly, they could soon find their data mine closed down. As a result, companies are now painstakingly detaching personal information from their useful data. For example, patient names are being removed from hospital data and the companies are looking more closely at use of generally encrypted data to improve their algorithms and to share them with hospitals, patients and doctors. These higher moral standards are certainly not (yet) being followed by everyone in China, but the innovation leaders have definitely got the message.

HUNGER FOR BIOTECH

In 2008, the Chinese government launched its 'Thousand Talents' plan, an attempt to lure the country's best and brightest scientists back to China to work in local research institutes.[206] Successful applicants received a starting bonus of 140,000 US Dollars and access to research funding of up to half a million US Dollars. In this way, 7,000 world-class experts have already been lured back to their homeland, 1,400 of them in the life sciences sector. Of the 2 million other expatriates who have returned in recent years, another 250,000 work in biotechnology. These returnees are known in China as 'sea turtles', a reference to the female of the species that after many years at sea uses the Earth's magnetic field to find her way back to her birthplace to lay eggs. The first scientists to return under the Thousand Talents plan discovered a Chinese pharmaceutical industry that was dominated by generic medicines. At that time, there was little or no research and development of new medicines in China. This R&D was done by the big pharmaceutical companies in the West. Even so, the certification of the Western products for use in China was slow and they were 'asked' to lower their prices if they wanted to be included in the system that oversees the reimbursement of medication costs to patients.

Of all the innovation sectors in the West, it is the pharmaceutical giants who complain most loudly that they have been unfairly treated by the Chinese government. Slow approval of products, protection of local brands, turning a blind eye to illegal copies: Western companies say all these actions put them at a disadvantage. But because the Chinese healthcare market is growing at 10 percent a year, with current healthcare expenditure representing just 6 percent of GDP in comparison with 17 percent in Europe, it is impossible for the Western companies to ignore China's massive potential. China represents the world's second largest pharma market and the one with the largest growth and profit.[207] China's answer is that its approach is necessary to give its huge population access to affordable medicines. Twenty years ago, affordable medicines were only available for a third of the Chinese people. This explanation fails to satisfy the Western pharmaceutical industry, but for China it represents a great humanitarian success. The dynamic confrontation between the ideas of the Western, capitalist, market-driven economic model and the Chinese, socialist, state-driven economy continues to cause friction. In reality, China today has a mixed economic system, but its fundamentally socialist ideology relating to the redistribution of wealth throughout its population in a balanced manner remains crucial in the health sector. On the other side of the coin, researchers and academics in China (in contrast to the West) can easily profit from their discoveries, because in this context China believes that a capitalist approach stimulates greater innovation. Sometimes China is market-driven; sometimes China directs the market. China is never the simplistic 'monolithic' place some experts describe.

The Chinese biotech 'sea turtles' who have returned to the shores of their homeland are learning that they have arrived back in a very different place from the one they left. In New Normal China, everything is much more focused on innovation. Universities are producing biotech doctors by the thousands every year. Billions of dollars, both public and private, are being poured into investment funds, both at home and even abroad. The approval procedures for patents, research funding and generic medicines are being drastically simplified. In mid-2018, the import tariffs on medicines were lowered. The passion for science and in particular biotech innovation is being further stimulated by state support at the highest level. In the most recent Five-Year Plan, the government set an objective that biotech should represent 4 percent of GDP by 2020 and that 20 of the existing 100 life science parks should have an output worth at least 1.5 billion dollars. Estimates suggest that China has invested 100 billion dollars in the sector to make this objective attainable.[208]

WILL CHINA SUFFER THE SAME FATE AS JAPAN?

From 1950 to 1970, Chinese women had an average of between five and six children each, with a dip during the famine years of the 1960s. Mao Zedong believed that more children would make China stronger (see figure 10).[209] At the start of the 1970s, China introduced family planning like most other countries, primarily by providing all its citizens with contraceptives, although coercive practices were also used. In just 30 years, the Chinese population doubled from 540 million to 1 billion by the early 1980s. In order to keep the number of the current generation constant with those of the previous generation, the replacement level of fertility worldwide is 2.1 children per woman. In 1979, China initiated its 'One Child Policy' to reduce population growth below replacement level, although in rural communities a second child was permitted if the first one had been a girl. In this way, population growth rapidly decreased to 1.5 children per woman, with experts suggesting that nearly 400 million births had been avoided.

Children born before 1970 will reach pensionable age before 2030, an elderly group that by then will represent 25 percent of the population. By 2050, this figure will have risen to 35 percent. Around 2035, the total population will have reached its maximum level of 1.45 billion, after which it will gradually fall back again to 1.4 billion. The working population will also fall, but not below a level of 800 million people.[210] China's challenge is to avoid becoming the new Japan, which 30 years ago, like China today, was set to become the new world leader in technology, but fell victim to its own demography. In Japan, almost a third of the population is older than 65 years of age.

In keeping with the Confucian tradition, and also enshrined in legislation, in China children are expected to look after their elderly relations. For young Chinese couples today, this means caring for five people: two sets of aging parents and their single child. As a result, 50

Figure 10

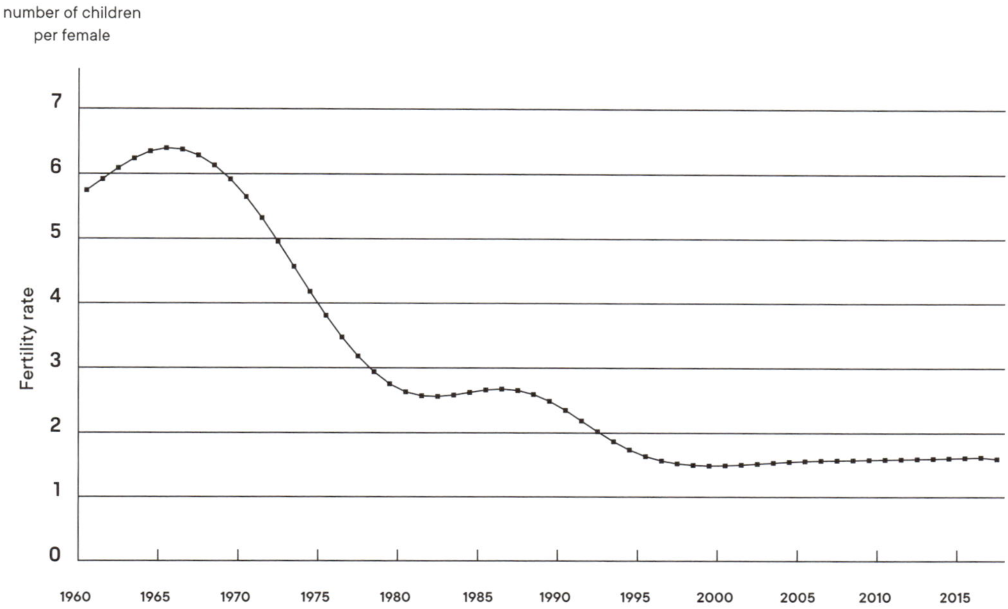

percent of pre-school children are raised by their grandparents and on average there are 6 percent more working women in Chinese families than in American ones. Both parents work in order to pay for the upkeep of their grandparents, who in turn take care of the upbringing of their grandchild. The pensions of the grandparents are insufficient to get by in a society that is becoming increasingly expensive. An ageing population and a shortage of pension contributions inevitably means that pensions will come under pressure and that the pensionable age will gradually be increased to 65 years. This will further increase the level of state debt, which makes it doubly important for China that care of the elderly takes place outside the framework of the hospital system. It is no coincidence that China is promoting healthcare technology that devotes greater attention to smart online learning programmes, targeted at personnel who are less well-educated than doctors, such as social workers and other carers. The ability of AI to support the social sector takes precedence over the fear of job losses that may be caused by it. Will we in the West be able to change our mindset in a similar manner?

HEALTHY CHINA 2030? [211]

Following the Chinese e-commerce and fintech explosions, I expect healthtech to be the next Chinese industry with the potential to redefine people's attitudes and behaviours worldwide. In other words, a step even beyond the more inspirational impact we have already seen in the security, entertainment, mobility and manufacturing industries. The conditions for creating disruption in the retail, financial and health sectors are the same: a billion dissatisfied customers who urgently want to improve their quality of life by embracing new technologies that free them from the imperfections of a badly performing service sector. In 2017, Chinese families spent 36.1 percent of their consumption on clothes (e-commerce); 28.5 percent on their accommodation (fintech) and other home-related items; 13.6 percent on communication and transport; 11.4 percent on education; and just 7.9 percent on healthcare.[212] During the next decade, this balance will shift significantly, with health and leisure time assuming increasing importance.

At the end of 2016, Xi Jinping announced the 'Healthy China 2030' plan, which aims by 2030 to have raised average health in China to the standard of the developed countries. This ambitious plan seeks to set in motion a movement that emphasises the importance of improving public health at all levels of society. The five areas of focus are healthcare, environmental management, the medical industry, food and medicinal safety. Typically for China, these 2030 objectives are highly specific and directive: a life expectancy of 79 years, infant mortality at 5 percent, etc. (see table 1). But the true significance of this strategy goes beyond mere figures and objectives. President Xi wishes to reanimate the entire health sector, with a master plan based on three core pillars:

1. China wishes to include a health aspect in all of the government's future policy initiatives, under the slogan 'Health in All Policies'. This relates primarily to the integration of health into the education system and the realisation of a transformation from sickness treatment to the proactive promotion and management of health (iCarbonX). In this respect, China wishes to make economic growth subordinate to the health of its people.
2. Although the government will continue to have a guiding role in health matters, China intends that from now on the entire population and the entire business community should be mobilised to work together for a Healthy China. Each individual citizen will henceforth be held responsible for his or her own health under the concept of 'My Health under My Control', while all companies are expected to behave in a socially responsible manner (CSR).
3. The health market must become the largest new motor for economic growth through the development of emerging industries such as age care, tourism, fitness and leisure. China wishes to make use of its cultural traditions like TCM to convince the population to spend more money on healthcare. In other words, this plan has a nationalist and socialist undertone, yet it remains primarily a means to stimulate the commercial potential of the sector, which is the main aim.

This type of holistic policy thinking is typically Chinese. Just as Chinese medicine looks at the whole body instead of specific symptoms, so the Chinese government approaches its health strategy by looking at the entire health industry and its position within Chinese society: education, culture, accountabilities, the market, short-term incentives, long-term problems, global impact, etc. Can we in the West not learn something from this? Should we not look again at our obsession with compartmentalisation, which sees large problems split down into smaller parts for which shared responsibilities can be allocated? The truth is that some problems in education, mobility, security and healthcare are simply too important to be left to each region, province, city and village to do their own thing. Such problems demand a total approach.

Table 1

Major indices of 'Health China 2030' construction

Major indices of Healthy China	Target date		
	2015	2020	2030
Health Outcome			
Life expectancy (years)	76.34	77.3	79.0
Infant mortality rate (%)	8.1	7.5	5.0
Under-five mortality rate (%)	10.7	9.5	6.0
Maternal mortality rate (/100,000)	20.1	18.0	12.0
Qualification rate of the national physique determination standard (%)	89.6	90.6	92.2
Health environment			
Ratio of superior air quality days in central cities (%)	76.7	> 80	-
Rate of reaching case III surface water standard (%)	66	> 70	-
Health service and health insurance			
Premature mortality from major chronic diseases (%)	19.1	17.2	12.0
Licensed doctors (assistants)/1000 residential population	2.2	2.5	3.0
Health expenditure personal/national health expenditure (%)	29.3	28	25
Healthy lifestyle			
Residents' health literacy level (%)	10	20	30
Population exercising regularly (billion)	3.6	4.35	5.3
Health industry			
Total scale of health services (trillion yuan)	-	> 8	16

© World Health Organization

HOW TO FEED 1.4 BILLION CHINESE?

China needs to feed 20 percent of the world's population with just 7 percent of the world's agricultural land. To make this possible, over the past 30 years China has tripled its use of chemical fertilisers. After completing my studies in 1997 my first job was with my brother-in-law, who ran a company dealing in liquid fertilisers and high-efficiency greenhouses. I was sent to check out the Chinese market. It soon became clear that the Chinese had an urgent need of fertilisers, but there was no interest for high-quality products and certainly not for our luxury European greenhouses which required a significant investment. All that concerned them was to boost their level of annual crop production by dumping any cheap chemical rubbish into the ground. After a year of negotiation and lots of strong drinks (baijiu) shared with both farmers and government officials, I decided that my heart and my liver couldn't take any more, and so I stopped.

It was only ten years later that China began to realise that food safety was a critical factor. Among many scandals, the most disturbing one in the eyes of the Chinese public was the notorious milk scandal of 2008, when milk powder for infants was contaminated with melanin, a product that is normally used to make plastics. 300,000 children suffered kidney damage as a result and, sadly, at least six of them died. This terrible incident seriously damaged China's reputation, not only as a food exporter but also as a local food producer and public trust in Chinese food brands sank to new depths. In the following year, hundreds of imported foreign brands replaced 50 percent of local milk powder brands on supermarket shelves. The same year, the Chinese government passed food safety legislation banning the addition of unauthorised additives, among many other requirements and standards. However, these steps did not solve the underlying problem. Every few months, new stories about disgusting new scandals appeared in the local media, from meat being mislabelled or sold long past its sell-by date, and potentially harmful substances being added to food. The most recent crisis of this kind broke in 2018, when it became known that in Shandong Province 250,000 defective DPT (diphtheria, whooping cough and tetanus) vaccines were administered to young children.

If there is anything that keeps the government officials in Beijing lying awake at night, it is incidents of this kind. China is currently faced with huge problems, such as mounting state debt, slowing growth, environmental concerns and trade restrictions, to name but a few. However, there is a reasonable expectation that these problems can be resolved with the right planning, the right strategy and the setting of the right priorities. But scandals involving food or medication are of a different order. They create distrust and potentially social unrest and the finger of guilt is usually pointed directly at government, which after a decade of similar scandals still seems unable to control the companies and enforce its own legislation. The Shandong DPT vaccine case was widely shared and discussed on social media, so that most Chinese citizens now no longer trust any Chinese vaccines as a result. For a planned economy (as we often refer to China), this was very definitely not planned and the local vaccine industry quickly collapsed. Further proof, if any were needed, that Chinese consumers direct the government, just as much as the government directs the consumers.

The food supply chain in China is complex and often involves a dozens of different suppliers before food actually arrives on people's plates. In particular, there are lots of things that can go wrong during the production and distribution phases, especially if standards are put to one side in the interests of competition. As a result, consumers in China have essentially lost confidence in the local food production system.[213] In 2008, just 12 percent of the population thought that food and medication safety was a serious problem. Today, that is more than 40 percent.[214] For this reason, since 2016 onwards many of the high-quality food producers throughout China have sought to find an answer using of technology, seeing this as a means to 'prove' their credibility. IoT and blockchain are now regularly used in China to allow Chinese consumers to instantly trace the history of the products they use. In 2017, Wal-Mart, IBM, JD.com and Tsinghua University set up the Blockchain Food Safety Alliance with the aim of bringing to an end the anonymity of the actors in the Chinese supply chain. In this way, blockchain is a confidence-technology that can take over (or supplement) the role of monitoring the food companies from the state, which has shown that it is not always up to the task. In fact, blockchain is now seen as a necessity for the smooth running of the supply chain for foodstuffs, products and medicines, as a result of which it will be much more rapidly implemented than in the West. For example, in the higher-quality Chinese shops and supermarkets, QR codes on packs of steak now detail the breed, weight, diet and farm of origin of the animal. Similarly, the Zhong An Insurance phoenix has developed a blockchain platform to monitor the full process trail on chicken farms by fitting a sensor to the ankle of each chicken, which records that chicken's number of steps, age, date of slaughter and transport locations. This data can be consulted by the consumer for each individual chicken, but at the same time the chicken farmers are also provided with information that will give them better insights into their breeding methods. As always, the data giants are not far behind. Alibaba prefers to focus on pigs, more than half the world's total of which — some 700 million — are bred in China. Using sound and image processing in combination with environmental monitoring via IoT and RFID tags, Alibaba's AI platform monitors the daily activities, health, growth and pregnancy of every sow and boar.[215]

There are four major trends in the food industry in China:[216]

1. The search for **'premium'** foodstuffs, such as wine or chocolate.
2. The increasing demand (as in the West) for more **natural and organic** foodstuffs. In these first two trends, blockchain plays an important role to guarantee the authenticity of products.
3. The **personalisation** of foodstuffs, a new trend since 2017 that has turned food retail upside down.
4. But the biggest trend is new and **different eating habits**, habits that are much closer to what we are used to in the West: snacks, individual packaging, on-the-go, click-and-collect, etc. The Chinese are increasingly unwilling to wait for their food and are also pushing Chinese producers hard in the direction of a 'quality revolution', with a greater emphasis on organic, traceable and healthy food. In 2017, the

Chinese government published a set of guidelines to develop a smart food supply chain by 2020. With blockchain, AI and IoT, China has the tools to make this happen and will soon redesign the food industry to better reflect its food supply and safety needs. Although I expect it will take until 2025 until the Chinese example prompts the West into corrective action in the health sector, I anticipate that this will happen much more quickly in the food sector. And it will be worthwhile: because Chinese consumers actively seek out what they perceive as more trustworthy brands, innovative Western companies in the food industry can look forward to a number of golden years in China. One casualty: the days of the small, local Chinese family restaurants, so familiar for the past 2,000 years, are numbered.

THE BIGGEST POLLUTER

In terms of waste processing, China is the biggest polluter in the world, in part because of a shortage of waste recycling technology. Moreover, China not only needs to dispose of the waste it generates, but until the end of 2017 was also the world's largest importer of other people's waste. Up to 56 percent of all the plastic in the world found its way to China.[217] In the past, this importation industry was a smart way to recycle primarily electronic waste, but not anymore. Because the richer Western nations paid well to have their waste processed or recycled, the waste management companies in China were too busy dealing with this foreign waste to do much about their own.

We all need to stop for a moment and reflect on this phenomenon. For decades, countries like the United States, England and Germany found it cheaper to put their waste on a ship and send it to China instead of processing it themselves. What's more, in this way they were also able to avoid the side effects of toxic air pollution and by-waste. Similarly, during this period the Chinese factories that represent China's biggest domestic polluters were producing products to a significant extent for Western consumption. So, whichever way you look at it, the West is partly responsible for a substantial part of China's pollution problem. There is no way that we can turn back the clock, but today's reality is that the world is becoming ever more dependent on China, and therefore also on Chinese pollution. China is the biggest polluter in the world in terms of total output, but one of the smallest polluters in terms of pollution per head of population, since 20 percent of the world's population lives there. This is not a reason to celebrate: the Chinese are now steadily getting richer, and the richer they become the more they will pollute.

CHINA SAVES THE WORLD

I believe that China is the world's best hope when it comes to climate change. Domestic considerations inside China may make it possible to achieve the international norms agreed in Paris and prevent the disastrous consequences of climate change and global warming before it is too late. The US has already withdrawn from this agreement, but China has surprised the world by doubling its commitment. Xi Jinping has displayed a consistent focus on the environment since he was appointed in 2013. This consistency has put China (and Xi himself) on the map as a new and responsible world leader. As a result, in recent years the Chinese ecology sector has received a huge boost, with many new rules, regulations, objectives, subsidies and other encouragements. Now that time is running out for our planet, the appearance on the scene of a strong figure like Xi Jinping is more than welcome. Of course, China is concerned first and foremost with its own problems, but thanks to the Open-Door Policy of 40 years ago, China's problems are now inextricably intertwined with those of the rest of the world.

If you walk around Shanghai, the streets are clean and tidy. But it hasn't always been that way. In the past, the Chinese threw everything into their streets and rivers, and if an unscrupulous factory boss could make more money by illegal dumping, he wouldn't think twice. Over the past decades, it seemed as if the country was simply too big to be controlled. But almost everyone in China is starting to realise that things cannot carry on like this, with the government leading the way. Nowadays, the approach of the central and local authorities is much more uncompromising. Inspectors storm into factories and won't hesitate to take strong action, and social media plays its role in monitoring and exposing flagrant cases. In 2017, tens of thousands of factories were closed and almost 100,000 individuals were prosecuted. At the end of 2017, an import ban on 24 types of waste was announced and there are plans to decommission 100 coal-fired power stations. By 2020, China aims to invest 360 billion dollars in renewable energy. The country is already the world's largest producer of solar panels, wind turbines, and electric cars. It has also built the world's largest hydro-electric power plant and is a leader in green energy loans.[218] Today, every company in the cleantech sector can earn a fortune in China, if it plays its card right.

But the most reassuring aspect of this 'green' story is not to be found in regulations, initiatives or even technology, but in the context in which these actions are being taken.[219] President Xi has added a new narrative to this story: the narrative of an eco-civilisation. Or to put it in the president's own words: 'Green mountains and clear water are equal to mountains of gold and silver.' With this pronouncement, he signalled that China would give equal priority to the 'twin' objectives of ecological and economic growth. In my view, the biggest problem facing China in terms of its environmental policy and enforcement is one of awareness, or in other words 'values and priorities'. Xi Jinping hopes to tackle this by a broad ideological approach. He talks about a 'smart society', in which the focus is set on the promotion of a more person-oriented society, which is driven by the population, but still under the absolute leadership of the Party. In this context, the top-down propaganda system that so often puts China in a bad light is now something the world badly needs if we wish to maintain our ecological balance. Is Xi Jinping, who The Economist has called the most powerful man in the world, the figure we need to save our planet?

What to Remember?

1 → **People trust overworked and sometimes corrupt Chinese doctors less than they trust the new technological alternatives.** Chinese hospitals are medical factories, with too few specialists to provide good healthcare to the entire population. Making use of the availability of data and cheaper medical personnel, the Chinese AI MedTech companies are quickly building urgently needed smart applications. Big players like Alibaba, Tencent and Ping An are taking the lead in the race to fully digitalise the medical sector.

2 → **Innovation and research in China are being transformed from state-sponsored and academic activities into fully commercial enterprises.** Western pharmaceutical companies and manufacturers of medical equipment are still years ahead of their Chinese competitors, but market manipulation by the state is giving local companies more opportunities to innovate. Traditional Chinese medicine and a more personalised approach are the trends that will characterise the Chinese healthcare of the future.

3 → **China has the ambition and the potential to become the world leader in biotech, particularly in the genetics sector.** The government is playing an increasingly responsible role in terms of ethical regulations and regulations relating to data privacy, both of which were urgently needed. The Chinese are dreamers and the next Bill Gates or Larry Page who will change the word might well come from China.

4 → **As a result of its 'one-child' policy, China is faced with a huge demographic problem,** with an increasing number of elderly people and a shrinking workforce. To cope with this, the entire medical sector will be upgraded through the 'Healthy China 2030' plan, which shares responsibility between the population and companies. Innovation in the health sector has been identified as a new motor for the economy and the sector will be transformed from a care sector into a more personal form of health management.

5 → **Chinese citizens have totally lost their confidence in the quality of local foodstuffs and medicines.** This is the worst nightmare of the government, which is encouraging countless innovation initiatives in the sector in response. Companies are increasingly turning in huge numbers to blockchain, IoT and AI as a means of restoring consumer confidence through greater transparency. China was once the world's biggest polluter, but is now the world's best hope of avoiding ecological disaster through its new policy of promoting an eco-civilisation.

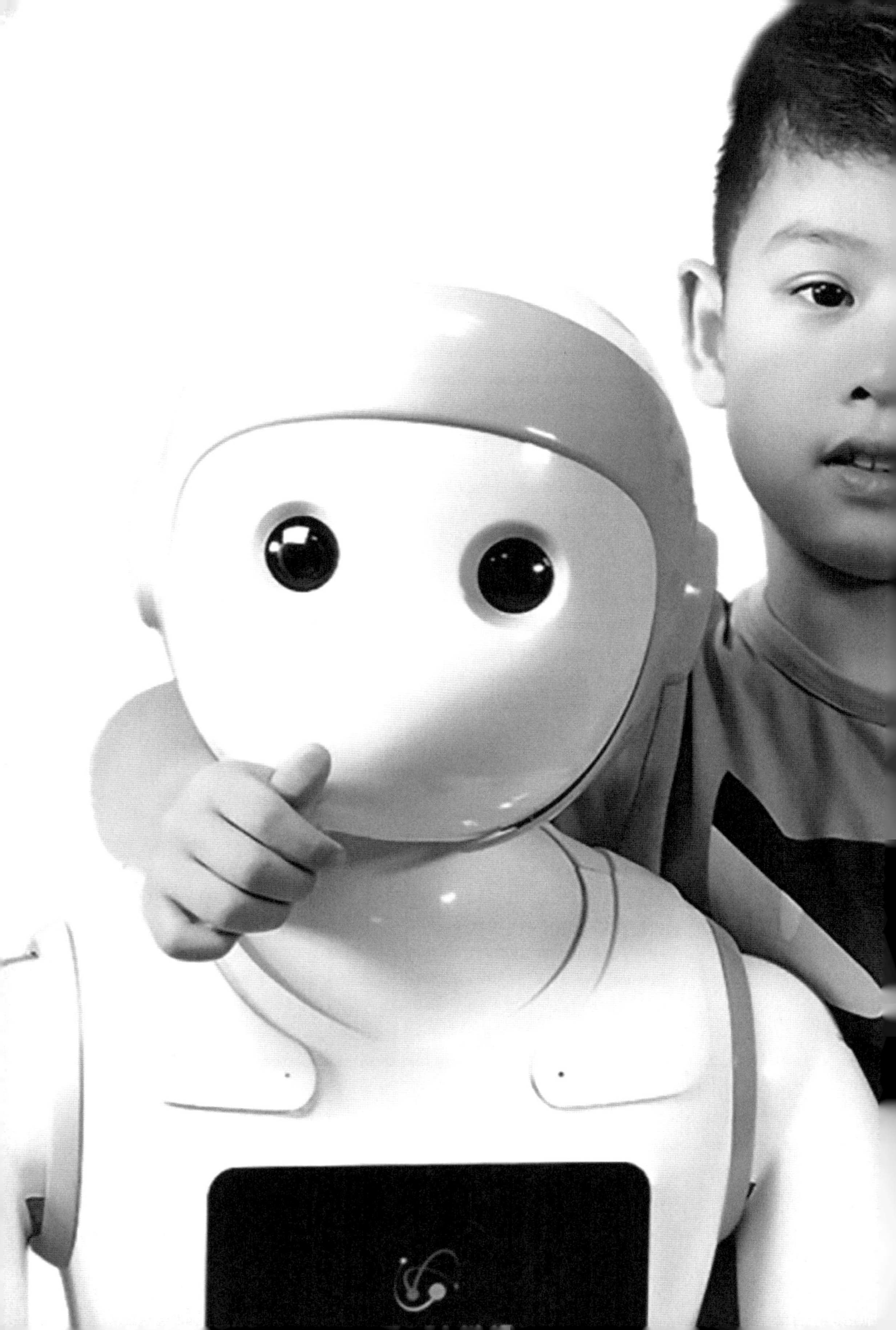

<
iPal is the intelligent humanoid robot made by the Chinese company Avatar Mind, designed for children and the elderly, either as a teacher or a social companion.

8

SMART EDUCATION

CHINA SETS THE STANDARD: FROM 2013 TO 2030

Finally, by 2030 I expect China to have replaced its present outdated system of education with technology-based **Smart Education**. What lessons can China, which currently has one of the most traditional education systems in the world, teach to educationalists in the West in the years ahead?

2013 2015 2017 2019 2021 2023 2025 2030

SMART EDUCATION

11 June, 2002 was a very special day for my wife and I. It was on that day that we went to an orphanage in the harbour city of Zhangjiagang (张家港). After a three-hour bus, we met our Chinese daughter for the very first time. She was nine months old when we first picked her up and held her, and she didn't like it very much. She had spent eight months in the orphanage. She looked even whiter than we did and only wanted to be picked up by her usual caregiver. After a very official photograph had been taken, we were guided to a room to collect her few clothes and other things. This room was arranged like a chessboard, with dozens of beds, in each of which a baby, almost like in a ritual, was given a bottle of sweetened milk in the hope of keeping them all quiet. All these orphans had been given the last name of Zhang (张), after the city where they had been found. Our daughter was called Zhang Shujuan (张淑娟). After a farewell dinner with the carer team, the final step was to go with her regular caregiver and the orphanage director to the office of the public notary in the provincial capital of Nanjing, where our daughter was given her Western name: Amelie Coppens.

Chinese adults are mad about small children and love to interact with them. In China, perfect strangers will play peekaboo with your daughter in the street, and waitresses in restaurants will carry her around during a meal so that you can eat in comfort. As young adoptive parents, we weren't very keen on this at first, but we soon got used to it, as in this way, we were able to continue our social life without really needing to always hire a babysitter. In Belgium, it is often taboo to connect with or admire other people's children in public (and not without reason) but I have come to believe that Chinese children receive more love, certainly in terms of quantity, than Western children. This is ironic because when most people in the West think about Chinese children, we imagine (again, not without reason) hard work, strict rules and even corporal punishment, but we don't see the love that is constantly lavished upon them. That love gives them the strength to move mountains.

WHO AM I?

Just months after Amelie's adoption, we moved to San Francisco, where I took up a new job at the headquarters of Wind River Systems, an American multinational. It had always been a dream of mine to work in Silicon Valley and this opportunity was too good to miss. However, the end of 2002 was not a good time to be in the Valley, because the internet and software companies were slowly bleeding to death. The atmosphere was one of gloom and doom and with each new quarter more of my new colleagues lost their jobs or were 'let go', as the Americans so quaintly put it. It was a daily sight to see someone with a cardboard box containing their personal effects being escorted to the main door by a security guard. It all seemed so cold and impersonal. This was something we had not gotten used to in China. Just a year later, my whole team was closed down and I was left the last man standing, trying to explain things to our bemused customers. At this point, I decided to resign. Now it was my turn to get a cardboard box and 30 days later my work permit expired, so that we were obliged to leave 'the promised land'. In fact, my wife was happy to go. She thought that China was much more interesting, more intense and more inspirational. It also seemed more genuine, bearing in mind the difficult period of often political, devious and heartless dismissals we had just experienced. And so I exchanged my long-anticipated American dream for a new Chinese one. Actually, my wife had not wanted to leave China in the first place, certainly not so soon after Amelie's adoption, but nor did she want to stand in the way of my ambitions. Now, she was happy to return. And America was not much fun for our daughter, either. Passers-by on the street always wanted to pinch her chubby cheeks, which she hated. Everyone in Europe and the States kept on telling us how lucky we were to have such a lovely little Chinese girl: pinch, pinch, pinch! In contrast, when we got back to China everyone kept on telling us how lucky our daughter was to have such good parents, before pulling up her socks so she wouldn't get cold. But this was no more to Amelie's liking than the pinching: all those Chinese faces staring at her really got on her nerves. So much so, that she increasingly began to turn her head away whenever they looked at her. For parents who both had an open attitude towards China and the Chinese, it was a bit of shock to discover that we now had a Chinese daughter who wanted nothing to do with the country and people of her birth!

MORE, PLEASE!

Because we were once again living in China, we thought that sending her to a local Chinese school might be the best way to change her 'anti-China' attitude. We also wanted her to learn the Chinese language, because that is not the kind of opportunity that comes along twice. By then she was six years old. Every evening she did her homework and the grades and teacher's comments in her exercise books were always good. Everything seemed to be going well, or so we thought. Two months later, her teacher phoned us to ask if our daughter could actually speak because so far she hadn't said a word! The other children and the teacher had protected her, because she had foreign parents, and she had even become a kind of mascot for the class! We promptly transferred her to another local school, but one with an international department for both foreign students and Chinese who held a foreign passport. In the new school we soon found that it wasn't so much the children who were the problem; it was the attitude of their tiger parents that was so very different from ours. Foreign parents often give their children a helping hand with their homework and only occasionally talk to the teachers after school. By contrast, Chinese parents are continually attending parents' meetings to demand that the foreign teachers give their children even more homework. Chinese children often receive additional tuition at home after school, frequently from these same school teachers, who are rewarded with gifts or cash payments in the hope that they will give their children an extra advantage. During the weekends there are also extra lessons in piano, violin or English (or all three!), for which there is no time during the week. If you ask Chinese parents why they put their children under such pressure and allow them so little time to play, they nearly always come up with the same answer: because China is so competitive, it would be irresponsible not to give their son or daughter every possible chance to succeed. Or as one Chinese father once said to me: 'In the West, children play, but after their studies become serious and do mundane jobs. In China, we do serious and mundane things as a child, but after our studies we can spend the rest of our lives playing.'

THE REFORM OF EDUCATION

China has the largest public education sector in the world: more than 500,000 schools, 260 million students and a literacy rate of 99.7 percent.[220] In 2015, the 'one-child' policy was officially ended, so that in future the number of children should increase if the policy has its effect. The government spends an average of 4.4 percent of GDP on education, but in 2018 there was a sharp increase in expenditure for pre-schools and universities. China has a very clearly defined national education strategy, which aims to have 16 of the country's universities in the world top 100 by 2030.[221] Today, according to the QS World University Ranking, there are already six: Tsinghua, Peking University, Shanghai Fudan and Jiaotong University, Zhejiang University and the University of Science and Technology. There might conceivably have been more, but many lose ranking points for their lack of thriving international departments. In other words, it is not purely out of interest in the West that Chinese universities invest in promotion to attract foreign students and professors. As far as the rankings for engineering science are concerned, there are three more Chinese universities in the top 100: Huazhong University of Science and Technology, Shanghai Tongji University and Nanjing University. In the general ranking, Peking University occupies 14th place with Tsinghua University in 20th position.[222]

In 2017, Premier Li Keqiang announced plans to modernise the Chinese education system as a means to modernise Chinese society as a whole. In 2009, China reached the status of a 'higher middle-income country'. But will China be able to escape from the middle-income trap and climb its way up into the league of the 'high income' countries, where the GDP is higher than 12,250 US dollars per capita? At the moment, the figure in China is

8,300 US Dollars. Since China is now likely to experience lower New Normal economic growth rates of 3.5 percent or less by 2030, it is not impossible that China will still not have reached its 'high income' goal by the 100th anniversary of the Communist Revolution in 2049. The trade war launched by President Trump is certainly not helping China, at least in the short term. For this reason, and to do everything possible to reach their target, the Chinese government has decided to invest heavily in education and innovation as key priorities. These reforms have introduced preferential policies and create investment opportunities across many aspects of education, including private education, online education, international schools, vocational education, pre-school, talent management, STEAM,[223] and technology integration. Technology, in particular, is receiving priority support. In his keynote speech, Premier Li Keqiang emphasised the importance of building larger and stronger industrial clusters around the implementation of Big Data, Artificial Intelligence R&D and applications, while simultaneously making progress in the internet-plus model in five key sectors: health, age care, education, culture and sport.

The proposed use of new technology in Chinese education will focus on three areas:[224]

1. Technology to help teachers and teaching, such as adaptive teaching via AI, VR/AR, 3D-printing, online education, sensors, etc.
2. Technology to improve student skills and innovation, such as STEAM, the maker industry and robotics.
3. Technology to improve school management and lesson quality, such as smart campuses and internet lessons.

China is preparing itself for a new era of experimentation in which technological tools for education will be tested in different schools before being rolled out across the entire country, if proven effective. The government has given the very highest priority to AI-supported education, in the first instance to eliminate the disparity in standards of learning between the cities and the countryside, but also because this kind of tuition makes it possible to keep the cost of education better under control by limiting the increase in wage costs.[225]

EDUCATION KILLS CREATIVITY

In the West, we generally believe that education stimulates our children to be more creative and to think more critically. This, we are quick to claim, is the strength of our Western education system and, by extension, of Western society. But the truth is throughout the world, including China, most schools continue to design courses of study that have barely changed during the past century, still largely based on learning by rote. This actually stifles rather than encourages creativity, whether in Europe or in China. Picasso said: "Every child is an artist. The problem is how to remain an artist once we grow up." It is not necessarily true that just because Chinese children study harder and are put under more pressure at school that their creativity will suffer vs. their peers in the West.

Outside of special academies of the arts, art, music and drama are increasingly regarded as secondary subjects, to which less importance is attached. I get the impression that children are now generally discouraged from taking risks and making mistakes in many of our Western schools. As a result, many of our young adults have become risk-averse. If creativity is the result of making things up, experimenting, taking chances, breaking rules, daring to be wrong, failing and having fun (as many educationalists claim), then I am certain that creativity is something at which the Chinese excel. I am the very last person to claim that the sometimes extreme urge to take risks characteristic of many Chinese people is inborn. I simply believe that the current education system worldwide kills creativity and stimulates our left brain over the right. As a result, I think we need to abandon the old stereotype that the Chinese are less creative, critical and inventive than we are.

CREATIVE CHINESE

Over the past 30 years the words 'Made in China' became a synonym for bad quality in many people's minds, so the updated slogan 'Created in China' is often greeted in the West with a good deal of disbelief and doubt. A small voice inside our heads continues to tell us that the Chinese can never be as creative as we are. But in my opinion, the idea that the Chinese are 'not creative' is the West's biggest self-deception regarding China. Creation and creativity are not something exclusively Western. All the world's peoples are creative, including the Chinese. In fact, during recent years Chinese entrepreneurs have understood better than anyone else that creativity can be very lucrative. If you don't believe me, look at recent prices for contemporary Chinese art. Sadly, despite clumsy efforts, the Chinese government does little to positively stimulate this creativity. This does not matter: the demand of the Chinese market and Chinese consumers for inventiveness and self-discovery has become so great that it can no longer be stopped. Hundreds of millions of Chinese have already achieved our Western standards of living: a home, good food, healthcare, stylish clothes, a car, education, a smartphone and travel abroad. And now they want more. They want to give meaning to their new personas. As a result, their desire for more creative experiences now has more urgency than ever before. And being Chinese means having a very deep well of ideas and history and culture to draw inspiration from, even as you focus on the future. When talking about creativity, many people often forget that China has built up a remarkably rich and deep culture over the past 3,000 years, preferring to remember instead only the grim years under Mao Zedong, when 'art for art's sake' was no longer tolerated, since everything in Mao's China had to serve politics and the people. Those days are gone, and China is a far more open and creative place than news reports would lead you to believe.

Today, the Chinese are increasingly searching for authenticity and meaning in their lives. These aspirations are being cleverly exploited by Western brands like Gucci and L'Oréal. China is the largest market for both of these companies. Four new trends are emerging from inside China that could turn the creative world upside down and redraw the map of global creativity, with China at the center.

1. **Cultural depth.** Chinese companies now want to create their own authentic brands with a strong and consistent narratives. The best market from which to gain an understanding of this trend is beauty products. What has happened in this industry in China is little short of a revelation. Modern Chinese culture often likes to search deep into the past for elements that are timeless and universal. In terms of make-up, this means going back to the colours that were typical of ancient China and which are embedded in Chinese astrology or tradition. Forgotten colours, but beautiful nonetheless. And it is the same in the world of wine. Quality wines from China and around the world are now evaluated in China according to their colour, aroma, pallet and body in symbiosis with Chinese culinary tradition and preferences. Into the development of new perfumes, the Chinese now go in search of fragrances that are unknown in the West, but are based on the natural herbs characteristically found in traditional Chinese medicine. As a result, some of the very best Western brands now have perfume laboratories in China, in the hope of finding new fragrance combinations for the China market, and potentially other countries. They know that the Chinese have a good nose for this kind of thing.

2. **National pride.** The Shanghai Fashion Week is held every year, with hundreds of Chinese store brands taking part. It is the place where independent designers can show off their new collections to the world. If you didn't know it, you would hardly believe that these brands are Chinese: unique concepts, clear design lines, beautifully finished. Some of the designers have studied in New York, others have worked in Paris or London. But now it is their moment to be discovered. The Chinese are becoming increasingly proud of their own culture. Creative artists such as fashion designers are starting to seek the recognition they deserve as many are now making a name for themselves in China and abroad. Having said that, Chinese consumers are still strongly attached to leading global brands, so that many of the most ambitious Chinese designers are still driven westwards. But change is on the way. When they shop, the Chinese millennials are becoming more and more interested in personal experiences and expressing their uniqueness. They no longer want to look as though they have just stepped out of a standard Western fashion magazine, they want to express their Chinese identity in a modern way. Chinese designers and young consumers will mutually strengthen each other in the years ahead and will turn China into a new trendsetter – not only in fashion -but in every creative industry.

3. **Creative technology.** FashionTech is the newest and hottest Chinese trend. It began with sport wearables, which, like most electronic devices, are made in China. But whereas Western brands seem most concerned to put more and more techno-

logy into their products, the Chinese brands focus on designing a better 'package' around their technology. Is a smartphone, Fitbit or digital watch a tech device or a fashion accessory? These two aspects are being increasingly merged and this is giving China new opportunities to challenge the Western brands. The idea of a blood pressure tracker in your watch or a heat regulator in your jacket may currently sound a bit geeky, but in the near future they will be the New Normal in China, and you won't even know that they are there. For modern Chinese consumers, comfort will become increasingly more important than the brand. This means that creativity in fashion will be first and foremost a matter of ease of use. If my Nike shoes no longer count my number of steps, I will switch to Li-Ning. What's more, new technology will make it possible for shoes to be personally designed, 3D-printed and delivered to your door within hours, all at an unbeatable price. This is where the creative genius of the Chinese will come into its own. It is no coincidence that Nike chose Shanghai as the location for its creative flagship store, the 'Nike house of innovation'.

4. **Mix of creative teams.** Most world-famous advertising and marketing agencies have had offices in China for more than twenty years, serving both Western and Chinese customers. Until recently, the creative directors and managers of these bureaus were always Europeans or Americans, or overseas Chinese who did not grow up in China. Today, things are different. You now see a growing number of mixed teams made up of local Chinese and foreign designers, who learn from and strengthen each other. Today, these local creative directors often have years of experience abroad and can speak perfect English. At the same time, they also have a better understanding of Chinese brands and consumers than any foreigner ever could. Chinese multinationals like Huawei or Lenovo have long worked with the world's top PR and advertising agencies. For them, money is no object; the necessary creativity is just bought in. But with each new iteration, there are more and more Chinese creative talent and designers in the mix. As a result, the difference between Chinese and Western creativeness is becoming blurred.

You can see this evolution taking place in almost every consumer market: from shampoo to cars, from bank products to telecom. In each case, the creative story is becoming more consistent, more universal and more simply told. I predict that before 2025 people worldwide will fall in love with this new generation of Chinese brands, and they will become part of our everyday lives. You can already see the initial signs of Western consumers falling for 'Created in China' with products like DJI (drones), Mobike (shared bikes) and Huawei (smartphones). And that is just the start of what will become a very long list.

THE SCHOOL OF THE FUTURE [226]

In 2016, Peter Diamandis of the Singularity University, the Silicon Valley thinktank, wrote Chronicles of Education, in which he set out the guiding principles for the schools of the future. Step by step, he explains the basic capacities, curricula, technologies and mentality that will be necessary to prepare future generations for an industry 4.0 cyber-physical world. In essence, Diamandis believes our children will need to possess five basic qualities: passion, curiosity, imagination, determination and critical thinking.

1. **Passion**. Millions of Chinese are full of passion and sometimes have frighteningly clear objectives and plans for their lives and careers. In the 21st century, they have countless Chinese role models — athletes, entrepreneurs, scientists, innovators — from whom they can draw inspiration.
2. **Curiosity**. The Chinese are by nature an inquisitive people, in part because in Chinese culture it is not impolite to ask personal questions. They think nothing about enquiring how much you earn or reading your newspaper over your shoulder on the train. It is almost as if they never lose the naive curiosity they had as children.
3. **Imagination**. Most Chinese have more than their fair share of fantasies and the patience to turn their imaginings into reality. We have already seen several examples of the long-term vision for which China is famous. The government is already planning for the year 2121 and Alibaba for 2101. The Chinese continue to dream bigger and bigger dreams, for which they are prepared to make bigger and bigger efforts.
4. **Grit/Persistence**. Persistence and China are almost synonymous. In my experience, the Chinese are still prepared to make huge personal sacrifices to get ahead in life. This same kind of extreme dedication and overwhelming hunger to succeed seems less common in Western countries. Jack Ma likes to tell the story of how he was refused a job 30 times. We are all familiar with stories of the many Chinese who work their fingers to the bone in factories to give their children and their families a better life. In China, like in Silicon Valley, failure is nothing shameful, whereas giving up is wholly unacceptable. Parents teach their children to try, try, try again and the highest form of success in China is to realise your dream through hard work.
5. **Critical thinking**. This ability to decide whether or not a statement or a line of reasoning is valid is cited by the Chinese who have studied abroad as an important difference between China and the West. Are these 600,000 returned students vanguard of a new generation of critical thinkers in China? Is it a coincidence that many of the founders of China's most innovative companies are returnees after studying abroad? Some cognitive scientists argue the opposite, claiming that repetition and memorisation are the foundations for building up a strong neural architecture, a network that serves as a basis for the stimulation of much more complex, creative and critical thinking later on. As it turns out, this theory has much in common with the widespread belief in Chinese culture that you cannot become a great artist in your own right until you have first copied the works of other masters.

Of course, these five basic capacities are not uniquely Chinese. In general, the West still offers a better educational environment for the development of critical thinking. But as far as the other four capacities are concerned, it seems to me that China prepares its children better for the future. At the end of the day, every child is different and some will do better in a Western educational environment than a Chinese one, and vice versa. This applies equally to Chinese children and Western children, many of whom I have seen do well in Chinese schools. My fear is that people in the West complacently conclude that we are better prepared to face the future because we are more critical thinkers.

According to Peter Diamandis, the entrepreneurs of the 21st century need to refocus on the importance of mindsets of individuals. He advocates the development of a mindset of optimism and abundance, in an environment where mistakes are tolerated. While we in the West are quick to condemn Chinese parents for putting their children under so much pressure and for 'robbing' them of their childhood years, it seems to me that the most universal values for creating a healthy family, company or society — hope, self-respect and respect for others — are steadily losing ground in Europe and America.

A 2013 study confirmed that there is no country in the world that has greater respect for its teachers than China, a status that is usually reserved only for doctors in Western countries. In contrast, teachers in most Western societies are increasingly seen as being on a par with librarians or civil servants, professions that generally enjoy a much lower level of respect. The same 2013 study also revealed that China is the country where parents are most likely to encourage their children to go into the teaching profession, whereas there is an urgent shortage of teachers throughout the Western world.[227] I am afraid that the growing lack of respect shown in the West towards people with knowledge and expertise will soon be revealed as one of the most serious weaknesses in our society, especially when compared with a Chinese Confucian model, which is grounded in respect for teachers.

A MINDSET FOR THE FUTURE

In the summer of 2015, we decided to send our daughter to school in Belgium. She was now 13 years old and we felt it was important that she should spend her teenage years with other Belgian children, with whom she was most mentally attuned. In China, her standard comment on the subject was: 'I am not Chinese; I'm Belgian.' To make the transition as easy as possible, we enrolled her in a public school in Ghent where there were already lots of other children from various origins or countries. What an eye-opener that was for our daughter, and for her parents too! There was huge tension and often physical violence between children from different religious or cultural backgrounds, and bullying was an almost everyday event. My daughter had never experienced anything like it before. There was little respect for others, not even for the teachers. When we expressed our concerns to the school, we were told that it was 'the spirit of the times' and that this is what we should expect in a 'free-thinking school'. After all, we were reminded, this was Belgium, and not a dictatorship like China! The children, apparently, had to be given the freedom to discover themselves and the world. But our daughter had already seen a lot of the world and she already knew clearly what she wanted from life and why. We stuck it out for two years and then decided to look for another school. Amelie is now spending the last two years of her secondary education in a relatively new school, which shares premises with the local art academy. It has turned out to be an excellent choice. She has blossomed and made lots of new friends in a safer and more respectful environment. But she also tells us that many of her classmates are often down or depressed. Everyone is struggling with his or her identity. True, she is finding the new school relatively enjoyable, but it is not exactly what you could call an inspiring environment. Is this the kind of hard world we are now living in? Is this the West's New Normal ... A society where hope is fading fast?

When I first travelled through China with my backpack in 1991, what most struck me about the Chinese people was their exuberant energy, determination and hope. Today, more than 30 years later, things have hardly changed. The Chinese still have hope. Hope in abundance. When I give talks across Europe about Chinese innovation, I mostly tell a positive story, because that is what I fundamentally believe. Innovation is only possible as part of a hopeful and constructive process. Sometimes someone in the audience tells me that he or she is fed up with the 'good news show' about China, almost as if I was spreading some kind of Chinese government propaganda. I reply that it is important to separate the propaganda from the real hope and opportunities that undoubtedly exist in China. 'The Chinese Dream' that Xi Jinping announced in 2013 was indeed carefully orchestrated propaganda, intended to rally the entire nation to create momentum behind huge state reforms that are necessary to move China forwards. Does this mean that the Chinese people never hear bad things about China and the world? It does not. They do hear such things — but they still remain fundamentally hopeful. Why? Because the power of good news over bad should never be underestimated. Stories about the most successful Chinese entrepreneurs are given a prominent place on social media. New discoveries and innovations are front page news. Reports about social progress are always given airtime on the state broadcasting channels. I simply repeat and underline this positive focus to my audiences because this is precisely how hundreds of millions of Chinese children, employees and entrepreneurs find the inspiration they need that will allow them to pursue their own Chinese dream. Finding the right mentality for the future will largely be a matter of finding the right inspiration — and inspiration is something they have no shortage of in China.

CHINA'S REAL WEAPON IS ITS CHILDREN [228]

In 2013 China put its children on the world map. Students from Shanghai high schools won the PISA test[229] for a second time. This is a test organised by the OECD in which half a million students from all over the world compete to see who is best in mathematics, the sciences and reading. High schools from Shanghai emerged as the winners in all three disciplines, with a lead of more than 100 points over most Western schools, which equates to a difference of three years at the age of fifteen. Chinese children are able to attain these results not merely because of the pressure they are put under at school, but because of the 2,000-year-old Chinese tradition of dedication to learning. Education is part of a cultural heritage that required the Chinese to study hard and pass extremely complicated imperial exams to qualify for public service, a path to success in dynastic China. The key content of the exams was the Chinese classics, with a strong focus on Confucius. This great philosopher, politician and educationalist, who lived during the 5th and 6th centuries B.C., once said: 'If you think in terms of a year, plant a seed; if in terms of ten years, plant trees; if in terms of 100 years, teach the people.' We now live in a knowledge society and China wants to become the world's greatest knowledge superpower, and the great teacher Confucius is still their guide.

Today's Chinese education system, like today's Chinese medicine, is a combination of traditional and modern elements. Traditionally, lessons still start with massaging of the eye-lids and stretching or singing, to open both the body and mind. To ensure maximum concentration, each lesson only lasts for 35 minutes throughout an eight-hour day. The teachers are each specialists in their own subject. They follow extensive training, at the end of which they are required to focus on a single discipline and a single age group, so that they perfect their mastery. More modern elements have now been added in the larger urban schools; by adjusting constantly the curricula and teaching practices; by allowing less good schools and students to collaborate with better ones; by being open to best practices from abroad; by making teachers' pay performance-based; and by giving children more time to play. The trend is now set, and the Chinese children of tomorrow will definitely not be the same as the children of yesterday. The most important transformation will be the introduction of technology into the classroom, which, unlike in the West, goes much further than digital agendas or learn to code. The Chinese view programming simply as the learning of another language, and that is precisely what it is. Chinese children now also learn things like how to take a cell phone apart and put it back together again, how to build a neural network and how to develop a personal interaction with the teacher via an AI robot.

THE END OF CHINESE TOYS

Robots look set to become the new parents in New Normal China. The parents of the Chinese children now attending primary school were born in the 1980s. This is a generation of parents that is simple, hopeful and curious. Most of their children, the lucky ones at least, therefore have two young parents and four living grandparents. The grandparents will generally have had hard lives, but now have high expectations for their only child and grandchild. Typically, the both young parents work long days to give their single child the best possible chance for the future. In these circumstances, robots are the ideal surrogate parents for the education, entertainment and monitoring of that single child. If you type in the search task 'educational robot' on Alibaba's Taobao site, you get 65 pages of product listings. On Amazon, the same term will give you a shorter list of almost exclusively Chinese robots. Chinese domestic-robot companies have clearly set their sights on children, who are focus for family spending. There is a highly lucrative market, but from a societal point of view it is even more important that this phenomenon is manifesting itself with a new generation of children who find AI-robots as natural as the iPad, smartphone or PlayStation. It is expected that in 2019 alone some 100 million AI educational robots will be bought in China.[230] It is also anticipated that within five years all toys in China will be intelligent and that the production of cheap plastic, non-interactive toys will basically end. Smart and affordable toys will be available for the entire population, not just the wealthy. Educational robots are no longer just a 'distracting gadget' in China, but are part of a fundamental revolution in the upbringing of children. This gives rise to essential questions about privacy and safety, but the trend is already unstoppable. These issues will need to be addressed, which will be a supremely difficult task for the government and its new privacy legislation (Smart Health).

The most valuable AI company in China (2018) is UBTech from Shenzhen. The CEO of this humanoid robot company, Zhou Jiang, has the same dream that Bill Gates once had about PCs: 'A robot in every house and the integration of intelligent robots in people's day to day lives to create a more intelligent way of living for everyone.' Their dancing Robo-dog 'Jimi' was chosen to herald in the Chinese Year of the Dog on national television in 2018 and their Alpha 1 robot holds the world record for the largest number of robots dancing simultaneously. UBTech has already made its mark, but Zhou Jiang wants to take things several steps further: 'At UBTech, we insist on looking on the robot as a future member of the family.' This dream begins with their strategy towards children and education. For example, their educational robots teach children STEM skills, including computer programming from an early age. You can compare this with playing with Lego, but with both hardware and software puzzle pieces instead of only plastic building blocks.

The start-up in the educational robot sector that intrigues me the most is Ling, founded by Gu Jiawei. Gu typifies the current generation of young Chinese start-up entrepreneurs. Having graduated in engineering in 2011 from Tsinghua University (the best university in China), he was trained in man-machine interactions at the world-famous Microsoft Research Lab in Beijing. Three short years later, in 2014, he was appointed as the principal AI architect at Baidu, where he led a team working on Google X type projects, ranging from self-driving cars to glasses to help the blind through facial recognition. Before his 30th birthday, he had worked on 21 projects, won 13 prizes, and had 13 patents and 7 publications to his name. In 2016, he founded Ling, raising 22 million dollars to get it off the ground. At the end of 2017, the company launched Luka, a book-reading AI robot for children. You ask Luka to look for one of the 40,000 books in his memory and he then starts to read aloud, stopping to ask you to turn the page of the same physical book in front of you. Very smart, but above all Luka is interactive and personalised. For example, Luka not only teaches children how to read but also corrects errors in their pronunciation. What's more, because schools (for the time being) still use lots of 'real' books, Ling has taken the pragmatic step of making the transition from printed paper to robots as straightforward as possible both for the schools and for parents. As a result, Luka is now ready to help train the next generation of geniuses, the future Gu Jiawei's of China.

LONG-DISTANCE LEARNING[231]

If you arrived in Shanghai in 2013 as a twenty-something Westerner, there was a 50 percent chance that you would be a teacher. You could easily earn 50 US Dollars an hour by giving extra English lessons to Chinese children, and the parents would have usually been ignorant of your strong French or Spanish accent (if you had one). At times, it seemed like the biggest foreign swindle in China since the Opium War. Chinese parents were so desperate for their children to learn English that you could get away with almost anything. On the corner of the street you could often see the dubious agents of the equally dubious language schools, dressed in cheap suits, offering private lessons from 'genuine' native speakers; Kindergartens advertised 'Genuine American English' in their ads. Chinese parents spend on average seven times more than Western parents on out-of-school lessons for their children, often amounting to 15 percent of their monthly income.[232] In the Chinese cities, education, not Gucci or Louis Vuitton, has become the new luxury, with summer courses for your children abroad seldom costing less than 5,500 US Dollars per trip. It goes without saying that this is still wholly unaffordable for the 800 million Chinese urban dwellers who have to make do with an average annual income of 11,000 US Dollars.

Clever Chinese entrepreneurs quickly saw that there was a market opportunity for online English courses. Companies like VIPkid, Yuanfudao, 17zuoye, NetEase Yudao, iTutorgroup and Hujiang are just a few of the most well-known EdTech start-ups, which have since grown into unicorns (or, better said, Chinese phoenixes). VIPkid, which focuses on 4 to 15-year-olds learning English online from North American teachers, is a classic example. Founded in the magical year 2013, it now has 500,000 weekly Chinese users and 60,000 teachers. Leaving aside the fact that the English these children learn is better than most Europeans, they also learn more about Western culture than we are ever likely to learn about China and its culture. The ability of Chinese children to find ways around the internet firewall to consume Western entertainment recently prompted Xi Jinping to demand a renewed focus on Chinese culture. Be that as it may, in 2018 there were 220 million online students in China, which is as many as the entire under-30 population in the European Union, and this in an EdTech market that continues to grow at 20 percent a year[233]. Most Chinese spend about an hour a day learning online. These lessons are anything but dull. Augmented reality and gamification are standard elements on the Chinese online education menu. If a student wants to talk about dinosaurs, VIPkid uses learning material from National Geographic to reanimate these ancient creatures. The teachers can also use virtual stickers and augmented reality to transform themselves into super-heroes or use virtual reality to take pupils on a museum tour in the far-away teacher's home town. Above all, however, it is the live video streaming that is the real driving force behind the explosion of online learning in China.

MY TAILOR IS NOT RICH. HE'S SMART

The most important factor of all is the use of AI. Interactivity and involvement are crucial in online education. At VIPKid they have collected tens of millions of examples of their students' speech patterns to train their AI algorithms to recognize facial expressions. In particular, they have taught these algorithms to analyse the movement of the eyes, because every student expresses him or herself differently. According to VIPKid, the new AI education will be able in the future to replace traditional classes of 30 pupils, providing a much more personalised approach for each pupil based on his/her personality, learning style and cognitive ability. The introduction of the first facial recognition cameras in Chinese classrooms to monitor levels of concentration might shock some people, but it is part of the programme to optimise a new teaching-learning process in China.[234] The days when we learnt our first English sentence by all repeating out loud 'My tailor is rich' are gone forever. Instead, we now have AI applications that are certainly rich, but also smart and tailor-made.

A company that goes a step further is Liulishuo (meaning 'speak fluently') from Shanghai. In their system, the teacher disappears altogether, which they say should help to solve the acute staff shortage in the teaching profession. Their AI teacher can teach hundreds of students at the same time, making language courses affordable for the entire population. Liulishuo focuses on speech recognition and the application of phonetics in natural language processing, which is one of the domains of Artificial Intelligence. This challenging task requires the computer to understand how sounds are produced, so that they can be analysed and used to help the student to read English texts, with real-time feedback being given via AI algorithms: your very own virtual, personalised AI mentor-teacher. In a field where helping a student learn a new language rapidly is not a logical earning model for a traditional bricks and mortar language school, Liulishuo has succeeded in cutting learning time by a third while providing the service at a third of the price. A dramatically more democratic approach.

STEAM AND MOOC

The Chinese people and the internet start-ups have already taken their first steps into the new world of online education. I expect that in less than ten years AI will have been integrated as a standard element throughout the entire Chinese education system. In 2018, the Chinese Ministry of Education launched an Artificial Intelligence Innovation Action plan for universities. The plan aims to train a new pool of AI+X talents by offering 100 new AI+X courses and creating 50 new AI academies, research centres and interdisciplinary institutes. 58 percent of all master graduates in China come from a STEM discipline, which equates to 4.7 million new and highly qualified STEM talents each year, or 37 percent of all STEM students in the world. India follows in second place with 2.6 million, while America is lagging far behind with just 600,000.[235] For me, this is the strongest signal that China (and probably India, too) will be the world's innovation leaders in 'the day after tomorrow'. This is not just because both countries have smart, creative and innovative people, but they have far more of them than anywhere else. At the same time, let's not forget the A in STEAM, which stands for Art, because this too will be given a more prominent role in China, although there is still a long way to go.

Because China is a country where the demand for content is many times greater than the supply, certainly in remote towns and villages, MOOCs (Massive Open Online Courses) have become the new format for the distribution of knowledge. This is a market where content is used as a weapon in the battle between start-ups, involving both local and foreign players like Udemy, Coursera and Udacity. Although the foreign programmes often have more and better content, the local companies are building up a lead by adjusting their models better to local needs. In this way, the unicorn Hujiang has turned many of its teachers into superstars, who can earn as much as 3 million dollars a year by offering result-driven content in an exclusive and personal KOL manner.

The opening shot for the EdTech race in China has been fired. In the first half of 2018, some 270 Chinese EdTech companies raised 2.22 billion dollars, which is as much as the full total for 2017.[236] The likely world market for 2019 is estimated at 190 billion euros, with an annual growth of 20 percent, of which 41 billion euros is expected to be generated in China.[237] However, I expect that we will soon need to radically revise our estimates about China's share in the market by 2025, because China will unquestionably take the lead during the coming decade. And the West? There is still time for us to learn from China's AI transformation in education — before it is too late.

SMART CHINESE

Far too often I hear people in Europe say that China's success mostly is based on 'skipping a generation', because they never had to surf on the previous wave of technological development, they were never held back by legacy systems, unlike in the West. They went straight to mobile payments because they never had bankcards; they went straight to e-commerce because shopping malls were rare, old-fashioned and inefficient; they went straight to smart security because there were no data privacy regulations to hinder them, and so on. The unstated assumption behind these comments is that 'this is a one-off transformation typical of developing countries, like Japan or Korea or India, and when China becomes more expensive, more complex and more regulated, the Chinese will lose their unique advantage'. In response, I try to explain gently that this is not a 'one off' event. There is such huge momentum, scale, resilience and vision in China that the Chinese will be able to keep on re-inventing themselves for decades to come. This response is often still greeted by eye-brows raised in disbelief. To explain the reasons for my confidence, I begin to talk about Chinese education. I observe that in Europe there are now attempts to have programming and entrepreneurship made a compulsory part of the curriculum, and that politicians and educationalists alike try to reassure the public that new technology will never replace the teacher. The truth is, however, that most of the tasks that are carried out by today's teachers can be done more optimally by technology, certain in matters of traditional knowledge transfer. In the West we live in fear of these things; the Chinese much less so. And that is one reason why they could ultimately outsmart us. That is the reason why Chinese society, with all its wonderful phoenixes, will continue its process of constant metamorphosis for many, many years to come. If the West is to stay ahead, we need to lose our fear for change and see the real benefits of new technologies.

Throughout my years in China, I made it a habit to do something completely outside my comfort zone at least once a month. The most recent outcome of this habit is the writing of this book. I imposed this rule on myself because it was my way as an entrepreneur to be able to compete with the super-ambitious Chinese who are always looking for new challenges and who never seem to be afraid. This fearlessness is what makes the Chinese so 'smart' in the sense of being ready for the future. It is not that they do everything so much quicker or better than we do, but they have an innate ability to visualise the world in 'the day after tomorrow' with great clarity and then move towards it step by step, starting today. And if they occasionally take a wrong turn, they just try a different route, always moving forwards and always full of hope. In this way, they are traveling together as a collective society towards an unknown but better world. And they have mapped out the milestones on the road to the future: a more efficient world by 2025; a more innovative world by 2030; a more highly developed world by 2049; a more harmonious world by 2121. A map to get to the world of 'the day after tomorrow'. It is this vision and belief that makes them smarter than us today, nothing else. Why can't we do the same?

What to Remember?

1 → **From ancient times, the Chinese have developed a Spartan approach to learning** that creates student-athletes loved and supported by their parents, trained by experienced and respected teachers, and strengthened by the steroids of new technology. Chinese children can only play once they have finished their schoolwork. In the West, we only work when we have first played enough.

2 → **The reform of Chinese education is an ambitious and necessary undertaking** launched by the government to allow the nation to escape from the middle-income trap and to eliminate the inequality between the cities and the countryside. They want to have the best universities and the best students in the world, and to get them China is making full use of the internet, Big Data and AI in all schools, with STEAM and MOOC as their main focus.

3 → **The Chinese are just as creative, critical and innovative as we are.** They are now making the transition from 'Made in China' to 'Created in China'. To make this possible, they are reaching back to their own cultural past, making more proud of their heritage and their country each passing year. At the same time, they are keen to learn about our Western approach to creativity, while investing their own brands with emotional narratives that have increasingly universal appeal.

4 → **The schools of the future must teach their pupils new concepts like passion, curiosity, imagination, determination and critical thinking.** Chinese children would seem to be in pole position in this respect and are better suited to develop the learning mentality of the future, which will be based on a willingness to take risks and be motivated by hope and inspiration. Chinese children are already preparing for their role in what will be China's century.

5 → **China's strength is its children,** who are raised with a potent cocktail of traditional methods and modern technology. Robots will be the new Chinese parents of the 21st century, online learning will be the New Normal and Artificial Intelligence will be the new electricity that powers the new teaching and learning tools. The Chinese will outsmart us, unless we have the courage to leave our comfort zone.

<
The Hong Kong-Zhuhai-Macao Bridge, the longest bridge in the world (55 km), connects Hong Kong with mainland China.

CONCLUSION

EAST-WEST, WHERE IS BEST?

Ever since Bill and Dave set up the Hewlett-Packard (HP) company after the second world-war, Silicon Valley has been synonymous with innovation and technological disruption. Intel intensified this process by defining Moore's Law, whereby the number of transistors on a microchip would double every two years, leading to a huge explosion in calculating capacity and a dramatic fall in the price of the chips. This propelled a new industry in personal computers, notebooks, internet and smartphones, so that the sector was soon earning billions in profits instead of millions. Bits and bytes were the new atoms. This trend attracted an entire generation of entrepreneurs to the unique environment of Silicon Valley, creating an enterprise culture based on a great passion for technology, a belief in change and an ability to adapt. This hotbed of innovation was also made possible thanks to being implanted in a society with the best universities, mountains of capital, successful mentors and a superior technological infrastructure. Silicon Valley gave the coding wizards an unfair innovative advantage in the largest market in the world: The United States.

But Moore's Law is now 'no more': its tenets simply no longer apply. Transistors are becoming so small that they have almost reached the boundaries of physics. Consumers continue to expect improvements each year, but Silicon Valley is no longer able to oblige them. Silicon magic is fading away. I firmly believe that the traditional cornerstones of our Western innovation model are crumbling, to be replaced by a new paradigm, in which repetitive work no longer has a central place in value creation. Economic added value will be increasingly created for people and decreasingly by people. In the world of 'the day after tomorrow', technology will live in symbiosis with humans to serve sustainable societal objectives. In this new process of creation, it is our uniquely human qualities that will be central to success: our social, creative and cognitive skills. New technologies will support our human brain to make possible the more complete satisfaction of our higher human needs: recognition, appreciation and self-realisation. Social, cultural, ethical and sustainability matters will take precedence over the pure pursuit of profit that typified yesterday's capitalist model. The transition towards a more qualitative and a more humane world will take place in both the West and the East. Companies in both Silicon Valley and Shanghai or Shenzhen can show us the way. The challenge we face is to make the mental adjustment to this New Normal as quickly as possible. I am convinced China can help us make this adjustment. We can already seek inspiration from the dynamic Chinese phoenixes, which operate in a culture with a strong and enabling social context; a consumer, data- and ecosystem driven culture, in close collaboration with a government with enormous resources and the ability to orchestrate long-term national plans that is seeking to create a more sustainable and harmonious society.

During the coming decades, China will further define the new norm for innovation in Asia. By 2050, Asia will generate half of the world's economic value, with the West accounting for less than half of Asia's contribution. The Chinese innovation model will have a huge impact on worldwide innovation, and therefore on every Western company as well. To remain relevant, every truly innovative company will be obliged to integrate three new standards into their operations, redefining them completely:

- A customer-centric innovation standard that focuses on the new type of consumer, who expects a personalised and relevant experience in a connected, enhanced and ready-to-use world.
- A technological innovation standard embracing, among other things, AI, IoT, 5G, blockchain, VR and AR, all of which are deployed within the framework of new data models and business ecosystems.
- A new standard for business organisation, based on entrepreneurship and speed in a new VUCA world full of red oceans.

Before 2030, China will make its mark on the economic world, industry by industry and country by country. It is already doing so in sectors like security, entertainment, e-commerce, finance and insurance; the first cars of a fast-moving Chinese train have come into view worldwide. During the next ten years, mobility, manufacturing, healthcare and education will follow. Only time will tell whether it will be Alibaba or Amazon, NIO or Tesla, Tencent or Facebook who has the strongest business model, but the winner will probably be a hybrid. Silicon Valley start-ups already look up to their Chinese counterparts for learning and inspiration, so why can't we in the rest of the developed world do the same? Most Silicon Valley VCs are no longer prepared to invest in companies that do not have a rock-solid China strategy and many Silicon Valley start-ups now have their hardware increasingly designed and developed in Shenzhen. On the reverse side of the coin, the big Chinese technology companies nearly all have a research establishment in the Valley. This double strategy, which involves parallel activities in both China and the West, looks set to become the New Normal for all innovative companies. In this way, you can get the best of both worlds and get access to the key global markets. The innovation winners of 'the day after tomorrow' will make optimal use of this 'China plus' model and will perhaps become our new competitors. For this reason, it is crucial that we start to draw inspiration from the new generation of Chinese innovator – today, not tomorrow.

RISE LIKE A PHOENIX!

The greatest challenge in learning about China is the need to first unlearn everything we thought we knew about the country and its people. The question that people in the West almost never ask about China is 'why'. It is only when we ask 'why' recent developments in China have become the New Normal that we will be able to fully understand. Throughout the book, I have tried to give answers to some of these 'why' questions. I hope this has cleared up a number of mysteries, misconceptions and confusions. It is only by looking at China more empathically and by understanding China in a realistic way that we will be able to gain more meaningful insights. But to be able to truly comprehend modern China and profit from its example, we first need to realise that our past image most people have of the country is no longer relevant. The Chinese companies that we regularly read about in the

Western media have embraced a new world, while we all too often still try to understand China in terms of the old world. It is not my purpose to argue that China is better, because that is not what I believe. What I want is for you to discover for yourself how different China is and how differently the Chinese think. I hope that my stories will have an innovative and inspiring effect on your own thinking, so that you can develop a deeper, richer and more accurate picture of the new China, and the implications of China's growing momentum for you, whatever you do.

Before I close, I would like to offer three suggestions that will help you to continue understanding China in the future as the country continues to evolve rapidly.

1. **Let go of your outdated image of China.** Forget about all the copy-catting. Forget the 2,000-year-old hierarchical structure of managers and bosses. Forget the image of China as either a communist or pseudo-capitalist country. Forget the lack of privacy and social responsibility. Think instead of the complex reality of China of today, which is never monolithic and is always adapting and changing. Think of the Chinese companies and entrepreneurs who from 2013 onwards have adopted a radical new approach with radical new objectives. Think of the Chinese consumers, who within a short generation have become sophisticated citizens of the world.
2. **Use the Silicon Valley model to understand China.** Like Silicon Valley, China is a place where money, large markets and top talent are more readily accessible; an ecosystem in which technology, infrastructure and an entrepreneurial culture make it possible to create the next Google; an environment of hope with a change mentality where 'think big' ideas can turn dreams into reality. The new China has all these things, from Beijing to Hangzhou and from Shanghai to Shenzhen, and in many other cities you have never heard of.
3. **Draw a new mental map.** What makes China more powerful than Silicon Valley is its state-of-the-art manufacturing companies, a visionary and generally effective government and unparalleled speed of execution. China's new tech innovators strongly resemble those in Silicon Valley, but their domestic market is many times bigger and they want to grow stronger and faster, using this triple dose of steroids to help them on their way. Try to disengage traditional limitations in your imagination, so you see the new China as an environment of truly unlimited resources, limitless opportunities, constant change and non-stop challenges, packed with entrepreneurs who possess inexhaustible energy, abundant expertise, a powerful collective mission and countless dreams.

My dream is that you, like the Chinese phoenixes, will be able to rise from the ashes of the past and re-invent yourself, using the inspiration of China as your example. I hope that this book will help you to start unravelling the mysteries of the Chinese puzzle, and maybe inspire you to buy that plane ticket to Shanghai or Shenzhen sometime soon. I hope that it will continue to serve you as a guide to give you a better grip on the future. Last but not least, as your guide on this journey into China's New Normal. I hope that I have been able to share with you valuable new insights, information and ideas. My ultimate wish is that China will become as fascinating, exciting and enriching for you as it has been for me during the past 30 years.

<
Amelie Coppens (age 6 years)
in Shanghai.

HOMEWORK

EIGHT INNOVATION MODELS FOR CHINA'S NEW NORMAL

Before our ways finally part, I would like to focus a little extra attention on eight of the Chinese innovation models covered in this book. These are eight models or ways of thinking that are significantly different from our Western way of innovation, but have given Chinese companies the wings to become so quick and so successful at innovating. I would invite you to allow yourself to be inspired by this Chinese methodology, so that you too will be ready to meet the challenges of our New Normal in 'the day after tomorrow'.

1

BE LOYAL TO YOUR CUSTOMER

Stop trying to make your customer loyal to you. Your customer is not loyal to you. Your customer is loyal to your loyalty to him. As long as you make him relevant, you will have his confidence. If you don't, he will no longer trust you — and will leave. It is your responsibility (and yours alone) to win and keep that trust. So, measure your loyalty to the customer, and not vice versa.

2

INNOVATE IN SMALLER AND MORE MANAGEABLE STEPS

Increase the tempo of your innovation by doing it in stages, like in a relay race. Design fewer daily sprints and don't run an ego-marathon. Don't set your innovation bar too high. Go from innovation to the market and then back to innovation, in a spiral that gets ever bigger and ever faster. Market success remains the best condition for the development of creativity or inventiveness, and not the other way around. Do not turn innovation into a culture, but see it as a survival strategy and a voyage of discovery.

3

BRING YOUR MARKET INTO YOUR COMPANY

Mirror your company and its organisation on the market. Transform your managers into hungry entrepreneurs within a micro-environment where no one fears change. Instead of being over-confident, bring the uncertainties of the market into your company. Let your innovation teams work together as if they were trying to get out of an escape room. Build a company culture of micro-collaboration, but with the necessary pressure cooker to succeed.

4

USE TECHNOLOGY AS A WEAPON, NOT AS A TRANSFORMATION PROCESS

Stop your digital transformation. New technologies like Big Data, AI, blockchain or IoT are not catalysts to prepare you for the new 4.0 industrial revolution. These technologies are the new world, offering new markets, solutions, models and customers. See these 4.0 technologies as a way to grow quick and earn money fast, not just as a means to increase your efficiency. Make yourself expert in at least one of the key new technologies.

5

INVEST IN YOUR ECOSYSTEM

There is no point in swimming alone against the tide if you can make use of the economies of scale that ecosystems offer: more customers, more money, better reach, better supply chains, greater capacity. Change your focus from industry player to ecosystem player. If you have the resources, build and grow your own ecosystem and invest in four things: your data platform, the integration of new services, smaller fast growth companies and co-creation with partners. If you don't have the resources, join someone else's ecosystem. Relinquish control and focus on the trust that your customers have in the ecosystem.

6

MAKE BUSINESS PERSONAL

By separating our work from our private life, we all live a double existence, and that can be very tiring. Is it not possible to approach our business in a more personal way? Trust is the strongest foundation for success. We spend more time 'retraining' ourselves than in building up relations with the people who hold our future in their hands: customers, ecosystem partners, bosses, etc. We have become the 'meeting generation', dependent on people we do not know all that well. Companies with strong social integration are often healthier and more dynamic. Make business personal again, because at the end of the day it is people and their relationships that determine company culture.

7

DON'T LIMIT YOURSELF: THINK BIG !

Stop trying to give innovation a 'framework', because doing this limits your chances of success. Don't start with a fixed budget, a brand, a timing or an objective. These boxes mean that out-of-the-box thinking is no longer possible. Imagine instead that you have an unlimited budget, lots of experts, a huge market and countless customers. It is this kind of thinking that makes the Chinese more out-of-the-box than we are. It is not that they are more creative; it is just that their box is so big that you can no longer see it. Expand your own mental box to accelerate your innovation. It is liberating to work for a fast-growing company, but this is only possible if you can first liberate your thinking — a chicken-and-egg problem that only good leadership can solve.

8

INNOVATE BY DOING

To innovate, we need to be able to 'think': critically, creatively, reflectively and with vision. But we also need other exceptional 'character' traits: curiosity, resilience, eagerness to learn, willingness to collaborate, passion about craftsmanship, communication skills, etc. In innovation, there is seldom a shortage of thinking, but often a shortage of character. Innovation is and remains a question of mastery, and in this respect innovation by doing is becoming increasingly more important than innovation by thinking. Think like the Chinese shanzhai to better understand what customers really want, so that you can respond quickly and flexibly to change and thereby develop disruptive ideas and innovations. Innovate and learn by doing.

TAKE ACTION

How different is your organisation from the Chinese phoenixes? Do you have a good understanding of how innovative Chinese firms operate today? Have you been to China to experience what is taking place for yourself? The markets in 'the day after tomorrow' will be governed by customers, data, smart technology, ecosystems, superpowers and fast entrepreneurs, so we all need to organise and learn how to innovate in a different way. These practices are already a reality in many leading Chinese technology firms today. The above eight models from China provide a good start. These innovation strategies can be super-effective for every Western company and will become ever more relevant and necessary in the new VUCA world. So now it is over to you... are you ready to act?

ENDNOTES

1 http://www.chinadaily.com.cn/a/201810/29/WS5bd6cef4a310eff3032853d4.html
2 https://www.marketwatch.com/story/china-has-9-of-the-worlds-20-biggest-tech-companies-2018-05-31
3 https://www.digitalpulse.pwc.com.au/startup-unicorns-fantasy-fiction/
4 https://www.thehindubusinessline.com/news/world/china-likely-to-surpass-us-in-rd-spending-by-year-end-report/article24076852.ece
5 https://eandt.theiet.org/content/articles/2018/12/china-continues-to-dominate-worldwide-patent-applications/
6 http://usawc.libanswers.com/faq/84869
7 https://www.slideshare.net/omohout/european-tech-scaleups-report-2017
8 Of course, this does not apply for people who already know China well or live there.
9 http://reports.weforum.org/human-capital-report-2016/learning-through-the-life-course/
10 https://www.pwc.com/gx/en/issues/data-and-analytics/publications/artificial-intelligence-study.html
11 https://technode.com/2017/10/22/china-vs-us-ai/
12 https://www.wired.co.uk/article/alibaba-city-brain-artificial-intelligence-china-kuala-lumpur
13 https://www.asianscientist.com/2018/02/tech/zhang-tong-tencent-ai-lab/
14 https://qz.com/1177465/forget-bat-chinas-next-generation-tech-giants-are-tmd/
15 https://borgenproject.org/water-pollution-in-china/
16 http://www.xinhuanet.com/english/2018-09/03/c_137441670.htm
17 https://danieljmitchell.wordpress.com/2017/06/15/a-lesson-from-china-on-poverty-reduction-and-inequality/
18 https://www.imdb.com/title/tt1798709/
19 A slightly pejorative name used by the Chinese for foreigners.
20 https://www.scmp.com/tech/enterprises/article/2134498/chinas-huawei-set-lead-global-roll-out-5g-mobile-networks
21 https://techcrunch.com/2018/08/13/new-defense-bill-bans-the-u-s-government-from-using-huawei-and-zte-tech/?guccounter=1
22 http://fortune.com/2018/08/07/5g-china-verizon-sprint-t-mobile/
23 https://www.scmp.com/business/companies/article/2025622/china-telecom-set-cash-mobile-data-and-internet-tech-analysts-say
24 http://www.chinadaily.com.cn/a/201807/23/WS5b558effa310796df4df8281.html
25 https://www.spglobal.com/marketintelligence/en/news-insights/research/china-wireless-on-the-road-to-4g
26 http://ncel.ie.cuhk.edu.hk/sites/default/files/1569647391.pdf
27 https://en.wikipedia.org/wiki/Schr%C3%B6dinger%27s_cat
28 https://newatlas.com/china-quantum-cryptography-communications-satellite/44965/
29 https://www.scientificamerican.com/article/chinese-researchers-achieve-stunning-quantum-entanglement-record/
30 https://en.wikipedia.org/wiki/Elections_in_China#Direct_elections

31 https://www.cbc.ca/news/world/great-wall-of-china-even-longer-than-previously-thought-1.1263111

32 http://www.cbsr.ia.ac.cn/users/szli/

33 https://www.sramanamitra.com/2018/08/10/billion-dollar-unicorns-yitu-cashes-in-on-chinas-growing-surveillance-market/

34 https://medium.com/syncedreview/chinas-yitu-battles-for-position-in-huge-facial-recognition-market-8887bcc87234

35 http://www.chinadaily.com.cn/regional/chongqing/liangjiang/2018-02/23/content_35764308.htm

36 https://www.prnewswire.com/news-releases/china-will-have-44-59-of-the-global-facial-recognition-market-share-by-2023-and-cloudwalk-will-become-the-biggest-winner-300695897.html

37 https://www.edelman.com/sites/g/files/aatuss191/files/2018-10/2018_Edelman_Trust_Barometer_Global_Report_FEB.pdf

38 https://www.whatsonweibo.com/open-sesame-social-credit-in-china-as-gate-to-punitive-measures-and-personal-perks/

39 https://hub.hku.hk/bitstream/10722/143448/2/Content.pdf?accept=1

40 https://www.andrewng.org/

41 https://www.chinainternetwatch.com/2054/tencent-active-im-users-close-to-800-million-social-network-qzone-over-600-million-in-2012/

42 http://chinafilminsider.com/new-chinese-laws-to-hit-streaming-broadcasting-of-foreign-content/

43 Ezra Vogel (2013). Deng Xiaoping and the Transformation of China. Belknap Press.

44 http://www.chinatoday.com.cn/ctenglish/2018/zdtj/201803/t20180301_800118954.html

45 https://www.theguardian.com/world/2018/nov/09/worlds-first-ai-news-anchor-unveiled-in-china

46 https://www.forbes.com/sites/niallmccarthy/2018/08/23/china-now-boasts-more-than-800-million-internet-users-and-98-of-them-are-mobile-infographic/#1f54dad57092

47 https://adage.com/article/global-news/china-sina-weibo-olympics/236616

48 https://www.dragonsocial.net/blog/social-media-in-china

49 https://find.xyz/map/the-rise-of-toutiao

50 https://www.theverge.com/2018/10/26/18026250/bytedance-china-tiktok-valuation-highest-toutiao

51 http://www.xinhuanet.com/english/2018-12/21/c_137689613.htm

52 https://www.fbicgroup.com/sites/default/files/CCFA2016_Top100.pdf

53 https://www.youtube.com/watch?v=PQDxyHBHqNo

54 https://www.cnbc.com/video/2017/01/25/jack-ma-on-how-amazon-and-alibaba-differ.html

55 https://www.tematicaresearch.com/china-and-india-dominate-mobile-payments-not-the-u-s/

56 https://www.businessinsider.com/mobile-dominates-singles-day-2017-11?r=US&IR=T

57 https://www.searchenginejournal.com/mobile-shopping-now-accounts-for-over-50-of-online-transactions-report/270623/

58 http://www.tomdoctoroff.com/

59 https://www.dragonsocial.net/blog/how-to-master-xiaohongshu-from-a-users-perspective/

60 https://yourstory.com/2018/04/pinduoduo-funding-tencent

61 https://techcrunch.com/2019/02/25/pinduoduo-crossborder-ecommerce/

62 https://www.china-briefing.com/news/chinas-crackdown-daigou-cross-border-e-commerce-policies/

63 https://www.warc.com/newsandopinion/news/chinas_gen_z_relies_on_social_media_for_shopping/39204

64 Tik Tok is known under the name *Dou Yin* in Chinese, which means 'vibrato'.

65 https://www.theworldofchinese.com/2017/04/virtual-gifts/

66 Kai-Fu Lee is the former CEO of Google China and Microsoft Research Asia: https://en.wikipedia.org/wiki/Kai-Fu_Lee

67 https://www.statista.com/statistics/467160/forecast-of-smartphone-users-in-china/

68 https://www.china-briefing.com/news/mobile-payments-china-foreign-businesses-china-adopt-strategy/

69 https://www.paymentsjournal.com/mobile-payments-use-in-the-u-s-lags/

70 https://www.cnbc.com/2018/11/06/starbucks-ceo-were-going-to-apply-to-the-us-what-we-learned-in-china.html

71 https://www.theguardian.com/us-news/2018/oct/17/trump-universal-postal-union-withdraw-foreign-postal-rates

72 https://asia.nikkei.com/Spotlight/Asia-Insight/China-s-tech-boom-leaves-wide-rich-poor-chasm

73 https://www.valuewalk.com/2017/09/chinese-people-enormously-invested-stocks/

74 http://europe.chinadaily.com.cn/a/201806/20/WS5b29ee73a3103349141dd4f4.html

75 http://www.hurun.net/EN/Article/Details?num=24DD41EE3B19

76 http://www.hurun.net/EN/Article/Details?num=2B1B8F33F9C0

77 http://www.hurun.net/EN/Article/Details?num=5A320E03FD31

78 https://www.ai-cio.com/news/chinese-vc-investments-tops-us-first-time/

79 www.prnewswire.com/news-releases/chinese-ai-startups-overtake-american-peers-for-venture-capital-investments-taking-away-us5-billion-300702606.html

80 https://www.vox.com/2018/7/29/17627134/income-inequality-chart

81 https://www.bloomberg.com/quicktake/chinas-debt-bomb

82 https://www.economist.com/leaders/2017/07/20/chinas-state-enterprises-are-not-retreating-but-advancing

83 https://worldview.stratfor.com/article/state-owned-enterprises-are-hard-habit-china-doesnt-want-break

84 https://www.bloomberg.com/graphics/2016-us-vs-china-economy/

85 https://www.forbes.com/sites/kenrapoza/2017/03/19/shanghai-housing-prices-completely-unsustainable/#410d104d326e

86 https://www.latimes.com/world/asia/la-fg-chinese-poor-ugly-20181226-story.html?fbclid=I-wAR2yeA5Q5JV-qTtRg-ZTIurYRUidYNmeJf3IaOaWN0fYIDJDdLpfmLYc0uM

87 https://www.bloomberg.com/opinion/articles/2018-07-19/china-s-economy-is-different-no-recessions-in-a-quarter-century
88 https://medium.com/wharton-fintech/fintech-in-china-an-introduction-6b11abd9cb64
89 https://www.barrons.com/articles/alibaba-and-tencent-and-the-coming-fintech-boom-1490424026
90 https://data.oecd.org/natincome/saving-rate.htm
91 https://www.datayes.io/
92 www.chinadaily.com.cn/a/201810/29/WS5bd6cef4a310eff3032853d4.html
93 https://www.mckinsey.com/featured-insights/china/what-can-we-expect-in-china-in-2019
94 https://www.researchgate.net/publication/323877493_How_a_Little_Ant_Challenges_Giant_Banks_The_Rise_of_Ant_Financial_Alipay's_Fintech_Empire_and_Relevant_Regulatory_Concerns
95 https://www.brookings.edu/blog/order-from-chaos/2018/02/08/whats-happening-with-chinas-Fintech-industry/
96 Also known as TenPay or Tencent Pay.
97 https://www.businesswire.com/news/home/20110707006596/en/Research-Markets-China-Third-party-Payment-Industry-Report
98 https://www.chinainternetwatch.com/25770/mobile-payment-q1-2018/ (in Chinese)
99 http://www.gov.cn/xinwen/2015-01/05/content_2800381.htm
100 https://techcrunch.com/2018/08/01/the-dramatic-rise-and-fall-of-online-p2p-lending-in-china/
101 http://www.globaltimes.cn/content/1116051.shtml
102 https://www.caixinglobal.com/2018-08-24/opinion-a-run-on-peer-to-peer-platforms-shouldnt-be-possible-its-now-happening-in-china-101318522.html
103 https://www.whatsonweibo.com/beijing-failed-protests-over-collapse-of-chinas-peer-to-peer-p2p-industry/
104 https://www.mckinsey.com/Videos/video?vid=5974784629001&plyrid=HkOJqCPWd-b&aid=9023A802-612C-425D-804C-61A3ACE523B2
105 https://asia.nikkei.com/Business/Companies/China-s-ZhongAn-goes-overseas-with-Japanese-deals
106 https://www.oxbowpartners.com/zhong-an/
107 https://www.crowdfundinsider.com/2018/08/137797-chinese-insurtech-zhongan-technology-launches-one-stop-claims-service-e-platform-for-insurers/
108 https://www.mckinsey.com/~/media/McKinsey/Industries/Financial%20Services/Our%20Insights/Digital%20insurance%20in%202018%20Driving%20real%20impact%20with%20digital%20and%20analytics/Digital-insurance-in-2018.ashx
109 https://www.cnbc.com/2018/03/06/amazon-could-become-the-third-biggest-us-bank-if-it-wants-to-bain-study.html
110 Deloitte report download: https://www2.deloitte.com/cn/en/pages/public-sector/articles/super-smart-city.html
111 World urbanization prospects — United Nations, Department of Economic and Social Affairs, Population Division (2014).
112 https://www.bbc.com/news/world-europe-38479439

113 http://www.uncrd.or.jp/content/documents/5917Presentation%202-High%20Speed%20Railways-Ms.%20Li.pdf

114 http://en.people.cn/n3/2017/1228/c90000-9309653.html

115 https://news.mb.com.ph/2017/10/23/chinese-high-speed-rail-amazes-world-with-china-speed/

116 http://www.chinadaily.com.cn/a/201808/02/WS5b623be8a31031a351e91899.html

117 http://worldpopulationreview.com/countries/china-population/

118 http://www.worldometers.info/geography/largest-countries-in-the-world/

119 https://www.quora.com/How-large-is-the-inhabitable-area-of-China

120 https://www.chinacheckup.com/blogs/articles/china-metro-systems

121 https://www.ft.com/content/dee63006-ded3-11e6-9d7c-be108f1c1dce

122 https://qpsoftware.net/blog/bike-sharing-china-mobike-ofo

123 http://mckinseychina.com/wp-content/uploads/2017/09/China-auto-Survey-2017_EN_FNL.pdf

124 https://www.aptiv.com/media/article/path-to-autonomous-driving-begins-with-consumer-and-adas-adoption

125 https://www.investopedia.com/articles/investing/051215/baidu-vs-google-how-are-they-different.asp

126 http://www.andrewng.org/

127 https://venturebeat.com/2014/07/30/andrew-ng-baidu/

128 https://singularityhub-com.cdn.ampproject.org/c/s/singularityhub.com/2018/08/17/baidu-alibaba-and-Tencent-the-rise-of-chinas-tech-giants/amp/

129 https://www.eetasia.com/news/article/18062105-apollo-chinas-autonomous-driving-program

130 https://seekingalpha.com/article/4160799-baidu-ai-city-dreams

131 https://medium.com/@fisher.jianyu.shi/breakdown-of-chinese-self-driving-car-industry-dd20deea7e73

132 https://qz.com/1250731/china-just-made-it-easier-for-self-driving-tests-to-take-place-on-any-road-in-the-country/

133 https://www.scmp.com/news/china/society/article/1952218/traffics-toll-road-accidents-kill-700-people-day-china

134 https://successstory.com/people/jia-yueting

135 https://medium.com/reputation-squad/2-chinese-tech-giants-jia-yueting-820d7624fc8a

136 https://www.mckinsey.com/industries/automotive-and-assembly/our-insights/savvy-and-sophisticated-meet-chinas-evolving-car-buyers

137 https://www.nio.io/visioncar

138 https://www.theguardian.com/environment/2016/sep/27/more-than-million-died-due-air-pollution-china-one-year

139 https://www.forbes.com/sites/salvatorebabones/2018/03/06/china-could-be-the-worlds-first-all-electric-vehicle-ecosystem/#6d9d19a6130f

140 https://www.bloomberg.com/news/articles/2018-07-06/china-is-said-to-weigh-further-cuts-in-electric-car-subsidies

141 http://www.asahi.com/ajw/articles/AJ201808230026.html

142 http://www.mining.com/chinas-ganfeng-grabs-sqms-stake-argentinean-lithium-project/

143 http://news.mit.edu/2017/will-metal-supplies-limit-battery-expansion-1011
144 https://www.japantimes.co.jp/opinion/2018/04/09/commentary/japan-commentary/control-battery-resources-key-ev-leadership/#.W4VpfZMzZZ0
145 https://qz.com/1083571/nine-years-ago-warren-buffett-put-a-bet-on-byd-then-an-unknown-chinese-cellphone-battery-maker
146 https://www.wired.co.uk/article/electric-car-sales-china-vs-tesla
147 https://www.dw.com/en/chinas-answer-to-climate-change-e-mobility/a-41232395
148 https://qz.com/1169690/shenzhen-in-china-has-16359-electric-buses-more-than-americas-biggest-citiess-conventional-bus-fleet/
149 http://www.china-briefing.com/news/2017/08/21/chinas-sharing-economy.html
150 http://en.people.cn/n3/2018/0308/c90000-9434399.html
151 https://www.youtube.com/watch?v=G9uPGoN0dvQ
152 https://www.bakermckenzie.com/en/insight/publications/2018/02/adoption-ai-chinese-courts
153 https://www.wired.co.uk/article/didi-chuxing-china-startups-uber
154 http://fortune.com/2018/01/19/uber-softbank-didi-worth-most-valuable-startup/
155 https://www.wsj.com/articles/chinese-app-meituan-raises-4-2-billion-in-ipo-1536819691
156 https://qpsoftware.net/blog/bike-sharing-china-mobike-ofo
157 https://mobike.com/global/public/HowCyclingChangesCitiesMobike.pdf
158 https://www.theguardian.com/uk-news/2018/aug/22/bike-sharing-scheme-mobike-threatens-to-pull-out-of-manchester
159 https://en.wikipedia.org/wiki/Li_Shufu
160 https://www.carlist.my/news/geely-fridge-maker-car-maker-just-12-years-who-are-they/44053/
161 https://www.forbes.com/sites/pamelaambler/2018/01/23/volvo-geely-the-unlikely-marriage-of-swedish-tech-and-chinese-manufacturing-might-that-earned-record-profits/#295707e54ecc
162 In Chinese: *(shǎjīqǔluǎn)*
163 https://www.nytimes.com/2007/08/29/business/worldbusiness/29labor.html
164 http://jefftowson.com/2017/07/massive-chinese-brainpower-is-the-next-really-big-thing/
165 https://www.cnbc.com/2018/12/24/china-is-reportedly-consider-ing-law-against-forced-tech-transfers.html
166 https://www.quora.com/How-many-employees-do-WeChat-and-Line-have
167 https://www.slideshare.net/haxco/hax-63822195
168 https://www.yicaiglobal.com/news/shanghai-has-largest-migrant-population-china-shenzhen-has-highest-ratio
169 https://www.youtube.com/watch?time_continue=23&v=_ng8xQ-SNGc
170 https://www.ipwatchdog.com/2018/05/07/rapid-changes-chinese-legal-system-attractive-venue-ip-litigation/id=96099/
171 https://en.wikipedia.org/wiki/Belt_and_Road_Initiative
172 https://www.digitimes.com/news/a20180828PD216.html
173 https://asianroboticsreview.com/home146-html
174 https://www.reuters.com/article/us-usa-trade-china-robotics/china-robot-market-growth-

to-slump-this-year-as-trade-war-weighs-idUSKCN1MS0L7
175 https://www.ft.com/content/6ff764e8-9a1c-11e8-ab77-f854c65a4465
176 https://www.bloomberg.com/news/articles/2018-03-06/china-s-economy-is-set-to-overtake-combined-euro-area-this-year
177 https://www.annelies-slabbynck.com
178 https://www.nytimes.com/2018/09/30/business/china-health-care-doctors.html
179 https://www.statista.com/statistics/279385/amount-of-hospital-visits-in-china/
180 https://www.thestar.com.my/tech/tech-news/2018/07/02/china-counts-on-ai-to-find-a-cure-for-its-ailing-health-care-system/
181 https://www1.racgp.org.au/newsgp/professional/china-wants-to-train-500,000-new-gps-by-2030
182 https://foreignpolicy.com/2018/11/30/under-the-knife-in-china/
183 https://sciencebasedmedicine.org/ibm-watson-versus-cancer-hype-meets-reality/
184 https://www.latimes.com/world/la-fg-china-ai-20180706-story.html
185 https://chinameddevice.com/seven-cancer-patient-diagnosed-every-minute-in-china/
186 https://en.wikipedia.org/wiki/China_Food_and_Drug_Administration
187 https://www.thecasecentre.org/main/products/view?id=120042
188 https://www.ft.com/content/104517b4-ba0f-11e1-aa8d-00144feabdc0
189 https://www.ft.com/content/ea032bba-5f33-11e8-9334-2218e7146b04
190 http://www.iberchina.org/files/2017/MGI-Digital-China.pdf
191 https://technode.com/2018/02/11/Tencent-medical-ecosystem/
192 https://www.prnewswire.com/news-releases/Tencents-wesure-forms-partnerships-with-20-insurance-companies-300752964.html
193 http://www.stockhouse.com/news/press-releases/2018/11/09/ping-an-good-doctor-s-wang-tao-internet-ai-will-reinvent-medical-services-and
194 https://seekingalpha.com/article/4163049-week-review-ping-good-doctor-plans-1-billion-hong-kong-ipo-mid-may
195 http://www.academypublication.com/issues/past/jltr/vol05/04/08.pdf
196 https://www.genome.gov/12011238/an-overview-of-the-human-genome-project/
197 https://www.genome.gov/27565109/the-cost-of-sequencing-a-human-genome/
198 https://www.wired.com/2017/05/chinese-genome-giant-sets-sights-uitimate-sequencer/
199 https://www.scmp.com/tech/enterprises/article/2188449/chinas-tech-billionaires-back-ethical-rules-guide-development-ai?fbclid=IwAR0Je7conA2JbHoNiFql2jdSdmEHN-rZu23IF-MNQvl3ZBfrZmB77GIw2GsE
200 https://www.asianscientist.com/2016/07/print/meet-chinas-first-biotech-unicorn-wang-jun-icarbonx-bgi/
201 https://rethinkresearch.biz/articles/icarbonx-aims-to-be-amazon-rather-than-google-of-digital-healthcare
205 https://www.theverge.com/2018/4/10/17222444/mark-zuckerberg-senate-hearing-highlights-cambridge-analytica

203 https://www.cnbc.com/2018/12/05/data-privacy-issues-may-be-capturing-more-attention-in-china.html
204 https://www.csis.org/analysis/new-china-data-privacy-standard-looks-more-far-reaching-gdpr
205 https://eugdpr.org/
206 https://www.nature.com/articles/d41586-018-00538-z
207 http://pharma.nridigital.com/pharma_dec18/is_china_the_next_great_hope_for_the_pharma_industry
208 https://www.nature.com/articles/d41586-018-00542-3
209 http://theasiadialogue.com/2016/05/10/fertility-trends-and-population-growth-in-china/
210 https://timesofindia.indiatimes.com/world/china/chinas-population-to-peak-to-1-45-billion-by-2030/articleshow/57603275.cms
211 https://www.ncbi.nlm.nih.gov/pmc/articles/PMC5898031/
212 http://www.stats.gov.cn/english/pressrelease/201802/t20180228_1585666.html
213 https://journals.plos.org/plosone/article?id=10.1371/journal.pone.0206793
214 http://www.pewglobal.org/2016/10/05/chinese-public-sees-more-powerful-role-in-world-names-u-s-as-top-threat/10-4-2016-9-38-34-am-2/
215 https://www.scmp.com/tech/big-tech/article/2178548/alibaba-uses-ai-speed-detection-pregnant-pigs-seven-times-boosting
216 https://www.foodnavigator-asia.com/Article/2018/05/24/Four-major-food-trends-driving-growth-in-China-Fonterra#
217 https://www.scmp.com/comment/insight-opinion/article/2126098/24-reasons-why-chinas-ban-foreign-trash-wake-call-global en https://www.theverge.com/2018/6/20/17484866/chinas-plastic-waste-import-ban-trash
218 https://www.weforum.org/agenda/2017/08/how-china-is-leading-the-renewable-energy-revolution
219 https://www.forbes.com/sites/jakehayman/2018/07/05/eco-civilisation/#74fd7cb164a3
220 https://www.oecd.org/china/Education-in-China-a-snapshot.pdf
221 http://en.people.cn/n3/2017/0117/c90000-9168026.html
222 https://www.topuniversities.com/university-rankings/world-university-rankings/2019
223 STEM and STEAM: Science, Technology, Engineering, (Arts) and Maths.
224 https://www2.deloitte.com/cn/en/pages/technology-media-and-telecommunications/articles/new-era-of-education-china-education-development-report-2018.html
225 https://www.scmp.com/tech/science-research/article/2115271/china-wants-bring-artificial-intelligence-its-classrooms-boost
226 https://www.diamandis.com/blog/back-to-school-edition
227 https://www.varkeyfoundation.org/media/2787/2013globalteacherstatusindex.pdf
228 https://www.wired.co.uk/article/china-artificial-intelligence-education-superpower
229 https://www.telegraph.co.uk/news/worldnews/asia/china/10494678/PISA-education-tests-Why-Shanghai-pupils-are-so-special.html
230 https://edition.cnn.com/2018/09/28/health/china-ai-early-education/index.html

231 https://www.edsurge.com/amp/news/2018-11-14-education-looks-eastward-snap-shots-from-beijing-s-global-education-technology-summit

232 https://qz.com/970130/asians-spend-15-of-their-family-income-on-extra-education-and-tutoring-for-kids-americans-spend-it-on-cars-and-gas/

233 https://www.chinainternetwatch.com/25683/online-education-k12-preschool/

234 https://www.telegraph.co.uk/news/2018/05/17/chinese-school-uses-facial-recognition-monitor-student-attention/

235 https://www.forbes.com/sites/niallmccarthy/2017/02/02/the-countries-with-the-most-stem-graduates-infographic/#24e57b91268a

236 https://medium.com/@EdtechChina/china-ed-tech-raised-2-22-billion-usd-in-2018h1-ec63c8e284d4

237 Statistics from iResearch and Decebo: https://www.scmp.com/business/companies/article/2109612/chinas-online-education-market-grow-20pc-annually-bolstered-new

Pelckmans Pro is part of Pelckmans Uitgevers nv
www.pelckmansuitgevers.be
Brasschaatsteenweg 308, 2920 Kalmthout, Belgium

Original publication: *China's New Normal. Hoe China de standaard zet voor innovatie.* (Pelckmans Pro, 2019)

Cover design: Stijn Dams
Layout: Inge Van Damme

D/2019/13955/20
ISBN 978 94 6337 184 1
NUR 801

If you would like to stay up-to-date on China's most recent developments, we welcome you to keep following innovative China on www.chinasnewnormal.com.

pelckmanspro.be
pelckmanspro.nl

pelckmanspro